The Tact of Teaching

SUNY Series, The Philosophy of Education

Philip L. Smith, Editor

The Tact
_of_ Teaching

The Meaning of Pedagogical Thoughtfulness

Max van Manen

STATE UNIVERSITY OF NEW YORK PRESS

Published by
State University of New York Press, Albany

Printed in the United States of America

For information, address State University of New York Press,
State University Plaza, Albany, N.Y. 12246

Production by Marilyn P. Semerad
Marketing by Theresa A. Swierzowski

Cover photo: Ghirlandajo (1448–1494), *Grandfather and grandson.* In discussing this well known painting by Ghirlandajo, Klaus Mollenhauer says: "The scepsis of the grandfather and the glance of the child—questioning and full of trust—stand in a certain relation to each other. It expresses an open, uncertain future, and a waiting for knowledge that is passionately desired, to become 'grown-up.' Between child and grandfather there lies a life of development, learning, and formative growth. In their loving relation they are together and true to each other, but with respect to the future, that they anticipate in accordance with their own abilities and possibilities, they are separated from each other." (Mollenhauer, K. 1983. *Vergessene Zusammenhänge.* München: Juventa Verlag, p. 95).

Library of Congress Cataloging-in-Publication Data

Manen, Max van.
    The tact of teaching : the meaning of pedagogical thoughtfulness /
Max van Manen.
      p.   cm. —(SUNY series, the philosophy of education)
    Includes bibliographical references and index.
    ISBN 0-7914-0667-9. —ISBN 0-7914-0668-7 (pbk.)
    1. Teaching. 2. Tact I. Title. II. Series: SUNY series in
philosophy of education.
LB1775.M425   1991
371.1′02—dc20
                                      91-11349
                                      CIP

10 9 8 7 6 5 4 3 2 1

to Judith, Mark and Michael

Contents

Preface

This text is written for beginning teachers who want to feel enabled and inspired for what is surely the most vital of all human
endeavors. It is meant for experienced teachers and child specialists who may be prompted to become more reflective about
their everyday professional lives. This book may also serve teachers who feel burntout or uncertain about their vocation and want
to reexamine their commitments. It is written for educators who
wonder if they have taken for granted their responsibility to children and ignored the real child. And not least, this is meant for
parents who have an interest in pedagogy: Parents are the original educators.

What are the makings of a good educator? A person may
have learned all curriculum methods and all the techniques of
instruction and yet be a poor teacher. How do thoughtful teachers act? What knowledge contributes to reflective pedagogy? This
book deals with such concerns, not theoretically but practically,
by addressing not only the head but also the heart, or, better, the
whole person.

In writing this text I have aimed for certain effects: Novice
teachers may feel that this book leads them to become more reflective but also provides them with experiences drawn from life
that make pedagogical reflection meaningful and possible in the
first place. Experienced educators may recognize in these pages
instances of their own experience and they may want to return
to those experiences in a thoughtful way. Most important, I hope
that this text helps us to give the welfare of our children higher
priority, to take young people seriously, and always to consider
educational concerns first from the child's point of view.

Some readers may feel that this text is too idealistic, that
there is a moral tone to it, that expectations of pedagogical
thoughtfulness and tact are unrealistic. I do not apologize for a
passion for children's concerns. But this passion is down-to-

earth, measured, and pragmatic; it is a part of our responsibility to children. In most of the literature about teaching and education, the intuitive side of life has been severely underestimated and neglected.

I offer a theory of the unique that knows how to address the particular case, the practical moments of teaching in which emotion, morality, and reason cannot be disentangled. All education is deeply normative, and precisely because of this ethical ground our pedagogical practice can be thoughtful and reflective. In all our interactions with children, we are constantly involved, whether we like it or not, in distinguishing between what is good and what is not good for them (in contrast, educational research is usually more interested in distinguishing between what is effective and what is ineffective). Yet even (or especially) the best educators temper their practice with the knowledge that we all often fall short and do not always know what is best.

This text is incomplete and introductory in nature. Of course, no text is complete, and a committed reader does not criticize a text merely from the sidelines. Rather, a pedagogically motivated reader tries to be productively critical. After all, the best pedagogical influence of the parent or teacher does not merely preach, criticize, or defeat; rather it is an influence that strengthens, that lives by example, that shows what it is like to be pedagogically strong.

The text is organized so that the reader may gain a sense of the continuity of the meaning and practice of pedagogy. But the various chapters can also be read separately, to measure them against real life, to prod further insights, to stimulate alternative interpretations.

In describing the pedagogical experience, I have tried to relate it to timehonored themes as well as to recent perspectives on the pedagogical traditions and educational thinking of Europe and North America. I have attempted to integrate these themes with what I see required of us as we near a new millenium. But above all, I have been animated as parent and as teacher by my personal relations with educators and with my own and other people's children.

Acknowledgments

I thank Judith and her students. I hope that this text in some way honors them, as well as those other teachers and students with whom I have worked and who have shared experiences with me.

Next, I wish to acknowledge the Dutch educator Martinus J. Langeveld. He died at the age of 84 on December 15, 1989; yet his work on theoretical pedagogy lives on. The spirit of Langeveld's phenomenological influence is noticeable throughout this text.

A special dedication goes to a memorable teacher, Ted Aoki, who possesses the teacherly tact of "letting learn."

I appreciate the helpful comments on this text by Larry Beauchamp, Terry Carson, Rod Evans, Bas Levering, Wilfried Lippitz, and Antoinette Oberg.

Finally, I am grateful to the Faculty of Education of the University of Alberta for awarding and supporting this work with a McCalla Research Professorship.

1
TOWARD A PEDAGOGY OF THOUGHTFULNESS

Introduction

What is a child? To see a child is
to see possibility, someone in
the process of becoming.

Jan's parents did not get along. Even at age six Jan knew this; it created tensions and sometimes an unpleasant feeling at home. Then, one day, her parents announced plans to break up their marriage. They decided for the sake of the children not to live too far apart; Jan and her brother could choose whether they wanted to live with their father or with their mother.

That was several years ago. The father has moved away. Jan now lives with her mother.

Jan is in sixth grade. The teacher finds Jan remarkably mature. Or is it that she seems so much more experienced than some of her other classmates? Every day the children spend half an hour writing in their individual journals. Sometimes children write poetry, sometimes they write a story, and sometimes they use the journal as a place to express their feelings and communicate to the teacher. At the end of the day the teacher takes all the books home and writes a response to each child. The teacher reads Jan's story: "Today I'm a little blue. I wrote a letter to my Dad last night and I really miss him. Usually Trisha will cheer me up but she's sick. I know my Dad misses me, but I just wish that I could be in two places at once or that I could live normally with parents that live together. I'm glad that now, when they talk on the phone, they sound more like friends, but that still doesn't change the fact that my Dad lives too far away. I

know I live normally — like I got my health and a loving family
... but then again, not really. I guess today you have one lonely
kid!" As the teacher responds to Jan with some thoughtful lines,
she is again amazed at herself. As a teacher she knows many
children like Jan, many worse off than Jan. But why does the
teacher in her always want to respond as a mother?

Compared to their parents and grandparents, young people
today live in a severely fractured world — families are less stable, divorce has become commonplace, neighbourhoods tend to
be more in flux and less community-minded, schools are less personal and more competitive, and peer groups set up conflicting
loyalties. Moreover, television, radio, newspapers, and other media rush images of adulthood into the living space of young children — images beset with violence, sexuality, drugs, global
crises and conflict. Many parents and educators feel uneasy about
the frenzied, intensely eroticized icons of some music videos on
the developing minds and bodies of young viewers. They believe
that children prematurely see and experience too much in our
consumer-oriented, information-based, and advertising-driven
culture. Technology, in the form of computers, video, and other
communication innovations, also radically alters the modalities
of modern living. Aspects of adult life that previously remained
secret from children until they had mastered more sophisticated
reading levels and until they had obtained access to more mature literature now have become dominant themes of the lives of
children. This has led some educators to suggest that the boundaries between childhood and adulthood are eroding and that
childhood itself, in its development phases, may be dis-
appearing.

It is this reality of change, complexity, plurality, fragmenta-
tion, conflict, and contradiction of beliefs, values, faiths, living
conditions, aspirations, and life-styles, that makes the lives of
young people today an experience in contingency. Contingent
life is indeterminate, unpredictable, subject to chance, impacted
by events and unforeseen circumstances. The youngster born
into the modern social world often must respond to early pressures and premature expectations to grow up faster than seems
possible or advisable. And yet, in spite of — or because of — this
contingency, the lives of young people are often full of stimula-
tion, interest, and challenge.

The modern child is born into a world that can be experienced, within limits, as a life of possibilities — though the possibilities are certainly not the same for all. Yet even children who are raised in situations affected by poverty, youth unemployment, alcoholism, drug abuse, prostitution, violence, crime, and other dangers of modern living nevertheless may be able to experience a certain openness of choice and possibility in life.[1]

The Possibility of a New Pedagogy

Unlike the ages when one knew, by being born in a particular social niche, what one was expected to become, whom one could count on, what one could do, present-day children must live with uncertainty. They must make active choices in their lives for fear of not becoming anything or anyone. The modern child must actively realize that he or she is born into a condition of possibilities. He or she *is* this body of possibilities. To become a person, to grow up and to become educated, is to transform one's contingency into commitment, responsibility — one must choose a life. This means that the vocation of pedagogy, of being educationally involved with children, is to empower children to give active shape to their life's contingencies.[2]

To be a contingent person can be seen both negatively and positively. Negatively it means that many present-day children are growing up in an uncertain world, a world with too many conflicting views, values and aims; this predicament can mean that children drift into (self-)destructive lifestyles. Positively it means that each young person must make choices and commitments in life, that they all must come to terms with their possibilities. The child is in a real sense the agent of his or her own destiny — at both the individual and the social level. So a new pedagogy of the theory and practice of living with children must know how to stand in a relationship of thoughtfulness and openness to children and young people rather than being governed by traditional beliefs, discarded values, old rules, and fixed impositions. The pedagogy of living with children is an ongoing project of renewal in a world that is constantly changing around us and that is continually being changed by us.

Indeed, as we ask ourselves what it means to belong to this

earth, we must seriously ask ourselves what it means to belong to our children. Living at the turn of a new millennium poses unforeseen and unforeseeable challenges to parents and to teachers and other professional educators. This does not mean, of course, that we should dismiss or abandon every valued cultural construction that appears presently under siege. For example, in a new age of commercialized social mores and more fluid interpersonal relations, the family has experienced difficulty maintaining its former cohesiveness. This does not mean that the more close-knit familial structure is or was wrong and that we should give up on the idea that children need, if possible, a mother and a father, as well as other kin relations, all playing active roles in the child's journey to adulthood. A new pedagogy must face the challenge of change but also be prepared to defend, or reconstruct in new forms, values and value frameworks that growing up seems to require.

Of course, life will be carried into the twenty-first century by new realities and new visions. Some of these realities will be exciting and positive experiments in human living. But we must recognize also that spheres of human intimacy increasingly come under strain from consumer, economic, bureaucratic, corporate, and political technologies and ideologies. The notion of education, conceived as a living process of personal engagement between an adult teacher or parent and a young child or student, may well disappear in an increasingly managerial, corporate, and technicized environment. How can educating and bringing up children remain a rich human and cultural activity?

This text is addressed to both beginning teachers and experienced educators. But the perspective and approach is somewhat unusual in that it takes the *in loco parentis* relation as a source for exploring pedagogical understandings and insights that maintain a holistic focus on the lived world of professional educators and children. In my ongoing conversations with teachers and young people I have been intrigued by the fact that when teachers and children talk of meaningful educational experiences, these experiences often seem to occur on the margin or on the outside of the daily curriculum experiences of the classroom. One should not make the mistake, however, of supposing that the pedagogical life on the margin of the "teaching/ learning process" is not fundamentally connected to the central processes of curriculum and teaching.

Remembering educators' in loco parentis *relation*

Even in these times of eroding parental and family influence, parents carry the primary responsibility for the child's well-being and the child's development. Does anybody have a right to diminish the rights and abilities of parents to be responsible for their children's welfare and growth? Yet we are living in an age when many children and young people experience very little parental support and influence in their lives.[3] Working parents who are largely absent, families in various stages of disintegration or breakup, single-parent families without adequate resources or child care, family violence and child neglect, poverty-ridden neighborhoods, alcohol and drug abuse, all are contexts for the lives of many children we meet in our schools.

At the same time there are children growing up in a variety of modern family settings, surrounded by a stable atmosphere of parent(s) and other adults who are present to them and with whom they share and interact in significant ways. Yet even these children are living in a time of crises and a sense of doom about the viability of the human race and the survival of the earth. Teachers are living with children who come from very diverse backgrounds and with widely varying experiences. These teachers exercise a responsibility *in loco parentis*[4] toward all those children entrusted to their care. Naturally, teachers are expected to educate these children in the various curriculum subjects. Other child professionals too have particular educational tasks. Their pedagogical responsibilities are associated with their specialized tasks as counsellors, school administrators, psychologists, child care workers, and so on.

The implication for teachers is that they are constantly being reminded to be mindful of their status *in loco parentis*. Professional educators, if possible, must try to assist parents in fulfilling their primary pedagogical responsibility. In other words, out of this primary responsibility of parents flows the teacher's charge as a responsibility *in loco parentis*. So what is relevant for the relation between parents and children may be informative for the pedagogical relation between teachers and students. As schools and other child care institutions have taken on more and more responsibilities previously dealt with within the family, professional educators need to become more reflective about what *in loco parentis* entails.

Indeed, the school, as a cultural-political institution, needs to come to terms with its *in loco parentis* responsibilities. The responsibility of the adult resides in children's need for a protective sphere in which they can develop a self-responsible maturity. The school institution also has legally defined *in loco parentis* responsibilities. The school's boundaries were traditionally commonly considered as a transitional space between the secure intimacy of the family and the more risky public openness of life in the outside world.[5] But in modern society we cannot assume that this secure family exists for the child; and to the extent that it exists, it cannot be assumed that this family "intimacy" grows out of the right kind of love for the child. And so, the *in loco parentis* responsibility of the school does not only consist in preparing the child for the larger world, it also consists in protecting the child from the possible risks of abuse and shortcomings in the intimate sphere of the family.

Some have argued that increasing selfishness and greed in modern society requires that professional educators develop caring school environments, for the sake of the children and ultimately for the sake of society.[6] Similarly, schools struggle with the task of preparing children, not only for the challenges and dangers of the larger world, but also for the demands of intimacy and moral responsibility that successful family life presupposes but that families find increasingly difficult to impress on their children. In other words, the institution of the school needs to orient itself increasingly to the norms of parenting that parents themselves seem to have forgotten as it were. While parents are excused, the schools are often accused of improperly preparing children for the responsibilities of their own parenthood.

There exist deep connections between the nature of teaching and of parenting, yet these connections are rarely explored. In the North American educational literature the parent is remarkably absent. It is as if in the minds of education theorists the education of children is not an integral part of the whole process of growing up. Even the English language reflects this separation between education (largely an institution process of teaching/ learning in schools) and child rearing (usually considered the process of parenting in and around the home). There is no single word in English that describes the entire moral, intellectual, physical, and spiritual complex process of bringing up children.[7]

Parenting and teaching derive from the same fundamental

experience of pedagogy: the human charge of protecting and teaching the young to live in this world and to take responsibility for themselves, for others, and for the continuance and welfare of the world. Moreover, there are other similarities often overlooked between the world inside and outside the school. For example, how often do educators tend to forget that the children who are before them in school are the same children they see in the street and that the way children learn in school is essentially no different from the way they learn at home or in the street?

Children are not empty vessels who come to school merely to be filled with curricular content by means of special instructional methods. Moreover, children who come to school come from somewhere. Teachers need to have some sense of what it is that children bring with them, what defines their present understandings, mood, emotional state, and readiness to deal with the subject matter and the world of the school.

Educators may be able to learn about pedagogy not only from what they share with parents but also from the differences between being a parent and being a professional educator. For example, like parents, teachers often develop deep affection and love for their students, they feel responsible for the young people in their charge, and they cherish hope for the children they teach. Eventually teachers have to let go of their children, and yet they may live on in the memory and in the lives of the students they have taught. Professional educators may need to reflect on the question of what is similar and what is different in these experiences between the pedagogical relation of the parent and the child, on the one hand, and the pedagogical relation of the teacher and the student, on the other.

In this text, I will constantly consider examples of the pedagogical experiences of parenting and of teaching in order to keep reminding ourselves of our *in loco parentis* relation to the children we teach. As parents and as teachers we need to keep open the question of the pedagogical meaning of our vocation, and we need to remain aware of the total life world in which young people grow up, learn and develop.

What do we look for in pedagogues?

Another obvious feature of the *in loco parentis* responsibility of professional educators is found in the expectations that parents hold for the teachers of their children. In everyday life parents look for certain qualities in the teachers of their children. What might those qualities be? Parents often have a difficult time articulating relevant standards. Generally they are concerned that the teachers "like" their child because parents sense that a positive affective relationship may benefit the child's school experience and the child's success in school. Parents' particular expectations are usually more concretely tied to the daily experiences their children have in schools and classrooms. Often expectations become more clear when things have gone wrong at school, when the child has been let down, hurt, neglected, misunderstood, misjudged, or mistreated.

In this text it is suggested that the following qualities are probably essential to good pedagogy: a sense of vocation, love of and caring for children, a deep sense of responsibility, moral intuitiveness, self-critical openness, thoughtful maturity, tactful sensitivity toward the child's subjectivity, an interpretive intelligence, a pedagogical understanding of the child's needs, improvisational resoluteness in dealing with young people, a passion for knowing and learning the mysteries of the world, the moral fibre to stand up for something, a certain understanding of the world, active hope in the face of prevailing crises, and, not the least, humor and vitality.

Of course, teachers of the young should know what they teach, and should take responsibility for the world and traditions which they share; moreover, they need to know how to hand over this world to the child so that he or she can make it his or her own world. In other words, pedagogical thoughtfulness is a multifaceted and complex mindfulness toward children. This is a tall order for any human being. And yet underlying this suggestion is a crucial question: Does a person who lacks any of these qualities possess the pedagogical fitness required for educating young people?

The idea and nature of pedagogical fitness as a certain thoughtfulness and tact is offered, described, and interpreted in this book in a manner that may contribute to the thoughtfulness and tact through which the reader can come to see, act, and interact with children and young people. This book offers a (self) reflective approach to teaching children. However, "pedagogical thoughtfulness and tact" are unlearnable as mere behavioral principles, techniques, or methods. So one will look in vain in these pages for simplified sets of effective teaching techniques, or for sure methods for managing classrooms.

Pedagogy is primarily neither a science nor a technology.[8] Yet it is often treated and researched in an empirically scientific way. Science and technology by their very nature cut knowledge off from experience by producing generalizations and technical principles that abstract from experience. This is quite all right in a field like engineering where students can learn the scientific principles of bridge building from an expert who in fact may never have built a bridge. Similarly, a technological approach to education assumes that teaching can be taught by means of generalizations and general techniques. Only recently has anyone recognized that education needs to turn back to the world of experience. Experience can open up understanding that restores a sense of embodied knowing.

Of course, it is not being suggested that aspects of teaching cannot be learned as special instructional techniques (for example, how to tell a good story, how to conduct a class discussion or seminar), or as organizational skills (for example, how to plan a stimulating lesson, how to organize a field trip), or as diagnostic competencies (for example, how to assess the child's cognitive abilities or school achievements). Yet, the essence of education is less a technical or production enterprise than a normative activity[9] that constantly expects the educator to act in a right, good, or appropriate manner. Accordingly, a pedagogical text like this one should not be composed and studied as if it were a technical handbook that specifies effective procedures for the productive management of learning environments. Rather, a pedagogical text needs to possess an inspirational quality together with a narrative structure that invites critical reflection and possibilities for insight and that leads to a personal appropriation of a moral intuition.

It is possible to learn all the techniques of instruction but to remain pedagogically unfit as a teacher. The preparation of educators obviously includes much more than the teaching of knowledge and skills, more even than a professional ethical code or moral craft. To become a teacher includes something that cannot be taught formally: the most personal embodiment of a pedagogical thoughtfulness.

The preparation of professional educators in institutions of higher learning tends to rely heavily on bookish approaches. But vicarious experiences provided by these texts tend to go to our heads, so to speak. Especially books that offer mostly "information," abstract concepts, and theoretical explanations and classifications may often be poor substitutes for the experiences provided by life itself. Pedagogy requires practical rather than intellectualized forms of knowledge. Through practical examples of experience, this text hopes to stimulate a reflective thoughtfulness and a sense of improvisational tact that actively speaks to our whole embodied being. As Dewey pointed out almost a century ago, it may be more important in the long term for educators to develop an orientation to children conditioned by ongoing reflection on the pedagogical meaning and significance of experiences in their lives, than to acquire an external set of behavioral competencies that enables one in the short term to improve "the mechanics of school management ... [but with which one] cannot grow as a teacher, an inspirer and director of soul-life."[10]

To write about pedagogical thoughtfulness and tact courts the dangerous presumption that one claims to know how to behave with moral superiority. By definition pedagogy is always concerned with the ability to distinguish between what is good and what is not good for children. Many educational thinkers are uncomfortable with this assumption, they try to pursue educational problems and questions in a value neutral or relativistic manner. It is wrong, however, to confuse pedagogical discourse with moral diatribe or preaching. Preaching is an act of moral exhortation on the basis of some unquestioned dogma. But pedagogy does not aim to deliver diatribe. Pedagogy is a practical discipline. On the one hand, educators need to show that in order to stand up for the welfare of children, one must be prepared to stand out and be criticized. On the other hand, pedagogy is a self-reflective activity that always must be willing to question critically what it does and what it stands for.

Becoming reflective about pedagogy as the practice of living

In this text there are two main thrusts. One is an attempt to rescue the idea of pedagogy from the wordmongers. For many decades the term "pedagogy" has been in disuse among educators in the English-speaking world.[11] Recently there has been an upsurge in the currency of the term *pedagogy* and the renewed popularity of this word may have something to do with the growing North American interest in West European philosophical, social, and educational theory. But present usage for the term *pedagogy* has added few new understandings to the field of education, and may have become little more than a new packaging of old ideas.

Second, this text aims to explore and offer a more experience-based interpretation of pedagogical reflection on the one hand, and of the practical pedagogical moment of teaching (and parenting) on the other hand. Indeed, it is the reality of these pedagogical moments that much literature has been trying to grasp and clarify under the labels of *reflective teaching, teacher thinking, the teacher as reflective practitioner, teacher as problem solver, teacher as decision maker, teacher as researcher.* Using the notions of pedagogical thoughtfulness and pedagogical tact, this book attempts to show that the interactive practice of pedagogy has a subtle and highly normative character. Pedagogical reflection plays an important part in the life worlds of parents and teachers with children; but the reflective nature of the actual pedagogical moments in parenting and teaching may differ markedly from the interactions of other professional practitioners, such as the medical doctor, with those in their charge.

Most books on education are agogical.[12] They direct themselves to the adults, to the parents or to the teachers, and not to the children. They preoccupy themselves with the question how educators (should) think, act, feel, and interact with children. But such a focus neglects two important considerations. First, this emphasis on the adult fails to consider how particular situations appear from the child's point of view, how the child experiences his or her world at home, at school, and in the community. From a pedagogical perspective the most important question is always, "How does the child experience this particular situation, relationship, or event?" Because this text deals with pedagogical tact, it must consider how things are for the child.

Second, an emphasis only on the adult's dealings with children neglects the direct and indirect influence that children have on adults, and especially on their parents. Many parents know how powerfully children transform the adults' sense of themselves, their priorities in life, and their preoccupations with the concerns of the world. Many teachers, too, experience the transforming effects young people have on their professional and personal lives. This powerful influence of children that transforms personal existence and that radiates throughout the life of the adult is what kindles the topic for this text: pedagogy.

2 THE CONCEPT OF PEDAGOGY

*Pedagogy is a fascination with
the growth of the other.*

Situations

David's parents have noticed that in the last year he has acquired
a nice way of articulating his words and a more reflective way of
engaging in discussions. They both like this change in David and
have commented to each other about it. In fact, the parents had
been joking about whether David was taking after "him" or "her."
Now they are returning from a parent-teacher meeting, and as
they drive home they are both smiling and thinking the same
thought: It is uncanny how David seems to have modelled himself after his favorite teacher this year. They noticed the subtleties in the same kind of clear speech, the same conversational
manner.

Ben gets a bicycle for his birthday. That day Ben climbs up
onto the bike while his father pushes, walking along holding the
saddle. Ben soon gets the knack of steering while negotiating a
precarious balance. His father runs beside the bike, just in case!
The next day, to his father's relief, that is no longer necessary.
Ben can now ride his bike by himself, while his father watches.
After a short while, even that is no longer needed. Sometimes
Ben and his father go for bike rides but now they derive a different, but still shared, satisfaction from their activity together.

The second grade teacher finally closes the book. She has
been reading to the class a few pages a day for the last two
weeks. But for Lucy the story is over all too soon. "It was so
beautiful — will you read it to us again?" she pleads. The teacher
takes the book from her desk and hands it to Lucy. "You want to
take this home Lucy and read it by yourself? I am sure you can
do it. You will enjoy it." Three days later Lucy returns the book.
"I finished it," she declares proudly. "Good Lucy," says the

teacher, "that was your first real book. Now let's see if we can find another one that you would enjoy."

The ten-year-old asks, "Mom, may I phone a friend to come over and play?" "Sure," says her mother, "but would you make your bed first so that your room will be pleasant to be in?"

A father tells his two boys, Mark and Michael, a bedtime story. The story happens to be about two boys just about their age. As they listen to the tale there is a certain stillness. Sometimes Mark, then Michael make a suggestion to give the story a certain twist, sometimes the one or the other asks a question. But this does not disturb the magic that envelops their quiet bedroom. As their father tells his story, faint smiles hover over the boys' faces, dreamy in the dark. They are wonderfully entranced, which is no wonder really. Mark and Michael recognize themselves in the stories.

Life is full of anecdotes like these. We could tell them all day long. Here are situations where older and younger people have certain experiences together. In fact, the anecdotes report very special experiences. We recognize them as the kind of relations, situations, and interactions that reveal moments of growth. And yet these are such ordinary examples. David acquires personal habits from his teacher. Ben's father teaches him to ride a bike. The teacher turns Lucy on to reading. A mother instills the value of esthetic order. The father of Mark and Michael helps his boys be more self-reflective.

What do we call these happenings? The situations are very different, yet they share something in common. We could refer to situations like these as "education," "child rearing," "teaching," "helping children develop and grow." Maybe one term seems to apply more appropriately to one anecdote than to the others. Yet we can see some commonalities: Each situation tells about something that transpired between an older and a younger person — a mature and a not-yet-so-mature person, an experienced person and a relatively inexperienced person. In each case there is a certain complexity of interactional influences. The older and the younger person influence each other. But the influence, that flows from the older to the younger person is of special interest here. It has the quality of opening up possibilities of being and becoming. And at the same time this influence is oriented in certain directions.[13]

We may notice some other features about this influence. Pedagogical influence is situational, practical, normative, relational, and self-reflective. First, the influence exercised by the adult appears situation-specific, often subtle, and apparently limited. This influence is never completely predictable or controllable. Furthermore, the influence mediated by the adult is formative — oriented toward the well-being and the increasing maturity and growth of the child. But of course we should be mindful as well that it is easy to overestimate the influence adults have over children, just as it is easy to overestimate the influence our parents had, and continue to have, over us.[14] Second, this pedagogical influence is always practical. Even as a theoretical discipline pedagogy is a practical endeavor. In living with children every situation requires a response from us. We cannot help but act. Every action (even non-action, negation, or withdrawal) must inadvertently be a pedagogical response. Next, whether we like it or not, every pedagogical action is normative: It shows how one is oriented to children and how one lives up (or fails to live up) to one's responsibilities. Pedagogical influence means not only that one is response-able but that in addition to this "ability to respond" one actually acts in a manner that is indeed responsible and thus morally accountable and defensible in terms of some pedagogical perspective, framework, or rationale. Fourth, by virtue of our biology and our culture we always stand in a potential pedagogical relation to our children: we have something to do with their birth, development and growth. Our responsibility to children makes us subject to or dependent on them — we experience the appeal that children make on us as a compelling order. In other words, children are dependent on adults, but in a deeper sense adults are dependent on children. Children show us what we are able to make of ourselves and of this shared world. Finally, this means that pedagogical influence is self-reflective: Pedagogical action constantly prods us to reflect whether we did things appropriately, right, or in the best way possible.

Influence is an intriguing notion. The term *influentia* originally referred to the emanation from the heavens of an ethereal fluid affecting human beings.[15] Since we all live under the heavens we are always under the influence. The almost inescapable and elusive nature of the spread and flow of influence may be the reason why the contagious epidemic raging in Rome in 1743 was called the *Influenza*. And even now the most common ailment is indeed influenza, "the flu," the influence. Influence, like "the flu," is something that we "catch" or that "catches" us — influence is something that we are overcome by, that takes over our body and mind.

Influence does not necessarily evoke the image of cause-and-effect relations; rather, influence may be something that is communicated among people who are present to each other. To experience influence is something that we suffer, that happens, that takes place, and so we speak about the influences of the Spirit of the Age, of the Word, of human affection and intimacy, of simply sharing and living together. Moreover, children do very actively participate in the shaping of their influence from the adult. Young people are typically eager to become independent and yet they also value influence. For example, there is mutual influence when one engages in conversation. So we should not assume that influence is necessarily manipulative or that influence reduces the relation between two people into a subject-object relation whereby the person of influence treats the other as mere object-to-be-controlled. Rather, influence is something that radiates or flows and may have very different consequences, effects, or significance. In a broad sense, influence connotes the openness of a human being to the presence of another.

With respect to culture and tradition everyone is always a late-comer and thus under the influence of what preceded. Not only the children who need education but educators too are under the influence of the past (and present), of tradition and culture. The question is, then, how is the educator able to develop a strong relationship with the sources of influence? We need to be neither iconoclasts who only rebel and tear down, nor iconolators who blindly submit to the monuments of their culture. A strong relation to influence may be the kind that wants to influence the influence. This means that the educator needs to be able to mediate the influence of culture and tradition on the lives of young people.

In order to explore, study, and describe the influences that are at the heart of the special interactions, situations, and relations between educators and students, parents and children, I will use the term *pedagogy*. Of course, not all influence between people is pedagogical (or agogical) in nature.[16] As suggested, every child and adult, is always influenced: by each other, by their cultural traditions, their language, their own biography, their socio-physical environment, and so forth. But only a certain kind of influence between adult and child is animated by an orientation to the good, to what is good for this child — meaning that this orientation has *pedagogical intent*. And the intention is to strengthen the child's contingent possibility for "being and becoming."

It should be noted, at this point, that some educational theorists find the notion of "pedagogical intent" repugnant.[17] They fear that the adult's pedagogical intent is really a disguised form of control, the exercise of power.[18] They argue that nobody can know what is good or not good for any particular child except the child. For one to have pedagogical intentions for a child implies for them that one keeps the child in a state of weakness and dependency. I would maintain, however, that even such a view has a pedagogical intent, having at its roots a concern with the child's well-being and authentic becoming. But we are living in an age where there is a general crisis of loss of values. And so, rather than risk making mistakes, many adults exonerate themselves from any responsibility by not risking themselves at all. It is true that the adult's intent can easily be misdirected and turn into a form of neglect or abuse. It is even more reprehensible, however, to leave children to scramble for themselves, abandoning them to the seductive and often tyrannical forces of the peer group or the larger society.

The pedagogical intent makes the difference

Pedagogy is concerned with
influencing the influence.

It is important to distinguish between situations with pedagogical intent and situations without it. Yet, from a pedagogical point of view, situations with no pedagogical intent may nevertheless benefit the child. There is little doubt that certain experiences can provide powerful influences on a person's education or growth toward maturity. Some influences benefit a young person's character or growth, other influences may actually be damaging to a person's positive development. For example, a severe illness or crisis can have the effect of strengthening a young person. A child loses a parent in a car accident, and demonstrates unexpected strength by becoming a support for the remaining parent. Another child has lived through the violence of intergroup conflict or war but turns this experience into a testimony of personal courage. Human suffering and struggle may contribute to fundamental growth in a person's character. And yet as adults we do not take credit for the positive effects of such experiences since they are not of our making; thus we do not call such happenings or experiences "pedagogical events." Pedagogy refers only to those types of actions and interactions intentionally (though not always deliberately or consciously) engaged in by an adult and a child, directed toward the child's positive being and becoming.

It may well be that, in the light of all the influences in a young person's life, the "educational" influences that come from the media and from the culture at large greatly outweigh the intentional influences from parents, teachers, or other pedagogically involved adults. In one way or another those many other influences contribute to the child's growth. What in all this influence is for the good and what is not? These are questions that may lead to never-ending pedagogical reflection and discussion. It is important to realize, however, that there are ongoing events and experiences in children's lives that are not of our making intentionally. In fact, many of our own routine, or otherwise "thoughtless" behaviors may influence children, for better or worse, in ways that we did not intend.

Not only the adult, but the child too has intentions, which are a source for the adult's involvements in the child's personal development. This means that the adult who is oriented to the child's intentions is oriented to the way that the child experiences the world and to the way that children experience the adults and their intentions in their life. The adult may feel deep love for the child and have the child's best interests at heart, but the child may not understand this. The child may not even experience the adult's presence and actions as loving or caring. What good is the adult's pronouncement of love and care when the child does not experience this affection?

The child's intentions also express themselves in the kind of person the child is and the way the child actively orients to the world. Parent's who have more than one child know how differently children come to us. Every child is unique and exhibits inclinations, sensitivities, modalities of being which soon express themselves in certain choices, interests, and desires. Any pedagogical intention needs to respect the child for what he or she is and what he or she can become. Pedagogical intent is aimed at strengthening as much as possible any positive intentions and qualities of the child.

Through play and work the child is actively involved in his or her own growth. The child's intent is complex since it is deeply intermingled with his or her feelings and daily projects. For example, the parent wants the child to go to bed, but the child is not sleepy and feels that the day is not over yet. There are many more interests to pursue, many more projects to accomplish. Or it may be the case that the child is reluctant to go to bed because he or she fears the darkness of the bedroom or the oppressive quiet of that awkward time when sleep refuses to come. And now the child's plea for staying up a little bit longer may lead the adult to suggest a bedtime story. In other words, the bedtime story not only becomes the adult's way of reconciling their different intents, it also becomes the occasion for addressing the child's desires, preoccupations, interests, fears, problems, or projects.

This example also shows that the adult's intentions are different from those of the child. The adult needs to take into consideration the intents of the child whereas the child's intents do not encompass those of the adult. In a sense, the adult's are oriented in two directions — the adult educates and knows and feels what it is like to become educated — whereas the child's intentions are oriented in only one direction — the child experiences being educated but is not responsible for educating others. Moreover the adult's intents may be more future oriented than those of the child.

On the one hand, the reflective awareness of our pedagogical intents enables us to make our pedagogical lives conversationally available: debatable, accountable, evaluable. And to the extent that we must assume responsibility for the child's as yet immature ability to be reflectively involved in his or her own educational process, we need to speak also for the child. Naturally the latter responsibility is an extremely sensitive undertaking, easily mishandled or abused by the adult. On the other hand, the living quality of the pedagogical intent is much more consequential than intent as an intellectual statement of any purpose we may have with respect to the child's situation or future. The pedagogical intent is also the expression of our fundamental experience of encountering this child as another person who has entered our life, who has a claim on us, who has transformed our life. In this latter sense, the pedagogical intent can be seen as a stirring responsiveness to which we find ourselves called in facing this child.

The question of intent is implicated in the very presence of children in our lives. In our modern society the whole issue of family planning and procreation has changed such that it now appears possible to make childbirth largely a matter of rational choice. The foremost question of intent then becomes: What do children mean to us? What do we mean to them? Do we want children? What do we want with children? What do they themselves want? It is likely that for most prospective parents the desire to have children is not really motivated by a true pedagogical intent. After all, one must first have some relation to a child in order to feel pedagogically involved and responsible. For many people the intent to have children may be motivated by a mixed or complex desire for generativity (to leave something of oneself behind), a concern for the world (to assure the continued existence of the human race), a yearning for personal fulfillment (to meet the cultural expectation of "meaning" in parenthood and family), a wish for security in community (to secure the support of offspring in dependent old age).

Not every interaction between parent and child needs to be deliberately oriented to the child's learning and growth. Pedagogical intent is a certain bent already implicit in the parenting or teaching relationship that the adult maintains with the child. For example, a parent asks a child to go to the store to get some milk. For the first time unaccompanied, the young child proudly goes to the store and returns with the milk and the correct change. "Well done," the parent says. "I am so glad you went; we were completely out of milk." The practical purpose of the parent was to get some milk in the house, and as it turned out this little errand to the grocery story became an opportunity for the child to take a small step toward independence. Here pedagogical intent is built into the very relation of living together in a family.

Of course, it is entirely possible that some parents neglect, abuse, or exploit their "parental" relation by permitting children's inappropriate, damaging, or immoral behavior or by getting children to perform unhealthy tasks. But in the latter case we know that the pedagogical intent has been perverted and then we place the term "parental" in quotation marks since the very meaning of parenting is at issue here.

But in any case it is important to locate the primacy of pedagogical intent in the experience of parenting. Educators have not sufficiently reflected on the pedagogical roots of parenting. In other words, they have to reflect on the meaning of teaching as standing *in loco parentis* to children. Therefore, the teacher too needs to come to terms with the questions why have children? what is the meaning of children in his or her life?

Educational programs and objectives reflect in an obvious way the pedagogical intent of our teaching children. The books we offer children, the environments we create for them, the experiences we help make possible — all these may reflect our pedagogical intent. We like children to acquire literacy in mathematics, language, science, social studies, music, the creative arts. We want them to acquire positive attitudes, a critical spirit, basic honesty, moral fibre. Because we are concerned with the growth of children toward adult maturity, we translate our hopes for our children's development into realizable aims and expectations. The notion of pedagogical intent expresses the desire of adults that their children fare well in life. Even without specific behavioral learning objectives, the activities of teaching are governed by pedagogical intent. The teacher of English discusses the structure of lyric poetry so that the students may derive satisfaction from reading such poetic literature.

Of course, it is possible for the teacher to violate the pedagogical intent of the teaching-student relation, as in the case of a physical education teacher who begins to care more about a winning sports team than about the physical well-being and development of the young people the teacher coaches on the team. Moreover, not all pedagogical intents have pedagogical effects. As adults we should be mindful that it is easy to suffer from mixed motives in one's pedagogical relation to children. In everyday life it is hard sometimes to distinguish between pedagogical intent and motives which are somehow tangled up in our own being: our personal life histories, our frustrations, victories, secret wishes, ambitions, fears, insecurities, desires, hopes. As a parent, do I want my child to take music lessons because it is good for my child or because I am vicariously fulfilling an old dream of my own? As a teacher, am I a tough disciplinarian because I believe this form of discipline is required for good learning or because I am uncomfortable with a gentler relation to the students I teach?

Most adults will admit that the way they treat their children has something to do with the way they were brought up themselves. As parents or teachers we never escape the influence of our own parents or teachers. On the one hand, this is the positive relation of generativity: Through our parenting and teaching we leave something worthwhile of ourselves behind in our children. For example, my parents may have had a love for reading and so they instilled this love for the poetic into my orientation to life. On the other hand, this parental influence can have negative life consequences for the child: our "parenting" may leave our children with burdens and curses. For example, my father's heavy drinking may have left me with memories of family conflict and violence. The question is always what do we do with our childhood memories and with the modalities in which these memories have incarnated themselves in our corporeal being? In the negative case we reproduce the burden and curse into the lives of our own children. In the positive case we transform our personal problems into something valuable. For instance, my father's indulgence may have become a lesson for me to value self-discipline and moderation in the manner in which I live my life and in the ways in which I try to be an example for my own children. Parents and teachers must be able to understand what particular experiences are like for children. But adults cannot understand children if they do not understand their own childhood.

The person I am is partly constituted by my life memories. Past experiences have been consolidated in me such that memories may unexpectedly appear in changing situations and circumstances. The past may have been forgotten, but it may also suddenly confront us again when the past becomes relevant for the present. The power of childhood and life memory attests to the fact that we are historical beings — we have life histories that give permanence and identity to the person we are.

Our identities are composed of projects that we try to work

out when we tell stories about our encounters, accomplishments, adventures, failings, accidents. But, of course, life itself is not a story. Just like literary stories, the personal stories we tell each other have thematic structures and artificial ends. In contrast, our lives are complex, ongoing and incomplete. Many of our life histories cannot be integrated into a harmonious whole. Our identities are layered and laterally segmented. As an adult I am not the same as I was as a child or as an adolescent. At home I am not the same as at school or as among my friends. And yet, in spite of this polymorphic and changeable nature of personal identity we also experience a permanent self-sameness at the core of our being. This self-sameness gives continuity to our character. The child becomes a youth, the youth an adult, the adult an old person, but the influences from our youth, and especially the influences of parents and teachers leave their effects.

So the pedagogical intents of our parents and teachers which ruled our young lives now are implicated, in often complex ways, in the pedagogical intents we hold for our own children. We need to realize that pedagogical intents are not simply intellectual convictions or curriculum plans and learning objectives that we have committed to paper. Pedagogical intents are involved in all our active and reflective distinctions between what is good and what is not good for a child.

Of course, many of the pedagogical decisions we make in life are the result of careful reflection. But in everyday life we often tend to live out these pedagogical intents before we have become reflectively aware of them. When we interact as teachers or parents with children we may be oriented in a particular way that expresses the pedagogical intent of our relation with them. For example, I may deal with a child in a particular situation in a probing fashion (How can I let her realize more deeply the significance of what she has done?); or in an exploratory way (I have tried this, now I'll try that); or in a more routinized manner (I must stay calm — I usually have more impact on him by simply overlooking this sort of thing). Pedagogical intents are expressions not only of our theoretical philosophies of life but also of who and what we are, and how we actively and reflectively stand in the world. Sometimes the child is aware of the adult's intents even though the adult is inattentive to what he or she is expressing through bodily behavior, gesture, or vocal intonation. The fulfilling of our pedagogical intents is beyond our grasp in a sense. Our influence falls short on the one hand, and it reaches further then we would expect on the other.

The vocation of pedagogy animates and inspires us

When children call us
they call upon us.

How does a woman become a mother? a man a father? How does a person become a teacher? There are obvious and immediate differences between the way a woman and a man experience the birth of their child. The way that children enter the life of a teacher is different again. One does not become a parent simply by deciding to become a parent. Neither does one become a teacher the day one has decided to enter teacher's college. Neither the fact of pregnancy nor the miracle of birth is itself the sufficient condition to make a parent. Just so, the moment a teacher faces his or her first class does not suddenly make him or her a teacher.

Initially one may only "know" oneself to be a parent or a teacher in a biological or legal sense. It is not unusual for a mother or a father to feel confused, to experience mixed emotions at the birth of the child. Similarly, the new teacher may not feel like a full teacher for some time yet. Rather, what makes a person a parent or a teacher is largely a matter of living and existing as a parent or teacher. In actually living with children, in its many small experiences, the awareness of oneself as a parent or teacher comes into being.

The experience of birth is often a profoundly moving experience for the woman and for the man — now she is the mother, now he is the father of this child. But to be a mother or a father one has to live as a mother or a father. And then, often quite gradually, the full measure of one's pedagogical being unfolds and makes itself felt in one's life. The point of this observation is that the common notion that one "decides" to be a teacher is probably just as inaccurate, experientially speaking, as the idea that one becomes a parent by "choice." Often parents find to their amazement that the transforming effect of children on their lives is much more profound than they had anticipated. Friends often say to new parents: "Your lives will never be the same again!" This may be true for beginning teachers as well. To the extent that they begin to live and act as real teachers with children, they may be touched by them in ways that they could not foresee. It is in this sense that we speak of teaching as a true vocation.

In present-day life, even in educational discourse, we do not hear people easily express themselves about education, teaching, or pedagogy as a "vocation" or as a "calling." Significantly, it is much more acceptable for someone to refer to teaching as a calling by means of a negative statement, by saying, for example, "I quit education because teaching is not really my calling." Yet, it may be important to realize that our lives with children will only be pedagogically meaningful when we feel animated or inspired by education as a calling. Interestingly, pedagogy is a vocation not just in a symbolic or transcendental sense. There is something about children that animates and draws us to them in a very concrete way.

Is it not amazing how, as a new parent, one becomes attuned to the sounds from the baby's room? Even parents with older or grown-up children will remember this. Even though the noisy conversation of guests may be all around me, I can hear my child stir in his crib in the distant bedroom. But what do I really hear? Crying? Calling? Does the sound of crying make me rush? Certainly, I may hear my child cry or call. But that is not "deeply" what I hear, when I say, "I hear my child awakening in her crib." There is something more fundamental that we hear in the child's calling. It is experienced as a certain power. It is the power this child has over one who can "hear."

Of course, it is not enough just to listen passively or indifferently to one's child calling or crying. The parent must heed the calling and act on it in some appropriate way. After all, being a parent means that one is protective and nurturing toward one's child. Being a parent means that one has a calling in life — a pedagogical calling. And similarly, being a child means being with someone who hears and heeds the "calling" that gathers this child and this parent into connectedness, into oneness. The pedagogical calling is that which calls, summons us to listen to the child's needs. The term "vocation" too carries the etymological meaning of calling *(vocare)*. Wherein lies hearing the calling?

As I listen again I do not hear anything. No crying. No fussing. My son has apparently gone back to sleep. I decide to make sure and check on him. As I quietly push the door open a bit I know how he will lie there. Snuggled up, peacefully I bet, in the corner of his crib. But what I do see is a face fully turned upward in surprised anticipation. A radiant smile, arms stretched out. There he stands! Not a word, not a sound. But how full of calling is this silence!

"So there you are, my little boy!" As I pull my child out of his crib toward me, am I aware of the calling of parenting? As I begin to undo the diaper to assess the "damage" I don't reflect on all of this. He and I, we are too busy with one another to permit the indulgence of such reflection. But now, as I attempt to recapture in writing the meaning of this experience, I do not doubt that at that time I knew the presence of something that was real and not difficult to recall.

But what is it that I call forth once again? Is it simply the feeling of deep affection for my child that I wish to recall? Possibly. But to name what is thus recalled *affection* or *love* is not really bringing anything to light. These terms both say too much and too little. What I recall of the experience of what it means to be a parent is itself a calling: A vocation calls. We speak of the "calling of a profession." But wherein lies this calling? We say, "the call of duty." "Duty calls with the voice of conscience." "Duty calls me to a task to which I know myself committed." But duty is not really something that calls. Rather, duty is the way something calls, just as care and affection called me to my child's bedroom.

How then is this calling experienced? Is it something that I can hear and yet turn away from, as some "parent" might do? But are such so-called parents real parents? What about a baby-sitter, a person who looks after children because it is a job rather than a calling? How would a disinterested baby-sitter have walked into my child's bedroom? How would the baby-sitter have greeted his reaching hands? Would this person hear the "calling" in a child's calling? For those who are deaf to the calling, reflecting on pedagogy as a vocation is just sentimental nonsense, or at best a useless exercise.

In his "Bearhug" poem, Ondaatje[19] describes how his child

from the bedroom has been calling him for a goodnight kiss. The father yells "Okay, I'm coming." But he was finishing something and then does this and that before he finally responds to the child's calling. As Ondaatje slowly walks through the bedroom door he sees his little boy: "He is standing arms outstretched waiting for a bearhug. Grinning." Ondaatje gives a marvelous poetic description of the way a parent hugs a child. But then, almost as an after-thought, two short lines end the poem:

> How long was he standing there
> like that, before I came?

In this wondering we detect the fundamental relation of pedagogical acting and reflecting. In life we continually act and interact with our children, but every now and then we do something that prompts us to wonder and reflect: Did I do that right? What was this situation like for the child? What was my responsibility here? What should I have said or done? Thus, pedagogy first calls upon us to act and afterwards it calls upon us to reflect upon our actions. Both living with children as well as reflecting on the ways we live with children are manifestations of our pedagogical being.

About the Idea of "Pedagogy"

There are differences
that make a difference.

Why should we use the term *pedagogy* in this text? Why do we not use terminology more common to Anglo-Saxon educational discourse, such as "curriculum," "education," "teaching," or "instruction"?

First, I like to use the word *pedagogy* to bypass a whole common array of assumptions and criteria for approaching questions of education. If we restrict ourselves to the usual terminology, we find ourselves encapsulated by ways of viewing phenomena of educating and bringing up children that restrict us to certain traditional questions. This is not to suggest, of course, that the more generally accepted concerns of educational thinking and theorizing are irrelevant and not worth considering. I simply want to use the concept of pedagogy as a key to unlock other phenomena of educational reality (such as pedagogical understanding, pedagogical tact, pedagogical situations and relationships) that are not commonly addressed in the North American educational literature.

The word *pedagogy* has recently come into wider usage, but the distinctive meaning of the term has been covered over and blurred rather than explored and articulated. Pedagogy is now increasingly equated, arbitrarily and vaguely, with teaching, instruction, or curriculum. And pedagogy is used to refer to specific approaches or methodologies in the literature on curriculum and teaching. For example one speaks now of a new "language arts pedagogy" and a "writing pedagogy" to describe curriculum innovations in those areas.

The term *pedagogy* is also linked to political programs, with feminist and other philosophical movements — thus there has been an explosion of references to concepts such as *critical pedagogy, emancipatory pedagogy, deconstructionist pedagogy,* and so forth. How does the notion of pedagogy differ from these specific categories? Very briefly I will comment on the different imports of the current dominant concepts.

Education is a complex concept, to be sure, and its various meanings and significances overlap with the notion of *pedagogy.* Both education and pedagogy are normative concepts. However, the term *education* in North America is mainly employed to refer to the teaching and learning of children and adults in institutionalized settings such as schools, colleges, and universities. In German and Dutch, the term *education* translates into *Erziehung* and *onderwijs,* respectively. In those languages pedagogy stakes out a wider domain of meaning. The European notion of pedagogy has a somewhat different emphasis, and includes the domains of parenting and education in general, as well as the specialized fields of counselling, therapy, psychological referrals, aspects of social work, and so forth. In other words, pedagogy describes all those affairs where adults are living with children for the sake of those children's well-being, growth, maturity, and development. Naturally, pedagogy includes school learning.

Curriculum is a notoriously ambiguous term. For many parents and teachers it simply refers to the courses of study which children can take at school. But the scholarly field of curriculum studies is extremely varied, including such interests as policy studies, curriculum evaluation, the hidden curriculum, and curriculum development, but also political, descriptive, and ethnographic studies of curricular phenomena and school realities, as well as other social and human science approaches.

An immediate difference between the notions of curriculum and pedagogy is that the former tends to focus on the stuff of education and on the organization, management, planning, structuring, selecting, justifying, and programming of subject matters and teaching/learning processes. There remains an inevitable positivistic flavor to the idea of curriculum (which is not meant as a condemnation). The term *curriculum* tends to orient us away from the young person toward the structures and phases of study at an educational institution. The term *pedagogy* by contrast tends to bring out the human or personalistic elements of education and childrearing.

"Instruction" is often mentioned in the same breath as "curriculum." At many schools of education the main so-called teaching departments are "Curriculum and Instruction." This designation is also used to describe the various course offerings in the different subject matter disciplines. The classic primer in curriculum and instruction is Ralph Tyler's famous *Basic Principles of Curriculum and Instruction*, which offers a model for curriculum development and instructional planning. *Instruction* is a more impersonal, less subjective term than *teaching*. It diverts our attention away from the personal human element in education. We might say that computers instruct, but people teach.

The use of *instruction* suggests a desire to stick to the more systematic, classifiable, and measurable interactions and interventions that educators use to implement the curriculum. "Curriculum and instruction" often imply a view of educating children that is a "producing" of planned teaching/learning outcomes and other educational objectives. Thus the language of curriculum and instruction tends to be biased toward those conceptualizations of educational problems and issues which assume that we can "make" children learn something and that particular curriculum organization and instructional procedures are more effective in this process than others.

"Teaching" is another category that appears to be related to the notion of pedagogy. Again, one difference is that pedagogy describes a wider domain of adult-child relations than teaching. The term *teaching* is usually applied to more formal influence in school teaching or in church teaching of religion. The term *teaching* is less commonly applied to parenting and other influences by adults on children.

Sometimes teaching is referred to as the content of the relation between a learner and some aspect of the environment. For example, bumping my head against something teaches me to be more careful next time. Or a bird may teach me something about the beauty of a song. In contrast, the notion of pedagogy always assumes that there exists a personal learning relationship between people, usually between an adult and a child.

Pedagogy is a useful term precisely because its currency in North America is still fairly rare. The *Oxford* dictionary says that in the English language the word "pedagogy" has pedantic overtones. So be it. I will adopt the word "pedagogy" here to avoid and possibly correct two dangers of the contemporary discourse in education: (1) to restore a forgotten or absent relation between adults and children, and (2) to remove some of the barriers that prevent "educational" thought from being truly educational.

Many educators, teachers and parents, are becoming aware that something has come between us and children. This is not to say that throughout history there have not been generation gaps and barriers between the worlds of adults and children. But our modern predicament is that the resources of educational theory and thought that were supposed to overcome those barriers have themselves become obstacles preventing appropriate educational relations between adults and children. So *pedagogy* is not just a term that we should use to say the same thing differently. Through the notion of pedagogy we should try to further our understanding of what is essential to the excellence of our educational lives with children.

Pedagogy orients us to the child

Pedagogy is the excellence
of teaching.

We may define *pedagogy* as a certain encounter of togetherness between parent and child, teacher and pupil, between grandmother and grandchild — in short, a relationship of practical action between an adult and a young person who is on the way to adulthood. But not all social encounters between adults and children are pedagogical. Sometimes we see parents or teachers who seem grossly inadequate, incapable, negligent, or even abusive toward the children entrusted to their care. We can see this in parents who seem to care more for the growth of their business or personal career than for the growth of their children. Or the parents who, unable to cope with the disappointments and stresses of life, take their frustrations out on their children. Or the teacher who is more interested in the scholarly developments of the knowledge he or she teaches than in the educational developments of the children for whom the teaching was intended.

How should we judge whether in a particular situation a teacher or parent interacts with a child in a manner that we could call "pedagogical?" If we set out to devise objective criteria for sorting the pedagogical from the nonpedagogical, we might soon be involved more with philosophy, politics, or theories of education than with the phenomenon of pedagogy itself. Pedagogy is ultimately a practical affair. Pedagogy must be found, not in abstract theoretical discourse or analytic systems, but right in the lived world, where the newly born is first held and gazed at by the new mother, where a father quietly restrains the child from blindly crossing the street, where the teacher winks at a pupil in acknowledgment of a task well done.

So *pedagogy* is not just a word. By naming that which directs us and draws us caringly to children, the word *pedagogy* brings something into being. Pedagogy is found not in observational categories, but like love or friendship in the experience of its presence — that is, in concrete, real-life situations. It is here and here and here, where an adult does something right in the personal development of a child. Regardless of what we think parents or teachers do precisely, pedagogy is cemented deep in the nature of the relationship between adults and children. In this sense, pedagogy is defined not only as a certain relationship or a way of doing, but also pedagogy lets an encounter, a relationship, a situation, or an activity be pedagogical.

All our pedagogical being with children is a form of speaking with them. Even when we quietly listen, raise eyebrows, nod encouragingly, embrace, turn away, or hold a child's momentary attention with a meaningful look, we may do so out of a pedagogical concern. In everyday situations where we speak with children, pedagogy occurs in the way we are with children.

Naturally there are technical aspects to pedagogical acting. Some teachers excel more than others at this craft of pedagogy — how to tell a captivating story; how to give a memorable lecture; how to conduct a critically reflective group discussion. Yet the essence of pedagogy is not this craft. In everyday language we may indeed speak of a teacher as being outstanding. But it is inappropriate to speak of excellent pedagogy, since pedagogy itself is already an excellence. In Aristotle's words, pedagogy is a "good" or a "virtue." Every educator must possess this excellence.

A teacher or a parent who lacks excellence lacks pedagogy. In other words, pedagogy may be defined as the "excellence of teaching or parenting" because it helps us to identify the essence of true child rearing and teaching. It orients us to the value, meaning, and nature of teaching and parenting. More pointedly pedagogy orients us (teachers, parents, counsellors, etc.) to the child, to the child's immanent nature of being and becoming.

Yet it is important as well to realize that a child's development, for better or worse, is a consequence not only of our pedagogical actions. There are many factors which influence a child's growing toward mature adulthood. Educators (parents and teachers) need to realize that their task is momentous, yet limited. We easily overestimate the influence we may have over children. But perhaps, just because our pedagogical influence is limited, we need to take it more seriously.

Pedagogy orients us to children, but in a manner different from the way that we may be interested in some object of curiosity or scientific significance. What motivates our pedagogical interest in children? Some people study or teach children simply because "children are so interesting!" And it is true that one may become a teacher, a psychologist, or an ethnographer of childhood and children's cultures because one is interested in children in the same manner that one may be interested in the astronomical puzzle of black holes or in the biological enigma of bee behavior.

It is not difficult to understand such intrinsic interest: the entymologist is oriented to the world of insects by a fundamental fascination, the astronomer to the stars because he or she is filled with wonder or curiosity about their nature. And ultimately the entymologist may feel close to unravelling the mystery of life, and the astronomer may come face to face with the meaning of origins, singularity, the infinite, even with the place of God in the universe.[20] No doubt some social scientists too cherish similar inquisitive interest in the nature of child behavior and development. Such interests can be deeply satisfying in a personal as well as in a scientific sense.

But what motivates a pedagogical interest in children? The satisfaction of pedagogy does not lie primarily in some intrinsic scientific curiosity, but rather in interest in the child's growth for the sake of the child. Or, to say it somewhat differently, my pedagogical orientation to children is animated, not by the "disinterested" attitude of "objective" science, but instead by my love or concern for children. And naturally, out of this pedagogical interest may spring questions regarding theories of child development or approaches to teaching.

Pedagogy is concerned with the child's self and development

The child's becoming
is a coming to be.

The proverb says that one is never too old to learn. Growth remains a human possibility throughout life. An adult can give new shape and direction to his or her being or identity at any age. For a child as well as for an adult self-knowledge is not so much an introspective process as a process of becoming. We learn to know who we "really" are when we become who we really are. And growing up is in many respects an active process of desiring, preferring, choosing, or tending toward some things rather than to others. We may notice this growth in a new relationship, a changed way of looking at things, different connections, altered affinities, the pursuit of an exciting idea, critique of established notions, distancing from what was close and familiar, or the support of a new cause. In other words, growth is visible in the new relations we establish to the world outside and inside of us. This growth may manifest itself through all the expressive media of the person's being: language and voice, intonation and facial expression, demeanor and gesture, ways of moving and walking, manner of dress and self-presentation. We see such changes of self occurring in adults who may have experienced a crisis or turning point in their career or life style, their religious or philosophical awareness, their marriage, their health or age.

However, in the child growth and learning are less a matter of a change of self than of a formation of self. The child is a human coming into being, "be-coming." And this emergence of self is tied to the special character of the world of the child. Even the young child is of course not a tabula rasa. Teachers are becoming more aware that what the child brings to school in knowledge, emotions, interests, feelings, skills, and understandings must be connected to what the child learns in school. But unlike the adult, the child has not yet developed a full complex of relations to the world. It is still not fully determined what understandings, habits, outlooks, tolerances and intolerances, views, moods, feelings, morals, idiosyncracies the child will develop. Will this young person become sensitive or hard, flexible or rigid, altruistic or egocentric, influential or powerless, healthy or disturbed, well-balanced or neurotic? Will the growing child experience himself or herself as a success or a failure, as productive or useless, as effective or ineffectual, as daring or cautious in human relations and in life? Will this growing person learn to enjoy to read books, appreciate music, maintain friendships, fight injustice, work with people, value education, write poetry, be active in politics, protect the environment, care for children? There is still an openness as to what kind of person this young person may become. And it is with respect to the question of this possibility and development of self that pedagogy finds its meaning.

Of course, for the educator the question is, what will I mean in this child's life? What will my part be in this child's development? A young child usually stands in a very close relation to one or both parents. This is true especially in those family environments where the child experiences a profound shelteredness, security, trust. This inward-directed emotional climate of intimacy sponsors outgoing interests, curiosity, risk, and independence in the child. Especially because the child experiences the benefit of intimacy and caring, it can seek and assert its own growing identity. Schools too need to offer young people a caring and supportive environment, not only because caring teachers and caring schools tend to reproduce a caring orientation in the students themselves, but also because a caring school climate sponsors the conditions for personal growth itself.

In the very young child the fundamental emotional affinity to the parent is so strong that the child tends to learn from its parents by becoming as like them as possible. This is not necessarily because young children experience themselves as undifferentiated from their parents (as older theories of child development asserted). The child is already a separate being. But the very young child stands in an affective sensual relation to the parent that is symbiotic, and thus quite different from, for example, the relation between the older adolescent and his or her parent or teacher. The very young child associates and identifies with the parent in a manner that is spontaneous, unmediated, involuntary. The child is as it were "overcome" by the parents.

As an adult, I embody possibilities, serving as examples for the child. Almost from the start I see the child trying on my gestures, my ways of seeing and doing things, my ways of reacting, my ways of spending time. As I see myself reflected in the child I am confronted by my own doubts. Is this the way I want my child to act and be? If not, is it the way I want myself to act and be? Soon I also see my child adopting or trying on ways of being and acting that seem to belong entirely to this child. The child is becoming a person in his or her own right, different from me.

Older children tend to stand in a more distant relation to adults. They may identify with a special teacher or an admired person by wanting to be like this person. A child who learns from others by imitating them is involved in a more voluntaristic manner in developing a personal identity. Similarly, an adolescent developing a sense of self by wanting to be unlike his or her father or mother is involved in a willing process of redefining self, re-identifying personal identity.

But in either case, the child may become my teacher. As the child tries on new possibilities through imitation and creation, I am reminded of the possibilities still open to myself. The child teaches me that as an adult I too can grow, that there are possibilities of living life differently. As I see my child grow I am given the opportunity to ask myself about the meaning of growth. Is all growth for the good? Is growth necessarily cumulative? Can growth sometimes mean that I have to unlearn something, that I may need to forget certain attitudes and behaviors? It is important to see that the child has a purer openness than the adult. The adult has already become a person with many habits, beliefs, values, feelings, and a history and memory of experiences. If, as adults, we want to try on new modes, to make something different of ourselves, to gain new perspectives, then we may first have to unlearn, unmake ourselves, or integrate new outlooks with our present deeply rooted views.

3 THE PEDAGOGICAL MOMENT

The Pedagogical Moment Expects
Something of the Adult

It is hard not to act,
but it is easy not to educate.[21]

Often, when professional educators employ the word *pedagogy* they use it to refer simply to teaching, and that is how the dictionary defines it. But the term *pedagogue* derives from the Greek, and refers not to the teacher, but to the watchful slave or guardian whose responsibility it was to lead (*agogos*) the young boy (*paides*) to school. Why did the Greeks refer to the task of accompanying the boy as *pedagogy* while distinguishing it from teaching? Are we wrong to equate teaching with pedagogy? Or does this question matter?

It is helpful to reflect on the term *leading* (*agogos*) in this respect. In a literal sense the Greek pedagogue had to lead the way to show the child how to get to school and get back home. But, of course, there would also have been a richer sense to this notion of leading. The adult had the task of accompanying the child, of being with the child, of caring for the child. The pedagogue would be expected to see to it that the child stayed out of trouble and behaved properly. This is a kind of "leading" that often walks *behind* the one who is led. The slave, or pedagogue, was there *in loco parentis*. This task we have assigned in large part to the professional educators at school — the teacher, the principal, the school psychologist, and the others. In this sense, pedagogy is something that was and is at the very core of the adults' relationship to the child.

Of course, we do not like to be reminded of the image of slavery, and in many ways our concept of society, of school and of childhood is different from those of the ancient Greeks. But to see that in the adult-child relation the adult provides a sense of protection, direction and orientation for the child's life is to invest the notion of pedagogy with a significance that still deserves our attention. The original Greek idea of pedagogy has associated with it the meaning of *leading* in the sense of accompanying the child and living with the child in such a way as to provide direction and care for his or her life.

Thus, from an etymological point of view, a pedagogue is a man or woman who stands in a caring relation to children: In the idea of leading or guiding there is a "taking by the hand," in the sense of watchful encouragements. "Here, take my hand!" "Come, I shall show you the world. The way into a world, my world, and yours. I know something about being a child, because I have been there, where you are now. I was young once."

But one must eventually grow out of (*educere:* to lead out of) the world of childhood. My world of adulthood becomes an invitation, a beckoning to the child (*educare:* to lead into).[22] Leading means going first, and in going first you can trust me, for I have tested the ice. I have lived. I now know something of the rewards as well as the trappings of growing towards adulthood and making a world for yourself. Although my going first is no guarantee of success for you (because the world is not without risks and dangers), in the pedagogical relationship there is a more fundamental guarantee: No matter what, I am here. And you can count on me.

In this sense, the significance of pedagogy is more fundamental even than the reference to its Greek origin. Giving children direction, care, and protection is a fundamental feature of adult life. It is hard to imagine a human society where children have not lived in some pedagogical relation to their elders — most commonly to their mother, father, and other family relations and friends at first, and also to teachers and to other significant adults. But rather than slide into abstract speculation about pedagogy as living with children, let us sketch a series of situations that are potential instances of pedagogical life we might recognize in our own everyday experience:

• Sandra has completed her work and she hands it with visible pride to her teacher.

- While reading out loud during the class reading lesson, Billy mispronounces several words.
- Stephanie suggests to her teacher that the class goes outside for physical education rather than have physical education in the gym.
- Michael asks his grandma, "Will you play this board game with me?"
- After introducing a new concept and assigning an exercise, the teacher notices that, again, Jimmy does not know what to do.
- Anton comes home from his first day in grade two and announces to his parents that he "hates" his teacher.
- Jane says to her father, "I do not want to hurt your feelings asking you this, but ... from now on would you and Mom mind knocking on my door first when you want to enter my bedroom?"
- Emmy fails to understand when the teacher is trying to get something new across to the students.
- Sue complains that Jack broke her pencil.
- Rob refuses to participate in the science lesson since he feels repugnance toward killing a living creature and dissecting it.
- All the children are applying themselves to their work in class, but David does not seem to be able to concentrate.
- The parents are worried because it is late at night and Willy complains that he has trouble falling asleep again.
- The teacher notices that Kenny has been untruthful again about completing his school assignment.
- The teacher has captured the attention of most children in the class, but Ben just does not seem to be interested.
- The teacher is generally happy with the behavior of the children in her class but Jerry has picked a fight with another child again.
- Kim is eight years old and she has wet her bed again.
- After ten years of lessons, Erin announces that she no longer wants to take music lessons or practice the violin.
- Chen has written poetry at school that is so powerful that it deeply stirs the teacher.
- Mary is in tears; she comes to the homeroom teacher and confides that she feels nobody in the class likes her.
- Mother discovers that her seven-year-old son John has taken money from her purse.

- The teacher notices how Allan takes time to buddy around with Keith after other kids have been teasing Keith and leaving him out of their games.
- Sook asks his mom if he can go to a movie, that many of his friends have seen, even though the movie has been rated unsuitable for children.
- By spring most children in grade two have gained some proficiency in reading but Chris seems to have made no progress whatsoever.
- Matthew is a ninth-grade student; the homeroom teacher is concerned that her colleagues have written him off because he is difficult and unwilling to make an effort in school.

We could go on indefinitely drawing pedagogically challenging examples from everyday life. But what constitutes the pedagogical nature of each instance? Let us first notice that each situation is pedagogically charged because something is expected of the adult, the parent or the teacher. In each situation an action is required even if that action may be non-action. That active encounter is the pedagogical moment. In other words, a pedagogical situation is the site of everyday pedagogical action, everyday pedagogical practice. The pedagogical moment is located at the center of that praxis.

Notice that in our daily living with children we often must act on the spur of the moment. The usual case is that we do not have time to sit back and deliberate on what to do in the situation. And even when there is time to reflect on the alternatives and what the best approach is for one to take, in the pedagogical moment itself one must act, even if that action may consist in holding back.

Of course, in the cases sketched above the pedagogical moments have yet to be fulfilled. For the pedagogical situation to bear a pedagogical moment, the adult must do something pedagogically right in his or her relation with some child or children. In other words, in each situation the adult must show, in actions, what is good (and exclude what is not good) for this young person.

The pedagogical moment is the critical concept in our pedagogical interest in children. We must give priority to the practical pedagogical situation because it is this pedagogical life, this living with children, that is a fundamental human fulfillment, a *telos;* and it is this pedagogical life that is the *raison d'être* of all talk about pedagogy. So we must make a distinction between two kinds of pedagogical practices: (1) actively living through pedagogical experiences, and (2) reflectively talking or writing about these experiences.

Thus, pedagogy first of all refers to our everyday living with children as parents, teachers, school principals, guidance counsellors, educational psychologists, child care workers, and so on. And pedagogy refers to our need to reflect on our pedagogical living with children. There is value in this pedagogical reflection and everyday theorizing. Pedagogical reflection is oriented toward understanding the pedagogical significance of events and situations in children's lives. It is oriented toward understanding the pedagogical goodness[23] of one's own or others' past actions with respect to the lives of these children.

The question is, however, how do teachers or parents act in these various kinds of pedagogical situations? On what basis should they act? From what knowledge does one act? What is the pedagogical element in this? These questions are the basis for this entire text, but we should first examine the common answers that such questions elicit.

Those who see education as essentially a scientific field of study may argue that most important are the basic facts and empirical knowledge produced by scientific inquiry into how children learn, and into the conditions that hinder or contribute to the processes of child development. Others who consider education primarily a moral endeavor may believe that basic values, goals, norms, and principles are fundamental for pedagogical acting, the determination of which values are important is an ethical, political, or communal enterprise. A third answer may be provided by those who see the success of pedagogical activity mainly as a function of the instructional and curricular methods and methodologies that guide the process of teaching the various subject matters and of managing classroom routines. Parents too can consult a number of self-help books that provide approaches for dealing with children at home (for example, methods of dealing with discipline, bedwetting, sibling rivalry, adolescent conflict, and so forth). And, finally, there is the perspective that argues that a person's pedagogical acting really depends on a philoso-

phy of life, of education and of human nature. Probably all these
views are in some sense correct: Factual knowledge, norms,
knowledge of teaching methods, and philosophical orientation all
are implicated in pedagogical acting. We shall review all of these
answers.

Facts and values are important for knowing how to act pedagogically

First, knowing how to act pedagogically in a specific situation
involves empirical knowledge and a sense of values, norms, or
moral principles. Broadly speaking teachers must have factual
information (for example, these students do not appear to know
their times tables) as well as a normative standard (for example,
grade six students should know their times tables by heart). It is
generally assumed that teachers plan their lessons and decide
what they will include in the curriculum on empirical and normative grounds. However, in life as well as in theory the relation
between facts and values in educational programs and practices
is complex. Educating children is neither simply the outcome of
an inductive process of empirically observing and describing
what children do and can(not) do, nor is education simply the
result of a deductive process of determining and prescribing
from general norms and principles what children should learn.[24]
Facts and values, neither in isolation by themselves nor in combination as empirical knowledge to which norms and values are
appended, yield educational theory or pedagogical practice.
While facts and values are important, the essence of pedagogy
and of acting in the pedagogical moment still lies somewhere
else.

(1) There are always empirical aspects to pedagogy, ascer-
taining the "facts" of a situation. Of course, these so-called facts
commonly involve interpretive judgments. They often include or
imply evaluative judgments. For example, we know from reading
specialists that with effort on the part of parents or teachers
many preschoolers are able to learn to read at a very early age.
Children can be early readers ... but should they therefore learn
to read at an increasingly early age? Conversely, we know that
many children have difficulty with advanced mathematical concepts in school. Some children seem unable to learn certain
skills ... but should we therefore refrain from trying to teach

them these difficult ideas and skills? Bruner once made the provocative but educationally powerful suggestion that almost anything can be taught to children at any age in some simplified but intellectually honest manner.[25] It would be very difficult to state in general terms what knowledge, values, skills, and feelings children of a given age cannot yet deal with. In the specific case, however, we have to make judgments about what children can/ should deal with. But it seems clear that because children can do certain things does not imply that they should therefore learn them — *should* does not follow from *can*! Similarly, just because children cannot do certain things does not imply that they should not try to learn these things — *should not* does not follow from *cannot*![26]

Let us look at the case of Matthew. Matthew is a difficult student and unwilling to make an effort in school. Matthew's homeroom teacher feels that her professional responsibility has been called on. She must do something about Matthew. On what basis would she or could she act in some pedagogically meaningful manner? Some factual information might require consulting the school psychologist or a social worker. For example, Matthew is from an underprivileged home. He has low academic self-esteem. His reading skills are inadequate. Matthew's parents show little interest in his school success or failure. Yet teachers believe that Matthew is intelligent. Tests show that he has been achieving below his ability. Usually, on the basis of such diagnostic empirical information, some recommendations for action are provided. The school psychologist might recommend a counselling program for Matthew. The school principal might recommend some system for monitoring Matthew's school attendance. The social worker might suggest a series of family visits. What is the teacher to do? Today she has Matthew in her class. Should she ask him to stay for a chat? What should she say? What would be appropriate in this situation? Does it not also depend on the kind of person Matthew is? How should the teacher involve Matthew? How should she approach Matthew?

(2) There is also always an ethical-moral aspect to pedagogy. Pedagogical action assumes that one tries to distinguish between what is good and what is not good for the child. For this reason the study and practice of pedagogy can never be "objective" in a scientific sense. Parenting or teaching children always involves value judgments. But sometimes these values are so

embedded in the culture and everyday life that they are hardly recognized.

For example, in the case of Matthew above, his homeroom teacher is concerned that Matthew misses too much school and that he may soon drop out. She feels that he might forego a high school diploma and thus narrow his choices in life. Obviously the teacher is making value judgments here. One is that formal schooling is important for children. Another, that finishing school is important for Matthew. Some of her colleagues argue that one should not try to keep adolescents at school against their wishes. Value positions are also implied in the various recommendations of the specialists: the psychologist, the social worker, the administrator.

But in pedagogical moments neither facts nor values can tell us what to do

Both empirical knowledge and ethical-moral principles are important in pedagogy; it cannot do without them. Yet the essence of pedagogy is neither. The pedagogical moment is the concrete and practical response to the question, What to do here? Dealing with the child in the specific situation is the essence of pedagogy. The question of "What to do?" cannot be inductively derived from the "facts." For example, the factual observation, "These students do not know the times tables" is not in itself sufficient to tell this teacher how to act during the next math lesson. Will the teacher assign the times tables immediately for homework? Will the teacher talk about the importance of knowing the times tables? Will the teacher practise a certain math drill in class? What exactly will the teacher say and do?

In Matthew's case the teacher knows many empirical facts about Matthew's circumstances, but these alone cannot tell her what to do. Similarly, the teacher is aware of various value positions regarding Matthew's situation. She herself holds certain moral values about the importance of education in a child's life. Yet the teacher's actions with respect to Matthew cannot be derived deductively from her ethical-moral principles about the value of school or formal education. Even if the teacher were convinced that the right course of action was to keep Matthew in school, then she might still wonder about actually what to do. In what way is Matthew at present part of the school? Should she talk to Matthew informally? Should she involve other teachers? Should she try to influence Matthew more indirectly?

Method and philosophy are important for knowing how to act pedagogically

Next, there is the tendency to define pedagogy only from the point of view of methods and of curriculum programs or educational philosophies. This tendency confuses pedagogy with certain teaching approaches or with programs of dealing with the behavior of children or of organizing knowledge for teaching. Of course, being well-versed in teaching methods and programs is an important resource for pedagogy. But, just as in the case of empirical knowledge and moral principles, action in the pedagogical moment is neither derived directly from some teaching method nor from some educational program or philosophy.

Let us look at the earlier case of Chris as an example. It is spring, but unlike the other children in grade two, Chris has made no discernable progress with reading. Here again, we speak of a pedagogical situation because the teacher and the parents feel that something must be done.

(3) Good teachers have learned many skills, techniques, and methods for helping children learn and for teaching children certain subject matter knowledge, values and skills. To a large extent what teachers learn in teachers' colleges in their courses dealing with curriculum and teaching is method-oriented: how to manage classroom routines, how to plan curriculum programs, how to motivate students, how to introduce new concepts, how to deal with the logical structures of certain subjects in a psychologically appropriate manner, how to diagnose learning difficulties, how to test school achievement in the various content areas, and so forth. Methods are pedagogically loaded. For example, a good science or language arts program can broaden a teacher's pedagogical perspective and resourcefulness. But the use of simple teaching techniques is usually more helpful for guiding the practice of teaching than it is a guide to increase one's understanding of what one does and what one has done.

So pedagogy is concerned with method. It may involve inquiring how Chris was learning to read — using a whole-word method, a linguistic approach, a phonics method, a combination of these. A reading expert might suggest trying a different approach with Chris. There may be advice to the parents about what to do at home with language, stories, and books. The parents may be complaining that Chris resists reading at home and they wonder if the reading specialist understands how difficult it is at home to turn Chris toward any form of reading. These are all method questions.

(4) Pedagogy is also concerned with philosophical considerations. There is merit in considering the larger philosophical perspective within which the education of a child is occurring. Chris's parents may have begun considering alternative programs. They have learned that another school with a basic skills program is very successful with its students in reading. Another parent tells them about a school where there is an excellent teacher who uses a creative whole-language program to stimulate reading-writing-oral language skills. And they are aware of a Montessori school that offers a more individualized self-activated reading program; and of a Waldorf school that adopts a flexible and organic program approach to reading.

Each program is based on a fundamentally different philosophy of education; each articulates different priorities in educating and bringing up children. So much conflicting advice! What are the parents or teacher to do? And if they come to some conclusions about a preferred course of action, how should they talk to Chris?

But in pedagogical moments neither methods nor philosophy can tell us what to do

Does the knowledge of various teaching-learning methods or different educational programs tell a teacher or parent what is good for Chris? No methods and programs in themselves can tell us what to do. They can stimulate our pedagogical thoughtfulness, but they cannot tell us what is good for Chris. And does Chris have a voice in the matter? Chris does not want to leave his friends at school. He would be upset repeating grade one and seeing classroom friends move on. Both methodological and program considerations are important for pedagogy, but the essence of pedagogy does not reside in either the method or the program.

In other words, the pedagogical moment cannot be derived technically from methods or from theories of reading, and it cannot be inferred philosophically from approaches associated with broader perspectives on education or child-rearing.

As we saw above, the essence of pedagogy manifests itself in the practical moment of a concrete situation. Theoretical knowledge and diagnostic information do not automatically lead to appropriate pedagogical action. In part, this may explain the fact that psychologists or other specialists may be able to provide much information about a youngster like Matthew, but such specialists may be at a loss in dealing with the child. Similarly, reading theorists or educational specialists may seem very helpful for reading methods or philosophies of education, while in concrete situations they may appear to be pedagogically quite awkward and incapable in actually doing something with Chris.

Let us look at another example. Mother discovers that her seven-year-old son John has been taking money from her purse. She is quite convinced that it was John who took the money, and she has strong moral feelings against stealing. But this still does not tell her what to do right now with John. Perhaps she will read some books on child rearing which give advice about children who steal. Would the advice suit the particular circumstances of this mother and her son John? Does John feel that he is stealing? What does taking money from his mom's purse mean to this boy?

What this really means is that we need to distinguish between pedagogy and other disciplines that may contribute to pedagogy but which should not be confused with pedagogy. Knowledge necessary for pedagogical action needs to be situation-specific and oriented to the particular child with whom we are concerned. In other words, pedagogy is context sensitive. In these sketches of everyday pedagogical situations, we needed to fill in the context in order to make the situations pedagogically meaningful and comprehensible. So, let us now take a different focus and consider some life stories that may prompt us to pedagogical reflection and interpretation.

Pedagogy Is Sensitive to the Context of Life Stories

Life stories prompt pedagogical
reflection.

Pedagogy as a discipline is always concerned with the question
of what one should know, what one should be capable of, what
kind of person one should be, in order to orient and deal practically with children in specific pedagogical situations. The problem is that it is usually quite impossible to deal with specific
pedagogical relations unless one has some understanding of the
context of the pedagogical moments in those situations. Teachers
who are pedagogically sensitive to children also tend to be sensitive to the backgrounds, the life-histories of the children, and
the particular qualities and circumstances of the children for
whom they have responsibility.

Here follow some anecdotes that teachers tell about their
children and about their lives as teachers with children. These
anecdotes do not necessarily describe situations in which something is immediately expected of the teacher, as in our example
of pedagogical moments. Rather, they describe the context in
which pedagogical action, such as teaching, occurs.

Missing. "He hasn't come home since he left school on
Friday," said one of the two policemen to the teacher. "At first his
mother thought that he might be sleeping over at a friend's place.
But when Kenny still hadn't shown up by Saturday afternoon she
got worried and started phoning around. I don't know why she
waited so long; the boy is only nine years old." "No one seems to
have seen him since Friday," the other policeman added, "and he
didn't check back home Sunday morning either. We still feel that
he may be staying with one of the kids from school."

"What other boys in your class does Kenny associate with?"
asked the first policemen. "Mostly with Darryl, huh?" The policeman jotted things down. "Address? Okay, we can find that soon
enough. Did you see him leave with this Darryl, by any chance?
Was Kenny playing with anyone else at school on Friday?"

"Well, we'll let you know if we can still round him up before
the end of the day. We understand you are worried too ... being

his teacher and all ... . But we'll do our best ... . Thanks for your help, anyway. And sorry for having to bother you on a Sunday." The law men left, leaving behind them an atmosphere of foreboding.

But in less than an hour there was a phone call. "We just thought we'd let you know that the kid has been found. Kenny, I mean ... . You were right. He was with Darryl. We found them camping out in a bushy area near the tracks. They had built a hut. You know, the kind of stuff young kids do. Apparently it hadn't really occurred to them that people might be worried about them.

Kenny said something about his mother's boyfriend. They don't seem to be getting along. I guess the little kid is quite a handful. And the ... what do you call it ... stepfather, he has started to take a belt to the kid, for lying. That worries me a bit. There is a fine line between discipline and abuse here, I suspect. Not that I don't believe in an occasional spanking.

Anyway, we found them as soon as we started to search the field ... . We'd first gone to Darryl's place. Apparently that kid hadn't come home to sleep, either. But we only found that out later from Darryl himself. At his house nobody had noticed that he had not been there. Hard to believe. And yet not surprising, since everyone in the house was staggering drunk. The kid had been missing for two solid days! But no one had missed him. A real shame."

Home. The new teacher has moved into a house close to the inner-city school where she has started a new job. She is planting some flowers in a window box in front of the house. A little boy comes by on a tricycle and he strikes up an animated conversation with the woman. "Hi, I'm Jossey. What's your name?" Then, out of the blue, he asks, "Do you have a mother? Where does she live? and is she asleep too?" The teacher explains that her father and mother live far away in a different city; then she inquires after Jossey's parents. "Oh, I don't have a father," he says. "And my mom, she is always sleeping." "Well, maybe you should wake her up because it is almost suppertime," suggests the teacher. "No she won't wake up. But don't worry, my big brother, Hank, looks after me. He gives me stuff to eat." "How old is your big brother?" asks the teacher. "He's six! Hank goes to school already," Jossey responds with obvious respect for his big brother.

When the next day the teacher tells the little incident to a community liaison worker, she nods and says, "Yes, I know these kids. The mother is an alcoholic." Then she adds, "It's sad. Such a nice little kid. So open and communicative now. But in a few years Jossey will have hardened and be forever beyond our reach."

Absenteeism. She is such a waif of a child. Small for a nine-year-old. Undernourished. Poorly dressed. And smelly! She hasn't had a bath for weeks. It is April already, and since Christmas Gail has not been in school for more than eight days altogether.

I have tried many things: phoning the mother (there is no father); getting the liaison worker to go out; calling social services. Finally, the social worker came to the school to talk with me.

"There isn't really anything we can do," she said. "We have threatened the mother. She promised that she will try to have Gail attend school. But the woman is really not in control. She claims that she cannot get her daughter to go to school. We could get the police involved and charge the mother. But she is on social assistance. So what good will that do? And removing the child from the home would not wash. It is just one of those cases."

My face must have shown growing anger. "Believe me," she sneered, "Some people you just cannot change. It is no use putting yourself out." Another teacher in the staff room, who overheard the discussion, nodded: "No point beating your head against the wall. We are here to teach, not to run after kids who don't show up." I became really annoyed. I could not believe that a social worker would give up on a child that easily. I also felt that they were mocking my naive indignation. I am still a new teacher in this school, and some feel that I am unrealistic or idealistic: You just do not expect of these inner-city children what you would at your nice suburban school where I had been teaching for many years.

Anyway, that was yesterday. Today was a fantastic day. Our fourth grade class competed in a music festival and we actually won first prize in choral speech. We beat three other schools. And you should have seen the difference in presentation. The kids from the other schools were all dolled up. And then there was our troop. Many of my children had dressed in their best. But we still looked like a pauper representation from the United Nations! Every possible social and ethnic group.

Yet those kids had a determination to win, and they did their utmost. In our practising I had never seen them so attentive, so keen. They really came through!

The principal was there to watch and take pictures. He had been skeptical about the wisdom of involving our kids in this kind of choral speech event. But I told him that, even if we did not win, it had already been worthwhile. I have seen a change in the children. They are learning to articulate and stand up straight when they talk to you; they look you in the eye rather than standing stooped and mumbling. And even when they are much older these kids may forget grade four but they will never forget the lines of our poem.

So the principal was almost more thrilled than we were at our victory. He is going to photocopy the Certificate of First Prize and laminate a copy for each child to take home to remember this by. That is when I took stock. Of course, Gail was not there, even though she had been at school the day before. And I had impressed on her to be there and help us do well in the competition. Even though Gail has missed many practice sessions, she is a bright little girl, and it is amazing how in her sporadic school attendance she can still manage to somehow keep abreast of what we are doing in grade four. So I said to the principal. "Too bad that Gail did not show up again. This would have been a good experience for her too — to be part of this group effort." And then he told me what he did not want to mention until later. They had gone over in the morning to get her to school. They found Gail at home. The mother was out but there was a man in the house. And the little girl? She was bleeding. She had been sexually abused by her Mom's boyfriend.

Choosing. It is recess time and I am on playground supervision. This means that I must forego a well-earned cup of coffee. But there are benefits. Walking among the children in the school yard tells me about their lives: their joys, moods, needs, strengths, and conflicts. Some things you just see by being there: Who is playing with whom? Why is Carl sauntering there all by

himself? Should I strike up a conversation with him? Or does he
need some time alone?

Already there are some kids hanging on my arm. Marie is
just content to hold on and walk with me, quietly. But Crystal is
chatting away. She pulls my arm, steps half in front of me, and
looks into my face. Am I listening? Her voice has a gossipy tone.
"Her parents are always fighting," says Crystal. I realize that Crystal is talking about Nicole, her best friend and grade four class-
mate. "Where is Nicole?" I ask. But Crystal ignores my question.
"And Nicole has told me a secret — she and her mom may be
running away soon. Please don't tell her that I let you in on the
secret." (I promise my oath of honor as a fourth grade teacher.)
"It was really weird," she continues. "Two cars pulled up at the
park where we were playing yesterday. The car doors flew open
almost at the same time. Nicole's mother was in the one car. Her
father in the other. Each was shouting for Nicole to come into
their car."

Crystal is silent for a moment. Her face reflects a strange se-
renity. Both Crystal and Nicole are so much alike, both children
of poverty, family violence, and abuse. "You know I felt terrible
for her," says Crystal. "I know that Nicole loves her mother so
much more than her father, who beats her. She is really scared of
him. And he beats her mom too. Anyway, Nicole's mother called
her to get into her car. She was yelling really loud. 'Quickly! Come
on! Quickly!' she cried. But you know, Nicole's father. He was
cursing and telling her to come with him. And oh, Nicole started
bawling too. For a moment she just stood there, looking at them,
crying. She was screaming really ... . Isn't it awful to have to
choose between your mother and your father?" Crystal looks
really distressed. "And you know what was so weird?" She halts
for a moment as if to add drama: "The car Nicole got into ... it
was her father's car."

Pedagogy asks us to reflect on children's lives

Pedagogy always looks to the
larger context.

What do we make of anecdotes such as these?[27] Admittedly, the
anecdotes are not happy life stories of children. But it is espe-

cially (although not only) in cases where we feel concern about a child's welfare that we are prompted to reflect on the meaning of those life experiences for that child. As an initial response we may simply feel distressed about the predicaments of some children. But this is a passive reaction, understandable but not very productive. Or we may feel the urge to make reflective sense of the anecdotes by considering the pedagogical significance of those experiences for the children involved.

It is a crucial feature of teaching that the educator understands a child's learning and development in the context of the larger biography of the child. Indeed, understanding the significance of these children's lives may go some way toward appropriate future pedagogical action in one's relations with such children.

In a way, the stories of Kenny and Darryl, Jossey and his brother Hank, Gail, Crystal and her friend Nicole, are all stories that call into question the meaning of what it is like to be a parent, what the significance is of family life, and what it means to be a child in our culture. These stories make us mindful that in our technologically advanced culture there are many radically different forms of life, different communities, different political realities, different family structures. Of course, there are people who may simply shrug their shoulders. "Sure, for many kids it's tough growing up in this society." Other people may grin mockingly about the naivety of those who would expect all children to grow up in "nice middle-class families. ... Besides, are there still such families?" This is the new age. There are children worse off in other countries. Think about the prevalence of child prostitution, street children; think about the ravaged images of children whose bodies are riddled by disease, starvation, or malnutrition. What does it mean to develop a theory of pedagogy in this context? Should pedagogical theory be able to be universally relevant to all children?

Thus, it is important to be aware of the larger context of our pedagogical interest in children when these children are neither our own nor like our own. We must not be naive and ethnocentric by assuming that we know what is good for children, all children, these particular children. And yet it would be equally wrong to refuse to address the pedagogical responsibility we feel when we are confronted by children in predicaments obviously not of their choosing and undoubtedly constraining their possibilities to become what they might want to be in a humanly desirable world.

Society may undergo radical postmodern changes, but the pedagogical fact is that children are naturally conservative: They need security, stability, direction, support. Do we understand what these needs mean and require of us? It seems that, in Canada and in the United States, governments and child care professionals are less interested in what children need than in what children are able to endure or tolerate. Many children eight or nine years of age have to care for themselves after school. Two decades ago this would have constituted child neglect. In the real world there are children who simply do not have parents, or who do not have parents who act like parents, or who lack a father or a mother in their family. But, in a humanly desirable world it may still be preferable for children to have both a mother and a father, or at least to have some person dedicated to take extraordinary and lifelong interest in them.

How can we understand the significance of having to choose between mother and father? This is a relevant question, since separation and divorce are the modern condition of family life — at least in North America. We sense the severity of such choice in Nicole's distress and in her seemingly incomprehensible choice. The child of divorce may be better off than the child of neglect, such as Darryl. But even a neglected child such as Darryl, usually lives in a natural, taken-for-granted relationship with his or her home and parents. In Darryl's case there is neglect due to alcohol abuse by the adults. And yet his immediate relation to his parents offers him a certain atmosphere of security and stability even if parental neglect threatens the security and positive family environment that the child needs. We should not forget, of course, that while a child may live in conditions that are objectively marked by instability, the child nevertheless may not suffer from feelings of insecurity. Also, it is the quality of security-insecurity that ultimately matters in children's lives. But how much do we know about the nature and pedagogical significance of security in children growing up in the modern world?

Psychologists sometimes argue that it is healthy for a young child to come to terms with the feelings that accompany parental neglect and abuse. And so they help to bring the experience of neglect to explicit awareness. This may be valuable in some sense. But to help the child articulate and reflect on the forms of neglect from which he or she suffers is to break through the natural immediacy with which he or she experiences life. Distancing may bring with it a new form of insecurity and discontinuity that things can no longer be experienced in a taken-for-granted way. It is the profound sense of insecurity that, as in Nicole's case, comes from having to choose between the parts of what seemed most natural and most stable — having a mother and a father both. In the case of some children, the insecurity is felt as a strange sense of loneliness in their awareness of the fragility of their relation to the mother and the father due to the broken family structure, while in Gail's case, the insecurity arises from having in some sense not really any parent at all.

So what we may learn from anecdotes such as these is the deep meaning that adults' presence may or may not have for children's lives. In the positive case, the presence of adults may make it possible for the child to experience a sense of safety, support, stability, and direction. These qualities are pedagogical themes that recur in the literature of child care and pedagogy. Yet knowledge of these themes does not enable us to make generalized judgments about how particular children experience divorce or loss. But understanding the pedagogical significance of security, support, and purpose for the child's healthy growth and development may allow us to interpret the meaning of those conditions in the specific life contexts of specific children. Reflecting on the life contexts of children, and on the significance of the values embedded within them, may help us to heighten our pedagogical thoughtfulness and increase the likelihood of demonstrating appropriate pedagogical understanding in our everyday living with children.

Children need security and safety so that they can take risks

Stefan is ten years old. When his parents "have words" with each other, or act angrily toward each other — as parents sometimes do — then Stefan goes off to some part of the house and cries. This has made the parents feel bad, and they ask Stefan why he gets so upset when his parents have some disagreement. "After all," they say, "we do not cry when you and your brother have a little fight." But Stefan says, "I cannot help it. When I hear you shout at each other, then I get so afraid that you are going to get a divorce — just like Tommy's parents." It is hard for children to feel secure in the modern world where divorce is so common. Some children do not ask, "Are you getting divorced?" but, "When are you getting divorced?"

Jim is an older fellow now; he has several children of his own. But he admits that he was a reluctant father at first, and he feels that it may have something to do with his own childhood. As a young child and throughout his teenage years he experienced a deep-seated fear of his father. To Jim his father was an unpredictable, sour, and ill-tempered man. "I was most afraid when he would get that 'look' in his eyes," Jim recounts. "Sometimes my father would get this strange look when he became angry. Other times, he would have this look when he simply opened the door. Just in the way he opened the door for them made my friends feel uncomfortable and unwelcome in our house. Therefore, I seldom brought friends home with me. ... And now, having kids of my own, my greatest fear is that my kids may distrust me in the way that I dared not trust my father."

Parents may sometimes feel that their presence does not make that much difference in a child's life. Parents who leave their children for long hours in day care tend to rationalize that it is more important to give small amounts of high-quality time to children than simply being around children most of the day. And parents who are separated or divorced may try to maintain a presence from a distance. But long-distance parenting is highly unsatisfactory for children. Children are concrete: If you are there you are there, if you are not then you are gone. In addition to spending time with children by being attentive to them, it is important to be present to them, to surround them with the secure feeling that you are there, present and accessible.

The notion of safety and security in modern life has become invested with heavy meaning. It seems that the sense of well-being associated with human safety is threatened in so many realms of daily existence: income, jobs, shelter, peace, health, the environment. Some adults may feel that they are cracking under the weight of it all. Others seem to celebrate the thrill of living in the constant play of risk and insecurity. For a child to grow up and explore the world in the context of security means that the child feels protected by the love and care of some adult(s). It is significant that the term *security* is associated with *caring*. Children who feel that somebody worries about them do not have to worry unduly themselves. The Latin *secura* means free from care, free from worry. The term *sure* is also derived from *secure*, meaning *safe*. Security brings a needed amount of surety, certainty, and solidity in our lives.

In providing a loving atmosphere of safety and security for their children, parents give and teach the very young something without which growing up and living becomes quite impossible. Parents who surround the child with intimacy, the relation of closeness wherein their presence is felt in a protective way, make available space and ground for being. They teach their children that the world can be experienced as home, a place for safe dwelling, a habitat in which human beings can be, where we can be ourselves, where we can have habits, our ways of being and doing things.

So to bear children is, in a broad sense, to provide place and space for them to live, to be. The child is carried, borne inside the womb at first, then it is born into the world where it remains, for a while at least, most helpless, dependent, in need of nurture, warmth, caressing, holding fast, and safe outside the womb. Conversely, it is in the experience of separateness, lostness, being without a bearing, without a sense of direction, without the security of safe ground, that the primordial nature of parenting can be intuited.

Children seem often caught in their desire to venture out, court danger, and engage in daring behavior, while at the same time they seek to free themselves of risk and uncertainty. Even as adults we often seem to be consciously engaged in the struggle between our desire to exercise our freedom by taking risks and our desire to enjoy security by reducing risk. Modern society has striven to reconcile certainty and security on the one hand, with freedom and risk on the other. But we have been less intent on developing the conciliatory creativity to face and resolve the contradictions and conflicts which inhere in that striving.

What kind of security do teachers need to offer children? Good schools share certain features with the family, such as a certain intimacy and security. The school provides the kind of in-between, transitional stage between the close intimacy of the

family and community on the one side and venturesome expo-
sure to the public world on the other. Students learn best, are
willing to extend and risk themselves in an educational environment that is experienced as safe and secure.[28] A school should
even be safe enough (like the family) for problems to be experienced and worked out, and to tolerate questioning, protest, dis-
sent. School administrators or teachers who try to avoid
problems and difficulties at all cost are pedagogically unrealistic.
To live as a young person is to live with difficulty. To be alive is
to be in difficulty. In fact, all adults do well to remain sensitive to
childhood's problems and difficulties.

It is common wisdom that nothing breeds success like the
experience of success. What makes a school insecure for children? We already know that uncaring schools produce students
who do not care,[29] and that caring schools can make a difference
in students' lives.[30] For example, students do best when teachers
show that they care by teaching in a personal manner and by
demonstrating that they believe in their students by setting challenging expectations. Of course, inappropriate or unrealistic
challenges can be experienced as negative and contribute to students' unnecessary and unhealthy stress under teachers who create overly competitive environments, overtest, overevaluate the
students by constantly relating every assignment and every
learning situation to the determination of grades and competitive
standing. Indeed, learning cannot be positive in schools where
testing madness reigns and where many students regularly and
inevitably experience failure.

Children need support so they can become independent

A teacher recently moved from a suburban school, where family
support is strong and positive, to an inner-city school where for
many children there is little parental support. The teacher is soon
touched by the affection she receives from the children at the
inner-city school. Every morning some kids come early and wait
for her to arrive. They are smiling and waving as she drives up,
opening her car door. Then they walk with her, carry her things,
and accompany her to the classroom where they just hang
around, talking, asking questions, and generally enjoying the
chat. After school, too, the teacher has great difficulty getting
various students to leave and go home. Do these inner-city kids
just enjoy school so much more than the children she used to

teach? After a few weeks the teacher realizes the answer. For so many of these children life at home is chaotic and frequently marked by violence, abuse, and neglect. At home there is really nobody to talk to. And many children basically learn to "grow up fast" and fend for themselves. Often the school is the only stable support in their young lives. This school and this teacher whom the children feel close to provide them with some sense of stability, steadfastness, reliability, and general support that they miss elsewhere in their lives.

Another teacher who had to move away from a similar inner-city school admitted that leaving the school gave her a feeling that she had never experienced in leaving other schools: the feeling of betraying the children. She felt in a sense that her leaving caused a crack in the children's experience of the school as a stable support. She knew that as a teacher she had been for some children the only person who was always there when they needed her. Throughout the years children would come and drop by even after they moved on to higher grades. Now, after so many years of teaching at this school, she felt she was abandoning children who needed the continuity of her presence.

The anecdotes are drawn from real experience, and yet these teachers do not mean to suggest, of course, that all inner-city children lack supportive home environments. Nor do they want to suggest that the wealthier suburban schools and families necessarily provide better child support for the development and education of children. It is sometimes the professional or career parents who give the least time and commitment to building a supportive family sphere for their children. Interestingly, "child support" has become a term applied in situations of parental separation and divorce. But of course child support is not just a matter of providing money for the necessities of life. To provide support to a child means that the adult is reliable and can be counted on to be there dependably and in a continuing way. This is no doubt a major challenge for many modern families and schools.

Children need direction from us to find their own direction in life

Should I suggest that Steve opt for the academic courses even though he may have to work very hard to be successful in an academic program? Which courses should he take? Should I persuade Inge to continue with the violin even though she would rather play with her friends instead of practicing? How much practice is appropriate for her? Should I let Dave quit school and take a job, even though he may later regret not possessing a high school diploma? If so, what kind of work should I encourage Dave to explore? Should I respond to Marlene who is constantly asking what she should be doing? Or, at the risk of her getting quite frustrated, should I encourage her to depend more on her own resources to decide for herself? Should I try to steer Jim's interest away from girls because he seems rather young for it? Should I encourage Karin to play with friends outside in the fresh air? Or should I let her stay inside again to read a book? Should I give in to the requests of the kids for a more relaxing afternoon? Or should I insist that we need to get a certain task accomplished?

Pedagogical action and reflection consist in constantly distinguishing between what is good or appropriate and what is not good or less appropriate for a particular child or group of children. In other words, pedagogical life is the ongoing practice of interpretive thinking and acting — on the part of adults, but also and especially on the part of the children who continually interpret their own lives and who constantly form their own understandings of what it means to grow up in this world. This does not imply, of course, that every single thing we say and do with children places us in a situation of moral choice. But it does mean that our living with children is oriented in certain directions and that, as adults, we are accountable with regard to the reasonableness or goodness of our influencing of children.

Some adults may feel reluctant to make it clear to children that they have a set of expectations that they value as important. Other adults may feel no hesitation imposing their definite views on children or young people. Some children experience no sense of orientation from their parents or teachers, and other children experience adult direction as tyrannical. But the children who are not guided by adults (because they are brought up in a permissive, an open, or maybe a negligent environment) may experience the lack of direction also as a tyranny — the tyranny of being abandoned to the sole influence of their peers and of the culture at large. The point is that all children should be able to expect from their teachers and parents a sense of involvement in life because all children need direction — if only the direction that confirms that the choices they have made are good choices.

But this pedagogical requirement to provide a sense of direction to children's lives poses the additional requirement of the adult that he or she stands continually accountable for the goodness and appropriateness of the orientations and commitments he or she makes in living with children in the home or the school.

Tensions and contradictions belong to the pedagogical experience

Life is full of contradictions, which means that it is full of tensions among contrasting principles: freedom versus control, security versus risk, self versus other, right versus wrong, real versus ideal, the interest of the person versus the interest of society, and so on. Especially in the pedagogical lifeworld this antinomic structure of experience is probably the foremost factor that prompts us to continually reflect on questions of how we should act with children and students. The conflicting feature of everyday life also seems to lie at the root of many of our pressures, problems, conflicts, and uncertainties in dealing with young people — in families, in schools, as well as in society in general. We may sigh, "If only these contradictions and tensions did not exist, then everything would be so much simpler." Indeed, many theories of education, many approaches to child rearing, many ways of organizing schools seem motivated by the desire to exaggerate the importance of one approach to life in order to reduce the tensions and contradictions that follow when contradictions are more appropriately seen as unavoidably contradictory life forces, values, or qualities. Yet, rather than decrying or trying to deny these antinomies, we should celebrate them. They are what gives life its dynamic impulse, its normative structure and moral nature.

One of the most fundamental conflicts in the pedagogical world consists of the tension between freedom and control. Associated with freedom are notions such as autonomy, independence, choice, licence, liberty, room, latitude. In contrast, the language of control is associated with ideas such as order, system, discipline, rule, regulation, precept, organization. All parents and all teachers know something of the tensions and pulls asso-

ciated with the antinomy of freedom and control. Often this antinomy is experienced as a crisis of order. To what extent should
child rearing or education be based on a sense of order? What
does "order" mean? What should we make it mean?

In education two models of child care have attempted to
reduce the conflict between freedom and control to a single value.
On the one hand there is the behaviorist model founded on the
theories of John B. Watson and his influential book, *Psychological
Care of the Infant and Child,* and on the other hand there is the
psychoanalytic and humanistic model of Benjamin Spock's *Baby
and Child Care,* which became extremely popular. The behaviorist model led to an authoritarian, unemotional, manipulative, and
controlling approach to bringing up and educating children. By
contrast, the humanistic model led to a more laissez-faire, permissive, loving, and soft orientation, giving almost total licence
and latitude to the child's wishes and movements.

In the literature of curriculum and teaching the basic antinomy of freedom and control has led to very different types of
school: those organized on the ideal of maximum order such as
the British "spanking schools" depicted in David Leland's film,
Birth of a Nation; and those that strive for minimum order, as
found in some examples of open education in the tradition of the
progressive education movement. Even the most recent dis-
courses in education raise this issue of order and control —
think, for example, of the implied valuing of order or control in
those who advocate "a return to the basics" versus the implied
critique and distrust of order or control in the model of "emancipatory pedagogy."

Therefore, it seems pedagogically problematic for the antinomy of freedom/control to be interpreted exclusively in favor of one
or the other. Children need both freedom and order in their lives.
They need controlled freedom as well as control that pushes freedom forward. An environment of high permissiveness and the almost complete absence of control ironically does not appear to
contribute to the kind of development of cooperativeness, gentleness, positive self-concept, and self-discipline in young people as
some have suggested. And a highly regulated environment of severe
rules, blind obedience, imposed discipline, and strong punishment
also has detrimental effects on the positive development of young
people. Both highly permissive and highly regulated environments

have been associated with destructive, conflict ridden, and disorderly behavior in young people.

So a difficult issue for teachers and parents is often the question of the extent to which one should actively intervene in a child's life or leave the child to his or her own devices. The dual role of actively guiding the child and of letting the child find his or her own direction is a constant challenge to pedagogical reflection. We try to be aware of this antinomy by, on the one hand, giving active direction to a child's life while, on the other hand, being sensitive to the requirements of letting go or holding back. Young people desire both independence and a sense of order from their teachers. As teachers (and also as parents) we need to learn, for example, that sometimes it is appropriate for us to help the child learn to do something new, while at other times it is more important to be patient and let the child work it out for himself or herself, even if this inevitably involves making mistakes or encountering problems.

There are endless contradictions, conflicts, polarities, tensions, and oppositions that structure the pedagogical experience. The child wants to do something him- or herself but the parent feels responsible to assist or restrain the child in order to avoid a dangerous or undesirable situation. An idealistic teacher has vowed never to say "no" to a child but finds it impossible to live up to this determination. An adolescent struggles with the tension between what she would like to be and what she is, between what she would like to be able to do and what she is capable of at present. A young boy wants a father but no one assumes this responsibility. Supper is on the table but the kids would rather eat junk food. Most parents or teachers know by experience the challenges that these antinomies pose to everyday living with children.

While life is full of contradictions, not all of these contradictory values are constantly at odds with each other. The landscape of our world is made up of regions of order and disorder; each order has its own disorder in the background, and this disorder creates the possibilities for a different order. As we travel laterally in and across these regions, we encounter and internalize different views, norms, truths, expectations, rules, and principles. For example, family life is differently ordered than life at school or at work. We are not quite the same with our friends as with strangers. We will tolerate, even enjoy, experiences through cinematography or literature that we would not find acceptable in other contexts. We learn to move easily in and between these worlds, each of which possesses its own order, limits, and disorder. A contradiction or tension in one region may not be experienced as a contradiction in another. Thus, we tend to experience contradictions more vividly within these ordered regions than between the regions of our landscape. And when we describe the tensions and contradictions that we encounter at home, at school, in the neighbourhood, in society at large, then these contradictions need to be described from below, from the concrete reality of daily experience (as well as from some critical theoretical distance above).

Pedagogical antinomies not only challenge us in daily living, they also require of us a reflective response. For example, we are often caught between the demands of our ideals and the demands of "reality": On the one hand we need to strive for higher values (such as unwavering honesty in social affairs, perfection in the accomplishment of a task, fundamental respect for the dignity of all humans and living creatures) and on the other hand we need to realize that life is complex, never perfect and that living requires compromise with pragmatism. No theory of pedagogy can satisfy if it does not offer a perspective for the contradictions of daily life. By identifying and clarifying the ordered and disordered norms and antinomies of the pedagogical life, we may find a basis for more thoughtful pedagogical action.

4 THE NATURE OF PEDAGOGY

The Conditions of Pedagogy

Are there certain conditions so essential to pedagogy that without them pedagogical life would be impossible? What does the vocation of parenting or teaching ask of us? When does a parent stop being a parent? When does a teacher stop being a teacher? Three fundamental conditions of pedagogy are discussed in the following sections: love and care, hope and trust, and responsibility. Is it possible to act as a real teacher if one is not oriented to children with loving care, trustful hope, and responsibility? Obviously these conditions are not simply "qualities," "attitudes," or "feelings" that we can will ourselves to possess. Some days I may experience a sense of responsibility for the children in my care while on another I may feel exasperated and negative about my work as a teacher. Yet we should rightfully have doubts about our preparedness to educate children if we have lost altogether our sense of responsibility, hope and care for them.

Pedagogy is conditioned by love and care for the child

Even with rational present-day family planning (from prophylactics to abortion), when a child is born he or she still very much enters our life as a stranger. We do not choose a child as we choose a friend, for the qualities that it possesses. Selection through childbirth of a child with a particular emotional or intellectual make-up even though this may soon become possible, seems inconsistent with the intentions of nature.

The miracle of motherhood and fatherhood is that the child who comes as a stranger, greeted at first with enthusiasm or perhaps ambivalence — this child is often loved eventually with a love that is stronger than the strongest affection between friends or lovers. Although "to parent" literally means "to create, to bring forth," many new parents who have "produced" or "created" a child experience their act of creation as a "miracle." Did I make this child or did this child make me? The parents do not so much choose the child as they are chosen by the child. We understand the bond of love between mother and child, between father and child is fused by a force that science can neither measure nor explain. This love is less an achievement of pedagogy than its condition. Often new parents are themselves startled by the unexpected effects the child may have on them. In this sense too the decision to become a mother or a father is really made in ignorance or naivety. "You'll never be the same again," friends and relatives say to the new parent. And after that ... once a parent, always a parent!

How does the professional educator, the teacher, meet the child with whom he or she will stand in a pedagogical relation? Again unlike a lover or a friend, the teacher does not choose his or her pupils. Unlike a parent, the children are not given to the teacher as if by divine dispensation. Unlike the parent, the teacher does not develop a bond with the child which is cemented with blood. Rather, much more simply, the teacher meets the children when they show up in class. But this encounter, too contains the possibility of a certain pedagogical eros that transforms the teacher into a real educator. The teacher meets the class, and, says Martin Buber, from this situation one can discern the "greatness" of the modern educator. "When the teacher at school enters the classroom for the first time, he sees them all there, grouped arbitrarily in their desks: He sees children who are big and small, coarse and finely featured; he sees sullen faces and noble appearances, ill-shaped and well-proportioned bodies — as if they were the representation of creation," says Buber. "And his glance, the glance of the educator, embraces them all and takes them all in."[31] In that gesture lies the vocation, the greatness of the educator. The pedagogical love of the educator for these children becomes the precondition for the pedagogical relation to grow.

There is still another difference between the affection of friendship or erotic love and the love that pedagogues have for the children in their care. A lover loves his or her love for what the other is. But a parent loves his or her child for what the child is *becoming*.[32] This is not to say that adults do not change or that loves and friendships cannot be enriched by the changes that the partners may undergo. It is nevertheless true that change frequently is cited as the cause of marital breakup or the falling out of friends. "We grew apart," is the expression one hears in these contexts. In contrast, a teacher's affection for a pupil, like a parent's affection for a child, is premised to a large extent on the value of becoming and growth, on the value this has for the developing identity, character, or selfhood of the young person.

It is true, of course, that a parent may sometimes sigh, "I wish my child would never change!", "I wish I could keep him like this!" or, "Why does she have to grow up!" These exclamations may be motivated by the anticipation of future separation, or by nostalgia, and the sense of time flying by too fast. But no normal parent will actually make a concerted effort to completely prevent a child from growing toward increased self-reliance and self-responsibility. A parent, like a teacher, loves a child as a person who is essentially in the process of becoming.

Of course, this does not mean that we do not value children for what they are now. The meaning a child has for me, as parent or as teacher, lies in the present. Obviously I do not know who or what this child will become; I cannot tell the future. Yet what is so fascinating about children is that we constantly see them becoming into their own, as it were. I notice signs of a new maturity: a personal way of talking, a new pleasant confidence or a disarming shyness, a surprising critical judgment, a hard-won ability, an unsuspected talent, a certain way of walking, gesturing, or moving the body — it is in many little things that we see a child learn and grow up.

Pedagogy is conditioned by hope for the child

We commonly say that to be a parent or teacher is to have expectations and hopes for a child. But *hope* is only a word, and a word soon becomes overworked, worn out, losing its original relation to our basic experience. So we must examine how living with children, at home or at school, is experienced such that we may call it *hope*, hope for children. Having hope for a child is much more a way of being present to the child than it is a kind of doing. Hope felt by the parent or the teacher is a mode of being.

In everyday living we entertain many particular expectations and desires: I hope my child will do well in school. I hope he can keep up with his homework. I hope my daughter will get over this pneumonia soon. I hope she will stay away from cigarettes and drugs. I hope my son will not give up his violin. These are the hopes that come and go with the passing of time. But children make it possible for men or women to transcend themselves and to say I hope, ... I live with hope; I live life such that I experience children as hope. This experience of hope distinguishes a pedagogical life from a non-pedagogical one.

The pedagogical interpretation of hope also makes clear that we can only hope for children we truly love, not in a romantic idealistic sense, but in the sense of pedagogical love. What hope gives us is the simple avowal: "I will not give up on you. I know that you can make a life for yourself." Thus hope refers to that which gives us patience and tolerance, belief and trust in the possibilities of our children. Children who experience our trust are thereby encouraged to have trust in themselves. Trust enables! Trustful hope is our experience of the child's possibilities and development. This trust enables the child to trust his or her own possibilities and development. Trustful hope is our confidence that a child will show us how his or her life is to be lived, no matter how many disappointments may have tested our confidence. Is this not the experience of parenting and teaching, as giving bearings and support to our children? Thus hope gives us insight into the deep meaning of pedagogy itself. Or is it pedagogy that helps us to understand the significance of hope? Like all great values, their ultimate meanings seem to merge.

Pedagogy is conditioned by responsibility for the child

It is not fashionable in these times to speak of pedagogy in terms of the authority that the adult carries with respect to the child. The idea of authority is easily associated with the notion of authoritarianism — which might actually be called the perversion of authority. Pedagogical authority finds its source and rationale in the value of pedagogy. It defines both the nature of the charge or calling of the pedagogue and of the pedagogical relation. This means that to the outside world the pedagogue (parent or teacher) can act with or on behalf of the child by referring to the moral responsibility he or she bears for the welfare and the development of the child. This responsibility is easily betrayed or corrupted.

When an eight-month-old baby cries rather than going to sleep, what does one do? Canadian newspapers carried a story of an Ontario pastor who justified the bruises on his eight-month-old baby's body by referring to the Bible, which he reportedly claimed "orders the spanking of young children."[33] In a sermon entitled "How to Raise Rotten Kids," he allegedly advocated that corporal punishment is justified by the Bible. Authorities laid charges that the spanking of the baby violated section 43 of the Canadian Criminal Code, which says that a teacher or parent may use only "reasonable force" by way of correction. The pastor and his followers claimed that, "It's the Bible that is on trial here." They argued that the issue at stake is religious freedom. In other words, the pastor grounded his parental authority not on his pedagogical responsibility to the child, but on his right to religious freedom. But the way in which one exercises one's pedagogical responsibility can only be justified on pedagogical grounds, not on a rational derived from religion, business, politics, or science.

Throughout history, and no less it seems in modern times, children have been exploited, neglected, and abused. Parents and other caretakers of children too easily assume that they have license to enforce tough discipline over children, to exert their will over children's desires, to inflict pain and mental anguish, and to control children by fear and punishment. The terrible examples of abuse have led child advocates to call for the emancipation of children from all forms of parental influence. Some advocates even assert that all pedagogical influence is really a disguised form of adult domination and control. For this reason, they say, we should recognize that children and adults are equals; therefore, we should bring about laws and educational practices for children which are governed by the same laws, principles, and behavior that govern adult life. However, parents or teachers and children are not equals. In fact, children are more than equal to parents and other educators. Because of their dependency on pedagogical authority, children in a sense call upon those adults to serve them. Pedagogical authority is really a designation of moral service.

The notion of authority is in itself not a negative idea. However authority is easily confused with its abuse — authoritarianism. By its very essence authority refers to a certain asymmetry, difference, unevenness, inequality, dissimilarity in the relation between two or more persons. To be in authority is to be in a position of influence. This is precisely the relation between a parent or teacher and a child or youth. But the adult can only have pedagogical influence over a child or young person when the authority is based, not on power, but on love, affection, and internalized sanction on the part of the child. Pedagogical authority is the responsibility that the child grants to the adult, both in an ontological sense (from the viewpoint of the pedagogue) and in a personal sense (from the side of the child). The child, in a manner of speaking, authorizes the adult directly and indirectly to be morally responsive to the values that ensure the child's well-being and growth toward mature self-responsibility.

These formulations are not merely theoretical; they are practical insofar as the pedagogue and the child are influenced and guided by the experiential manifestations of pedagogical authority. For example, an adult who sees a child in need, who observes a situation of child abuse, or who responds to a child's interests and questions may actually feel motivated to do something, to help or assist the child. In this sense we may say that the adult is prompted to act on the sense of responsibility that comes with the experience of authority. And now something interesting happens: The adult who is oriented to the child's vulnerability or need may experience a strange sensation — the true authority in this encounter rests in the child and not in the adult.

We might say that the child's presence becomes for the adult an experience of being confronted with a demand for his or her pedagogical responsiveness. So the child's weakness turns into a curious strength that the child has over the adult. Thus, in more ways than one, pedagogical authority is granted by the child: in the form of an encounter that the adult experiences with his or her responsibility for the child, granted more concretely by the child, first on the basis of its trust and love, later on the basis of critical understanding. This means that the adult, who is invested with authority by the child's granting of it, needs to be the critical consciousness for the young child about his or her needs and his or her grant of authority. In other words, the adult must be critically self-reflective in the child's interests. Only gradually is this critical facility assumed and practised by the growing young person.

The Nature of the Pedagogical Experience

To explore further the meaning of pedagogy, we need to ask what it consists of, how it is structured. In what ways do we experience pedagogy in everyday life? In other words, what is the existential structure of this experience? In its most elemental form we may make a distinction between pedagogical situations, pedagogical relations, and pedagogical actions. Pedagogical situations are those circumstances or conditions that constitute the site of pedagogical actions and that make pedagogical experiences between adults and children possible. Pedagogical situations in turn are constituted by special affective pedagogical relations between adults and children, to which both the adult and the child bring the necessary requisites. Pedagogical actions are the experiences between pedagogues and children, in which both adults and children are actively and intentionally involved and through which a special influence flows from the adult to the child.

The pedagogical situation

Parenting and teaching involve human experiences that are always situation-specific. But not every situation in which we as adults find ourselves with children is a pedagogical situation. For example, a convenience store owner who caters to young people may be less interested in them than in the profits from their purchases. In contrast, a teacher who sees the children hanging out near such store, filling up on potato chips and pop, may be less content with such situation. It may prompt the teacher to do a lesson on health and nutrition. In other words, a teacher may want to do something with such a situation and turn it into a pedagogical situation where the children might come to some useful realizations about their life-style or eating habits.

The notion of "pedagogical situation" is a fundamental category of pedagogy. What is meant by "situation"? We always find ourselves in some situation. In general, "situation" may be defined as "the totality of particulars with respect to which one must act."[34] When we ask after a person's "situation" we may refer to the position, condition, or circumstance that the person occupies. But "situation" is more than a descriptor or objective datum about a person's place. In everyday life we employ the expression, "You have to understand his situation." And with this expression we do not just mean that one must take account of all the facts and factors that have a bearing on someone's position — it especially means that one must be able to understand the situation from the existential perspective of that other person.[35]

Thus, with respect to a child or children, we must be able to analyze, grasp, and understand the child's situation. Secondly, as educators, we are expected to act with respect to the child's situation in terms of our own situated relation to the child. Thus, the pedagogical situation is a situation for the educator (parent, teacher), because it is the educator who must act in a pedagogical, educational manner. Of course, there is an important difference between understanding a situation and being able to act in a situation. Some adults may show great insight into children's lives but be unable to act pedagogically on the basis of their understanding. Moreover, the way the adult sees or experiences a situation may not be the same as the way a child sees or experiences it.

More precisely then, what is a pedagogical situation? And in what respect does it differ from other kinds of social situations in which people find themselves? Much of education at home and even in schools takes place without conscious and deliberate planning. It is just a fact of life that, to become self-responsible persons, children need to live side by side with those more experienced and more mature than they are. Natural growth occurs within the realms of housekeeping, social interactions, play, sports, daily tasks, work, and so on. Situations of growth are those in which children benefit in some manner from the circumstances that exist. But at the same time, there are and always have been forms of pedagogical acting (parenting, teaching) which are more intentionally structured and more reflectively oriented to certain norms, standards, and ideals. So the pedagogical situation is created through the intention of the educator — through the way that the educator is attached to the child, through the way that the educator "belongs to" the child.

The pedagogical relation

A second way of approaching the question of the structure of the pedagogical experience is to focus on the special relation that exists between adult and child in a pedagogical situation. In pedagogical situations the adult and the child do not just happen to be in the same spot; rather, they are together in a special way. They are together in an interactive unity that constitutes a relation, a pedagogical relation.

The school, the classroom, the home, the family are typically the places or circumstances that sustain pedagogical relations. And the people that stand in a pedagogical relation are the teacher and the students, or the parent and the child. But it is also true that sometimes teachers and parents do not live up to the requirements of the pedagogical relation: "Can I go out and play with my friend?" "Sure, but don't keep walking in and out. And please, don't bring your friends here. I've just vacuumed." "Can I go out and play with my friend?" "Sure, but first finish your homework." Both situations are typical. The first parent does not necessarily love the child any less than the second parent. Yet the relation is different. In the first case the priority is the clean floor. In a way the parent is saying, my clean floor is more important to me than you and your friends. In the second case the priority is a certain value: the child is reminded that there are certain tasks in life that need to be fulfilled before one plays. If the child is responsive to the parent's appeal, then the pedagogical relation functions.

The pedagogical relation is best described as that between the parent and the child, or between the professional educator and the student when that relation is pregnant with certain qualities. For the young person, the pedagogical relation with the educator is more than a means to an end (to become educated or grown-up); the relation is a life experience that has significance in and of itself. Our relation to our mother, father, a teacher, or someone else in whose presence we experience real growth and personal development, is possibly more profound and more consequential than the experience of friendship or romantic love. We may always feel indebted for the rest of our lives to a parent or to a teacher, even though the material that we learned from this person may have lost its relevance. In part this may be due to the fact that what we "received" from a great teacher is less a particular body of knowledge or set of skills than the way in which this subject matter was represented or embodied in the person of this teacher — his or her enthusiasm, self-discipline, dedication, personal power, commitment, and so forth.

In the pedagogical relation — in the experience of being a

father, a mother, a teacher — a part of our life finds its fulfillment. Therefore, the German educator Nohl said that the pedagogical relation is not merely a means toward an end, it finds its meaning in its own existence; it is a passion with its own pains and pleasures.[36] Similarly, for the child the pedagogical relation is a part of life itself, and not merely a means for growing up — if it were only for that, the pedagogical relation would last too long. In other words, the respect, love, and affection between adult and child finds its meaning in their own enjoyment and satisfaction with each other in the present, rather than in any future benefits.

Parents intuitively know how crucial for the child's development and learning is the pedagogical relation that exists between their child and the teacher. Parents are often quite concerned that the teacher like their child and that the child like the teacher. To be sure, the pedagogical relation is not simply a relationship of affection or friendship. Children may like a teacher ("he is funny and always tells jokes"), but not respect the teacher to a degree conducive to pedagogical influence ("I liked the teacher but I did not really learn much from him"). The same is true for the relation between parents and their children. A father looks back over his life and realizes with regret that, although he was a good provider for his family, he did not really experience a fatherly relation to his son and daughter. Maybe he was too busy with his career. Maybe he approached his children with the same detachment that his own father maintained with him. Maybe he simply never was drawn into a fatherly relation to his children. Now his children are grown up, and in some respects it is too late to develop the personal relations a father can have with his children.

The pedagogical relation is always (to some extent ambiguously) a double intentional relation. I care for this child — for who this child is and for who this child may become. If the relation is not characterized by this double direction, it is no longer a pedagogical relationship. A mother has thrown her entire life into her daughter's musical career. The girl is only nine, but her future is set. She is not going to be anything but a concert pianist, if the mother can help it! The mother has sought out the best teachers and the best instrument, and she will not let a chance go by for her daughter to prove herself in local competitions. The mother sees to it that the girl practises three hours a day and that she takes additional lessons to develop compatible musical skills. As far as the mother is concerned, the daughter is already performing on the stage. The mother is so preoccupied with what will be that she can only see the child's possible future; she is unable to see the child's present life and needs. In other words, the child's real childhood experiences are sacrificed for the adult's image of the adult that the child is to become. This scenario is common. Some children are able to live up to parental pressures and eventually fulfill their parents' dreams. Others are not able to fulfill such expectations and may develop a hatred toward the skill as well as toward the parent.

Of course, sometimes children themselves may develop a love for a musical instrument, a sport, a dance form, or some other activity that sets them on the path of fulfillment and a possible career. They become obsessed by their interest and spend all their free time in its pursuit. Now the parent may be the one who, while nurturing the talent, keeps things in check.

There is also the other possibility. The parent is so in need of the child's dependency that the parent cannot let go, and does everything to keep the child a child — small and dependent. This is the case where the child is denied the opportunity to grow, to acquire new experiences, to assume self-responsibility, to take appropriate risks.

The pedagogical relation is an intentional relationship between an adult and a child, in which the adult's dedication and intentions are the child's mature adulthood. It is a relation oriented toward the personal development of the child — this means that the pedagogue needs to be able to see the present situation and experiences of the child and value them for what they contain; and the pedagogue needs to be able to anticipate the moment when the child can participate in the culture with fuller self-responsibility.

The pre-reflective or primitive form of the pedagogical relation is already found in various relations of everyday life — in the conversation, in helping another, in every event where a certain influence toward formative growth is exercised by one person with respect to another. The pedagogical relation differs from these everyday formative relations in that the pedagogue reflectively mobilizes his or her conscious desire and will to give direction and shape to such influence. But only when such intentions are responded to by the young person can the pedagogical relation come into existence.

In the earlier German and Dutch literature on pedagogy, the pedagogical relation was described as an intensely personal relation between an adult and a child.[37] We may confirm this quality of the relationship in the intimacy of the parent-child relation, where the parent's love and affection for the child are met by the child's feeling of trust and need for closeness, security, direction, and the simultaneous desire for independence and self-responsibility. However, this close and personal relation is much less easily achieved by teachers, especially by high school teachers who may be dealing with an average of 150 students a day. In other words, institutional organizational constraints of the school as a formal place for educating young people require that the pedagogical relation between parent and child differs in several aspects from the relationship between young people and the professional educator even though he or she stands *in loco parentis*. Of course, there are those who will argue that "realistically speaking" professional educators have only one charge, simply to "instruct" the students assigned to them in the curriculum subject of their expertise. However, the latter hold an unacceptably simplistic view of their educational responsibility and of what it means to educate young people.

We must ask, then, what pedagogical relation is possible between a teacher and the students in his or her charge? First, we need to emphasize that the relation of teacher to students differs from the parent-child relation in a fundamental respect in that it is always a triadic relation: It is a relation between teacher and student which both are oriented to a certain subject matter (mathematics, language, science, for example) and to the world with which this subject matter is concerned. The parent – child relation tends to be more diadic: primarily a person-to-person relationship. But, of course, parents too are teaching their children to live in this world. Another obvious difference between the pedagogical relation of teachers and parents is that the teacher – student relation is temporary (even though a child may remember an outstanding teacher for life) while the relation between parent and child is lifelong.

First, then, the pedagogical relation between teacher and students differs from other possible relations an adult may have with a child, such as friendship, commerce, etc. A pedagogue, as teacher, would speak inappropriately of his students as "my friends" or as "my customers" or "clients" (even though the language of commerce has curiously come to pervade discourse on educational theory). The teacher's pedagogical relation is a relation *in loco parentis*. The teacher is oriented to students in terms of orienting the students to the subject matters that give school learning its pedagogical significance. In turn, the students need to accept the pedagogue's charge as "teacher"; otherwise the learning process loses its footing. It needs to be realized as well that the pedagogical relation between teacher and student cannot be compelled or coerced. A teacher cannot force the student to accept him or her as teacher — ultimately that recognition must be won from, granted by the student.

Second, the pedagogical relation between teacher and students requires a two-way intentional relationship. The teacher intends the students to learn and grow with respect to the kinds of things that the teacher teaches. In turn, the students need to have a desire, a willingness, and a preparedness to learn. Without this "readiness to learn" nothing of consequence will be learnt. Naturally, to some extent the teacher can interest a child or young person in certain subject matters. But we need to consider that "readiness to learn" is a complex matter that entails more than cognitive maturity or motivated readiness.[38]

Third, the pedagogical relation between teacher and students has a special personal quality. The teacher does not just pass on a body of knowledge to the students, he or she embodies what is taught in a personal way. In some sense the teacher is what he or she teaches. A mathematics teacher is not just somebody who happens to teach math. A real math teacher is a person who embodies math, who lives math, who in a strong sense is math. Similarly, students do not simply store knowledge they learn; each student always learns in a particular, personal way. Each child gives personal shape to his or her understanding and to the way that he or she comes to understand things. Each child internalizes values, performs skills, forms habits, and practises critical reflection in ways significant and unique for this particular child. The teacher may be teaching a class of 35 students; but it is always important to remember that all learning is ultimately an individual process. It is a great challenge for teachers, therefore, to mediate the subject matter they teach in a personal way and to involve themselves personally with students. This does not mean that the teacher necessarily has to maintain one-to-one relations with every one of his or her students (especially in high school this would be an impossibility), but it does mean that the teacher is there in a personal way for those students.

Pedagogical action

The notions of pedagogical situation, pedagogical relation, and pedagogical action are interrelated. A pedagogical situation and a pedagogical relationship come into being through pedagogical action. I wrote earlier of pedagogical moments when the adult does something right in pedagogical situations and relations. On the one hand, only if we act in certain ways with young people do we create pedagogical situations and establish pedagogical relations with them. On the other hand, situations and relations between adults and children need to possess an active pedagogical quality for the adult's behavior to be pedagogically meaningful.

Pedagogical action may be quite subtle; it may even consist in holding back, in apparent non-action. But if the child does not experience the adult's actions and intentions as caring in a pedagogical sense, then the adult obviously does not have a pedagogical relation with this child. For example, a father who is accused of child abuse or neglect may claim that he deeply loves his children, but if the children do not experience this love, if, on the contrary, they feel indeed rejected, neglected, or abused, then the father's claim has no pedagogical significance. It is pedagogically essential always to ask how the child experiences the situation.

But understanding how things are from the child's point of view is not sufficient for pedagogical action. For example, there are many children who love their parents even though they are abused by them. There are various forms of abuse that children suffer from at the hands of adults. It is important to spell out what child abuse looks like since it is indeed the negation of pedagogical action. First, there is physical abuse that can range from occasional spanking to the battered child syndrome. Physical abuse means that the adult pinches, shakes, bites, strikes, smashes, punches, knocks down, throws, beats, hits, kicks, lashes, burns, chokes the child. All physical abuse of children is for many people profoundly repulsive and demeaning, although some parents and teachers would maintain that the occasional thrashing is "healthy" and "good" for developing a child's discipline, especially when other means do not yield results (i.e., obedience, conformity, etc.). Physical abuse is often visible in scars, bruises, broken bones, burns, brain damage.

Second, there is mental or psychological abuse that consists in scolding, swearing at, condemning, finding fault with, threatening, scaring, oppressing, confining, locking up children. Psychological abuse may range from such behavior as ridiculing a child in front of classmates, consistently denigrating the child's accomplishments, confining the child excessively to his or her room, leaving the child alone in a dark house while the parent goes out, burdening children with excessive demands, and so forth. Mental abuse is less easily recognizable, although it may be seen in children who are overly fearful, anxious, aggressive, withdrawn, nervous, callous, malicious, mean, brutal, or insensitive to others.

Finally, there is passive abuse through neglect that fails to provide children with needed love, attention, care, and proper food, shelter, and clothing. Passive abuse is also to continually ostracize, exclude, or ignore children for whom one is responsible — for example, by never being available to the child, by being totally indifferent to what the child does, hears, or watches, by letting young children roam the streets late at night, or by allowing children to engage in dangerous activities. Children who suffer from passive abuse may never learn to realize their full potential and take advantage of the possibilities that life holds for them. Children of neglect more easily become victims of life's contingencies — they may drift into exploitative relations of emotional dependency as a result of a need for the love and affection that they never experienced in their childhood.

In a way, it may seem easier to show what pedagogical acting is not than to state what it is. Physical, psychological, and passive child abuse are the exact opposite of pedagogical action and we need not concern ourselves here with examining the extenuating circumstances that may sometimes make child abuse, if tragic, nevertheless understandable. Sometimes it may be possible that because of family histories, economic circumstances, or mental ill-health some parents and teachers are not capable of dealing with children in a pedagogical manner — at best they merely cope with children. The term *coping*, of course, sometimes refers to handling the everyday ups and downs of living, but it is not enough if we fail to act or try to act as true teachers or parents as a positive influence on our children.

Pedagogical action mediates the influence of the world. Almost everything in life leaves its mark on a child's character: home, street, language and customs of the child's world, its music, technology, television and radio; almost anything that happens during a child's waking hours, and even what happens in dreams may have a consequence. To live is always to live under the influence of the world. The world influences the child as well as those pedagogically responsible for the child. In the midst of all those influences stand the parent and the teacher. But the parent and the teacher are unlike the other influences in that he or she is oriented to the child in a special manner. There is a single-mindedness, an intensity, a personal quality, a consistency to the pedagogical orientation that can make the parent or teacher more influential than the conglomerate of influences impinging on the child from the larger culture.

Strictly speaking the pedagogue tries to avoid directly influencing the child in the sense of making the child learn or do something because this denies the child any practice in self-control. Someone who says, "He made me do this!" has thereby refused to take responsibility for his or her actions. In contrast, pedagogy is the art of tactfully mediating the possible influences of the world so that the child is constantly encouraged to assume more self-responsibility for personal learning and growth. To teach is to influence the influences. The teacher uses the influence of the world pedagogically as a resource for tactfully influencing the child.

Yet, in the end, the parent or teacher is a lone figure. He or she may feel powerless in guarding the child from negative influences. Of course, the power of the educator is limited. Even in the best of circumstances one cannot be sure that children will arrive at desirable understandings or positive attitudes about some aspect of the world as mediated by school subjects — be it math, literature, social studies, science, art, health education, or personal life skills. But this recognition of one's limited influence and significance in a child's education and personal growth also suggests the need to trust the child's ability to make a life for himself or herself.

Finally, we need to ask, Is it possible to act always and consistently in a pedagogical manner with children? Should we realize that as teachers and as parents we make mistakes and fail in our dealings with children and young people? Indeed, we cannot avoid making mistakes with the children we teach. Sometimes we think that we have done what is best but discover to our dismay that we misjudged, that we fell short, or that we acted in ignorance. At other times we simply have bad days and cannot help but make mistakes or fail in our pedagogical responsibilities. The term *mistake* originally meant to take wrongly, to misunderstand.[39] It is obvious that educating children is an endeavor where the possibility for misunderstanding and for taking things wrongly is constantly imminent. *Failing* carries the meaning of falling short, losing power, being in default or found wanting.[40] What teacher does not feel at times that he or she is falling short and losing the power that makes teaching and pedagogical influence effective?

If teaching was merely a technical enterprise, then good teachers would rarely make mistakes, since teaching (like plumbing) would consist of applying technical knowledge and skills upon which an expert could be relied. What good is a plumber who keeps making mistakes, misconnecting pipes and causing leaks and floods? But the essence of an educator does not lie in technical expertise but in a complex of pedagogical qualities, as suggested in the introduction of this text.

It is easy to see how on any day we may fall short of the demanding requirements of pedagogy: Nobody is perfect. At times we feel crabby, bitchy, gloomy, or glum; we have difficulty with being patient, sympathetic, or tolerant; we may have a hard time simply getting through the day without showing that we are struggling with a major depression. Sometimes pedagogical action may indeed consist in "acting" — keeping up appearances in spite of the frustrations that plague us. The point is that our efforts and desires to do the best we can (knowing that it is not always good enough) are still animated by pedagogical intent and by a sense of pedagogical responsibility. For example, I may be irritated by my son or feel disappointed in his behavior, but that does not fundamentally affect my deep sense of responsibility for him.

It frees us to realize that it is impossible as pedagogues always to act right: to teach impeccable lessons, to be wise and fair, to explain difficult concepts with ease, always to keep the whole child in view, to be an inspiration to students, to understand perfectly a child's needs, to help students through deep learning difficulties. We must accept our personal limitations as well as the limitations inherent in the realities of everyday living with children. How else could we go on teaching and parenting children without being devoured by guilt, regret, and remorse over our constant mistakes and failings? More than many vocations, the task of educating young people is particularly demanding and consuming of a person's spirit.

Moreover, the structure of modern society, the pressures of institutional workplaces, and the conditions of the professional life of teaching (and of the life of parenting) are such that feelings of frustrations and failings are a constant concern. What teachers (and parents) need to do is to create conversational communities with others (with other adults, but also possibly with the children) to be able to discuss and address their experiences. Some of these communities spring up naturally in school staffrooms or even in the hallways (in door openings or behind the closed doors of classrooms). Other conversational communities may need to be created purposefully in special designated times and spaces.

5 THE PRACTICE OF PEDAGOGY

Pedagogical Understanding Is Sensitive Listening and Observing

"My parents do not understand me!" "My teacher does not really care about me at all!" "Why does nobody know how I feel?" "Why doesn't my teacher understand what difficulties I have with this?" "Teachers just teach at us rather than trying to find out what *we* think!" "Why can't the teacher be more helpful in preparing us for the work?" "Why do all teachers always pile up homework on the same day?"

What parent, what teacher has not heard complaints like these from children? These are complaints that raise the issue of the meaning and significance of pedagogical understanding.[41] Young children and especially teenagers often feel that adults misunderstand them or, worse, that they make no attempt at all to understand them. From the point of view of the adults these feelings are not surprising because so often adults are genuinely puzzled about the behavior of children and young people.

To the extent that parents or teachers are confident that they really do know their children it may come as an even greater shock when suddenly this confidence appears totally unfounded. When the child unexpectedly does something that seems completely out of character or when the child fails at something that seemed to lie so squarely within his or her competence, then our pedagogical understanding is called into question.

Therefore, what could be more fundamental, more essential to the task of parenting and teaching than exercising pedagogical understanding? What could be more important than to have a sense of what things are like for a particular child and what is necessary to help young people to stand more fully, more strongly on their own two feet in a moral, aesthetic, social and vocational sense? We need to ask what is the nature of pedagogical understanding and pedagogical perceptiveness, and in what respects does it differ from psychological, sociological, and other forms of understanding? For this we need to take as our starting point the request of the child to understand him or her first of all from the subjectivity of his or her experience. It is immediately clear that pedagogical understanding is not a simple skill. Rather, the structure of pedagogical understanding is complex, containing reflective as well as interactive elements. In other words, it requires of the adult that he or she hold back as well as know how and when to actively engage the child.

Can pedagogical understanding be learned? Probably all parents and teachers can increase their resourcefulness in pedagogical understanding. It depends on their willingness to really listen and on the kind of thoughtfulness of which they are capable. To children it may often appear that even when adults ask them about their experience the adults are not really interested in listening to them. For example, the adult asks, "Why did you do that?" or "What did you do that for?" But this question is rarely meant to provide an opportunity for the child to be heard. More often the adult has already made up his or her mind in judging the child. Often the "why" is meant to reprimand the child, even though the child's response — if only the adult would really listen — might make the adult more thoughtful and understanding about the child's world.

Pedagogical thoughtfulness and pedagogical understanding are closely related. Someone who is generally thoughtful is more likely to demonstrate real understanding of another person in a particular circumstance than a person who is relatively thoughtless. Pedagogical thoughtfulness seems to be a reflective capacity. With pedagogical understanding, however, there is an emphasis on seeing what is significant in the concrete situation. A frequent feature of pedagogical understanding is the ability to perceive and listen to children — and there are different ways of perceiving and listening, depending on the circumstances.

Pedagogical understanding is always a kind of applied understanding. Later I will propose that pedagogical understanding is realized in practice through what we may call "pedagogical tact." *Tact* describes what one actually does in pedagogical understanding. Sometimes this pedagogical understanding must be instant—a kind of embodied knowing—and other times there is time and space to reflect in coming to a pedagogical understanding. Nevertheless, there are no rules governing some automatic translation from understanding to tactful action. The translation is accomplished by tact itself. Ultimately pedagogical understanding and pedagogical tact are aspects of the same process.

Pedagogical understanding is always concerned with unique and particular circumstances. Pedagogical understanding is interactive. It is not an abstract, detached form of understanding that must then be translated into practical action. Pedagogical understanding is itself practical understanding: a practical hermeneutics of a child's being and becoming in a given situation. Pedagogical understanding is concerned with what is best for a child; in other words, it is normative, it is oriented toward the idea of the good—the good of the child.

Thus, it would be impossible to develop a set of rules or skills for pedagogical understanding. The requirements of each situation are different. Situational contingency arises from the incredible richness of meaningful elements that characterize any situation: We are concerned with a particular child or group of children, with a unique life history, with a particular preoccupation or systematic problem, in a specific situation, with a certain set of relationships, governed by a particular emotional climate. Each opportunity for pedagogical understanding is unique. Yet we may be able to identify some aspects of that praxis that at one time or another define the nature of pedagogical understanding.

The structure of pedagogical understanding can be examined by teasing out some of its aspects. Those aspects involve (1) non-judgmental, (2) developmental, (3) analytic, (4) educational, and (5) formative understanding. Each of these forms of understanding may be at play in the mindful concern with the child's growth.

However, it is important to realize that these forms of understanding do not necessarily add up to pedagogical understanding. They derive their meaning from various domains of life. Each is associated with a different practical discipline. The attempt to understand another person becomes pedagogical in nature when it is driven by a pedagogical orientation. Non-judgmental understanding involves the open listening that often occurs between friends or in certain therapeutic settings. A professional author too may be interested in understanding other people to help develop characters for a new novel. Developmental understanding is usually associated with the practice of the counsellor or psychologist. Industrial psychologists may use their expertise in developmental understanding to identify individuals who may serve the corporation better if provided with special training or with different job responsibilities. Analytic understanding is used on a troubled conscience or deep unsettling problems. For example, the priest or minister needs special skills in analytic listening to detect individuals' troubles. Educational understanding is exemplified by the educational acuity of the teacher. The teacher is able to listen for and perceive the state of intellectual, emotional, and moral development of a young person. But the athletic coach may use his or her ability to grasp the educational potential of a young person to assure a winning team, not necessarily for the good of the young athlete. Formative understanding is probably closest aligned to the notion of pedagogical understanding. The parent is most inclined to maintain a view of the whole child and of the total development of a child.

Non-judgmental understanding

The fundamental exemplar for non-judgmental understanding is friendship. Non-judgmental understanding involves a listening that is receptive, open, sympathic, authentic, facilitative. A good friend is a person whom we sometimes need to listen to our stories, our turmoils, our befuddlements, our commotions, our grief, our frustrations. Confiding in a friend helps us get rid of bottled-up feelings, tense emotions, unresolved guilt feelings. A friend will just listen without making things worse by passing judgment.

Children also need to be listened to, without critical or negative judgment. Confiding in another person whom the child trusts helps clarify things. Yet passive listening does not satisfy; it is not enough to be merely open and receptive. Non-judgmental understanding becomes pedagogical understanding only when it is intended to foster responsible self-awareness, self-understanding, a personal sense of direction and how one ought to deal with life. Non-judgmental pedagogical understanding is still characterized by a certain intentionality. Such listening/understanding knows when to be silent, where to support, and how to phrase a question that helps clarify the significance of the shared thoughts and feelings.

The teacher notices that Sven is not behaving as usual. When Sven leaves the grade twelve classroom at the end of the day he lingers, seems absent-minded, and is abnormally quiet. The teacher has nodded encouragingly to Sven, but he has turned away his eyes as if he were too embarrassed to acknowledge the teacher's friendly gesture. So when all the kids file out of the classroom and Sven appears to dawdle, the teacher calls his name. When they are alone in the room the teacher says, "I do not want to probe, Sven, but you seem bothered about something; it makes me unhappy to see you like this. Is there anything you would like to talk about? Can I be of help to you?" At first Sven shrugs and shakes his head. But then he tenses up with emotion, bites his lips, and barely audibly he whispers, "I do not know what to do. I don't know what to do." For a moment there is quiet. The teacher does not press on with further questions but takes Sven gently by the shoulder and sits him down at a desk. They are both seated. While the teacher quietly waits, Sven haltingly begins to share the details of his predicament.

One element of pedagogical understanding is the ability to become aware of the inner life of the young person. For this the adult first of all needs to be able to listen to the child in an open, warm, and receptive manner. Young children and older youths communicate their feelings and self-understandings about their lives in a variety of ways, and it is the task of pedagogical understanding to encourage children to express themselves, to talk about anything that concerns them, and to let them know that their feelings are acknowledged and respected. The adult must be able to listen in a way that is non-judgmental, not directed to the adult's interest. Yet it is an active listening.

Eight-year-old Michael approaches his father, who is busy with something. It is clear from the expression on Michael's face that something is the matter. "Well, Michael, what's up?" his father asks. But before he can say another word, Michael starts sobbing. "Come on, Michael, tell me what is wrong" his father says consolingly while he pulls Michael towards him. But Michael just continues crying. "Did you have a fight with your brother?" Michael shakes his head. "Did you hurt yourself?" No. "Did you have an accident or something?" No. "Are you in pain?" Michael shakes his head again. Well then, what is it? asks the father. "It is none of those things," says Michael, "I feel so sad." "So sad?" Father is getting a bit alarmed. He begins to suspect that something more serious may be wrong with Michael. And as the thought crosses his mind he looks Michael over a bit more carefully. Could he be sick? But there seems nothing unusual about Michael's appearance, except his tearful face. "Michael, I am getting worried. Can't you tell me what is the matter?" The father urges. "I feel so sad about the owl," Michael stutters. His father feels a faint sense of relief as he queries "The owl? What owl?" Michael begins to sob again with renewed vigor, at the mere thought of explaining. But then he says, "I just finished reading *Owls In The Family*, and the ending is so sad." Now the father is really relieved. "I know what you mean, Michael. I have often felt sad while reading a book. The story must have really touched you." Michael nods. "It is sort of beautiful to feel touched by a story, don't you think? It helps you know your own feelings and what is important to you." Michael nods again and asks: "Can I read you the last page?" "Yes, I would like that, Michael," his father says.

Non-judgmental listening is oriented to perceiving and understanding the subjectivity of the child's feelings, the child's emotions, the child's way of making sense of things. Sometimes it is just enough to be available to the child. At other times the adult may need to help the child to express himself or herself by prompting with questions: "How do you feel about that?" or by acknowledging certain feelings: "You must feel frustrated in encountering such difficulties." All the while non-judgmental pedagogical understanding senses how this listening may contribute to the child's increased self-knowledge and self-responsibility.

Developmental understanding

The classic practitioner of developmental understanding is the child psychologist or school counsellor. Such specialists possess the theoretical resourcefulness to understand the kinds of developmental, familial, cultural, and social patterns that characterize a young person's life. For example, developmental understanding involves knowing something of the pressures the oldest child may experience in a family, or the kinds of influences that the peer group may exercise over an adolescent. Psychologists have diagnostic skills and they may have insight into typical stages of cognitive and moral growth, and the phases of life that young people go through. Similarly, sociologists may have special knowledge of the trappings of youth subculture, the habits of drug-users, or the behavior of children of divorce. And they may know conflict models of family relationships, as well as various systems of therapeutic intervention.

But it is not enough to be knowledgeable about general developmental psychology and the sociology of youth, and it is not enough to be able to diagnose cases through tests or to be able to classify or analyze the behavioral stages of young people. Models of expert advice or therapeutic intervention are not helpful if this knowledge is mostly external and academic. One may be an excellent scholar in psychology but be completely incapable of helping people in psychological need. Developmental understanding becomes pedagogical understanding only when the pedagogue knows how to help a particular child overcome obstacles in concrete situations, or how to grow more mature. Expert psychological or sociological knowledge is helpful only to the extent that developmental pedagogical understanding can explain the circumstances of unique situations while maintaining a view of what is best for a child. In other words, the generalizations of psychology, child development, school ethnography, sociology of youth, and anthropology of childhood are only pedagogically relevant to the extent that they can function as theory for the unique, as theory for the particular case defined by the concrete circumstances of a specific child's life.

Moser is a counsellor-teacher at Eastside, an academic high school. Most of his students in their final year are quite aware of the importance of doing well, since their marks and their final examinations are considered in college and university admissions. However, Moser is concerned about certain individual students who do not seem to have this attitude toward school and learning.

Joss is an example. He is repeating grade twelve after dropping out midstream last year. The way Joss dresses and presents himself identifies with the outlandish features of certain youth subcultures. Although Joss came back to school of his own accord, he often skips classes, and he rarely turns in homework assignments. Moser suspects that Joss is into drugs, too. Some teachers have already complained about Joss' poor work habits, and as his counsellor Moser has been forced to consider denying Joss the right of further attendance in those classes. Other teachers have commented that at least while he is in class he appears motivated to participate well.

However, among the teachers there is no unanimity about Joss' real problem. Some see his behavior merely as a phase that some kids go through, and possibly come out of, once the realities and pressures of the outside world present themselves. Some feel that Joss has fallen in with a bad crowd and that there is little the school can do to help him. Some point to his poor relationship with his parents and feel that Joss is reacting negatively to his upbringing. Some offer still other views of the "problem" of Joss. There are many views of the problem, but few if any workable solutions. Of course, any one or all of the interpretations may have merit in explaining Joss' behavior.

Moser has Joss in his English class and also is assigned to him as a counsellor. It is true that Joss often expresses himself negatively about parents, but not necessarily his own parents. Joss prides himself in having several friends who have been "kicked out of their homes." When the topic under discussion in literature class allows it, he expresses himself strongly about the fact that many street kids are forced to make it on their own in life. "I know some of them, and they do not need their parents to look after them." Sometimes it is not clear whether Joss blames the parents or whether he just admires his homeless friends for their resourcefulness and their philosophy of life. His relationship with his own parents is also ambiguous. They obviously are concerned about his welfare, and Joss recognizes that. Yet he seems to need to push himself away from their parental influence. The counsellor Moser is uncertain what role he should play in Joss' negative attitude toward learning at school.

School counsellors tend to be well aware of the uniqueness of each case they encounter in their task. Once one knows the circumstances of each individual youth it often becomes difficult to simply apply the rules of school policy.

Analytic understanding

Those who exemplify analytic understanding are the priest, minister, or spiritual mentor. These are the professionals who know that in many people's lives there are darker sides, the things we may feel ashamed talking about because we consider them bad, evil, unworthy, despicable, wicked, naughty. And we may also hesitate talking about secret fears, grief, feelings of inferiority, weakness, or frustrated ambition. Some of these darker materials are hidden away in the further recesses of our awareness so that we have difficulty seeing how they manifest themselves in everyday life.

In the view of certain religious communities human nature has been considered fundamentally evil and great pains have been taken to exorcise wickedness from the young who are all "born in sin." In contrast, the more modern view tends to see young children as innocent, good, and pure. But consequently, we tend to overlook the possible trouble oppressing a child — felt as guilt over bad behavior, transgressions, sins, regrets, but also fears, doubts, or negative feelings toward others — hatred, envy, jealousy. Analytic understanding helps liberate the child from such dark stirrings by identifying and helping him or her to face the meaning and significance of specific troubling emotions.

But it is not enough to act as confessor for sins. Analytic understanding becomes pedagogical understanding only when it is intended to help a child form a strong conscience and spirit, a sense of personal courage. These qualities are not necessarily achieved by the priestly gesture of divine forgiveness. Analytic pedagogical understanding aims to convert negative or harmful hidden feelings into positive forces for personal growth. Sometimes it is helpful to try to rectify causes of pain or, if this is not possible, to resolve that a problem needs working out in a concrete and practical manner.

Danny refuses to go to school because he is sick. In the early morning and during the week he complains that he does not feel well. But later in the afternoon and during the weekend, when friends come over, his ailment has subsided and he feels well enough to play. His complaints are non-specific. "I just feel I am coming down with someting," he complains to his mother. But he cannot locate the problem. No, it is not his head, nor his stomach. No, he does not feel nauseated. He just does not feel well. Not well enough to go to school. So Danny has stayed home for a few days.

When things don't change, his mother begins to suspect that Danny is "schoolsick." And she starts probing to see if there might be something about school that upsets Danny enough so that he does not want to go. It is only the third week in September, and initially Danny was very eager to resume school after summer vacation. Mother asks, "Is there anything you want to talk about Danny? Is there anything wrong with school? Does it have anything to do with the teacher? Or do you not get along with the other children?" From Danny's face she can see that she has touched a sensitive spot. "They are all ganging up on me?" he cries. "They are calling me names, and they tell me that I have to give them money." Mother inquires who "they" are, and Danny identifies several boys. "You should not have to feel afraid going to school Danny; is there nothing you can do to stop them? Would you like me to phone the teacher or the principal?" No, Danny does not like that. "They would think that I am a mommy's boy." The next day Danny feels no longer sick and he goes off to school. When he returns home later in the day his mother has to repress her impulse to immediately ask Danny about his day at school. She admits to herself that she had been worrying about Danny's being bullied. But Danny does not mention anything upsetting. At bedtime she asks in a casual way about Danny's trouble with the gang. "Oh that?" he says off-handedly, "I dealt with it." Mother frowns, "you dealt with it?" "Yes, they came after me again, but I looked the leader straight in his face, and I said, 'If you mess with me then you better know that I am pretty good at Karate,' and then he backed off. They are actually not such bad kids. I played soccer with them in the afternoon." "Well," says Mother admiringly, "I can see that you know how to stand up for yourself."

It is sometimes astonishing to an adult how small conflicts or occurrences can carry such huge weight and meaning for the child that it can even make him feel sick (or feel so bad that he pretends to be sick). Was Danny intimidated into feeling sick by the aggression of some of his fellow students? Was his sickness a result of not feeling able to deal with the troublemakers? It is not always easy to identify what the trouble is that preoccupies the child. But in this instance Danny seems to have come to terms with negative feelings of defeat, fear, or meekness. His mother has given a positive significance to his active resolve to face his troubles, by praising him for his ability to solve things himself. To grow up means that you learn to stand up for yourself.

Educational understanding

The fundamental example of educational understanding is displayed by the teacher. Educational understanding is based on an understanding of how a child experiences the curriculum, and an appraisal of the strengths and weaknesses in a child's learning. The pedagogue needs to know how to assess a child's present abilities as well as potentialities.

But it is not enough to diagnose or evaluate a child's state of education. Educational understanding becomes pedagogical understanding only when it is oriented towards working out what it means for this child to be and become an educated person in his or her evolving life. So educational pedagogical understanding must go beyond a diagnostic or evaluative assessment of what a child possesses or lacks. It also must be able to appraise strengths or weaknesses, academically speaking, in a child's educational achievements, including his or her social and emotional development.

Travers is a bright student and a formidable debater. He cannot do wrong in the eyes of the debating club coach, since he is the star of his school-team. The social studies teacher, too, is aware of Travers' eloquence. In class discussion, when historical or contemporary issues are discussed, Travers seems to derive great joy from attacking any possible issue and trying to effect a clash of views with whoever has uttered an opinion. On the one hand, the social studies teacher has to admire Travers' oratorical skills. Travers' class involvement often contributes to an animated atmosphere and lively discussions. You can always call on Travers for a well-articulated argument no matter what the issue is. He will debate the affirmative as strenuously and as persuasively as the negative. He always argues the other side. The teacher and all the kids in class have come to know Travers. Frequently, when he challenges something that the teacher or one of the students says, they just smile and pass over it: "There you go again, Travers!" On the other hand, the teacher does wonder about Travers' real commitments. While Travers is always ready to start up a debate, he is curiously indifferent about his personal commitment to any cause, no matter what its social or human relevance. Rather, he seems to enjoy debating for the sake of debating and for the sense of victory it provides him. He mockingly calls himself "amoral, above all morals, as long as I am having a good time!" But the teacher wonders: is Travers with his love for argument just a kid who is seeking attention? does he have a need to constantly prove himself superior? Or is he already so cynical about life that he cannot believe in anything? Today, the teacher is surprised because one of the students, Ronene, hits exactly at this point. There is a discussion in class about "the morality of euthanasia," and she stops Travers in mid-sentence and asks, "But what do you really *believe*, Travers? How am I supposed to respect a person who seems to shift his position so easily from one day to the next?" Of course, Travers is ready with an answer, "We are not discussing the respectability of my person, but rather the soundness of my point of view." Ronene shakes her head and mutters something like, "What a jerk." Now the teacher steps in. She says, "Let's stop the debate here and let each of us individually write a short essay on the topic under discussion. Understand, you are not arguing for or against any particular point of view, rather you are to clarify how you would personally answer the question of the meaning of death by euthanasia as a human phenomenon. You are to address neither another person nor a particular policy, but rather the meaning of euthanasia as it would be relevant for you if it were to affect your own parents or someone for whom you care deeply."

The teacher forces the students to move beyond the class discussion as a topic for practising one's skill at arguing a point of view to a situation where each student, including Travers, must show some sense of responsibility for the view he or she holds. Of course, the experience of teachers is that most kids of high school age usually will be quite emotionally involved in most class discussions. Travers is not the typical case. In life, cynicism tends to set in with adulthood. But this teacher is aware of the dubious value of Travers' significant skills for the development of a personal sense of responsibility and commitment. From Travers' essay the teacher may gain some insights into Travers' relation to his parents. The teacher already knows that Travers is from a well-to-do background, that he has been provided with many material advantages, that he is an only child, and that both his parents are deeply involved with professional careers that may have left them with little personal time for Travers. The task for the teacher is to apply her pedagogical understanding of Travers in a manner that helps Travers to integrate his academic accomplishments into a mature and socially responsible self.

Formative understanding

The fundamental source of formative understanding is the parent. It is really the primary form of pedagogical understanding. Formative understanding is based on a full and intimate knowledge of a child's life and what is unique about a particular child. By "full and intimate knowledge" I do not mean knowing every factual detail about a young person's life. Rather "full" means that one has a sense of the deeper and significant aspects of a child's life, and "intimate" means that one stands close enough to the child that one is animated by a strong sense of personal responsibility for the uniqueness of this particular young person. Formative understanding is involved in rearing or bringing up children. There is a strong sense of what "up" means for parents. Generally parents, and teachers, want their children to do well, to be successful, and to be happy in life.

But it is not enough to want one's child to become happy and successful. Formative understanding becomes pedagogical only when it is able to self-reflectively separate one's own parental (or *in loco parental*) motivations and agendas of success for the child from the immanent sense of what is good for this child's becoming a self-responsible and mature adult. Naturally, formative pedagogical understanding is not only exercised by the parents. Anyone who stands in an *in loco parentis* relation to a child would have the child's growing maturity in view. But few educators maintain close enough relations to many individual children over time that they gain a full understanding of each child's evolving life history and career. Nevertheless, formative pedagogical understanding is what children need from significant adults in their lives if they are to receive good guidance and support when it matters.

Sue is visibly upset when she throws her report card on the table. "I am so dumb! Why can't I get better marks when I try so hard?" Her parents, themselves teachers, glance at each other. They know that their daughter is not a star student. To be sure, it could be a lot worse. In most subjects Sue is hovering just above or below average in comparison to her class mates. And it is clear that Sue is a conscientious student who usually works hard for an average mark on her school exams. However, the parents realize that with this kind of report card many doors to higher education will be closed to Sue. They would so much have liked her to have the option of a professional career for which a strong academic background is an absolute requirement. The parents feel torn between the desire to put more pressure on Sue to achieve what may well be impossible for her, and the realization that it would not be fair to burden her with their parental ambitions. They are deciding that Sue has to make her own life choices, and it is the task of the parents to support her in whatever is possible and best with regards to Sue's life career.

This is the great challenge for all pedagogical understanding: to stand close enough to the child to want what is best for the child, and to stand far enough away from the child to know what is best for the child. It is usually easy for parents to stand close to the child who is after all their own. It is often more difficult for parents to set enough distance from the child to see the child as an independent being, to prevent confusing their own goals and desires with the goals and desires of the child. It is just the other way around for teachers. Teachers usually stand far enough away from the child to gain some objective view of the child's strengths and weaknesses. But teachers may find it more difficult to feel close enough to the child to make a real emotional and intellectual investment in the child's highest possibilities.

Pedagogical understanding is facilitated by trustful sympathy

Pedagogical understanding is required in situations where we feel called upon by the child to do something. Such situations that daily confront us have been referred to as "pedagogical moments." A distinguishing feature of pedagogical moments is that something is expected of us. We have to do something, even if that is holding off for the moment. Of course, one reaction is to simply ignore the child and to go about our adult business as if we have no pedagogical responsibility. Why should I have to listen to a child? What do I have to do with this child's life? Indeed, this is the course some adults take. But for others, disregarding a feeling of responsibility to children is just not possible. A child calls upon me for help and I feel I must act responsively and responsibly to the child. "Feeling called upon" is therefore the deeper significance, the life-meaning of being an educator, a parent, a pedagogue.

No quality is probably more essential for the practice of pedagogical understanding than our capacity for trustful sympathy. Pedagogical understanding often occurs as an immediate grasping of what is going on with a child. To have a sympathic capacity means that one is able to discern the subtle signs in a child's voice, glance, gesture, or demeanor. Sympathically we sense what an experience is like for the child, or what mood the child is in — frustrated, stimulated, sad, bored, joyful, adventurous, fearful, gloomy, interested. In maintaining a sympathic orientation to children we are infected by the same mood, the same feeling, so that an even closer relation is formed between ourselves and this child. With this interpretation I assign greater significance to sympathy than we ordinarily do in everyday life where it is often merely used to express a sentimental feeling of external support or distant concern.

Sympathic understanding goes beyond empathy.[42] To practise empathy (literally, *in-feelings*) suggests that we transfer something of our own mind and life into the body of the other person, that we feel ourselves into a child's experience without necessarily being touched by it. From an empathic vantage point the child can remain an object for our observation and analysis. This is sometimes seen as a strength, since the empathic observer can put himself or herself in the other's shoes while remaining detached and emotionally neutral or indifferent to the interests and subjectivity of the other person. But empathic understanding of people who differ markedly from ourselves is sometimes hard to conceive of since we may have difficulty in transposing our own inner life into the other person. Moreover, pedagogy usually requires a stronger and more personal understanding on the part of the educator than empathy allows.

In contrast, sympathy (literally, *with-feelings*) presumes not so much that we vicariously live in the other person but that the other person already lives in us, that we recognize the experience of the other person as a possible human experience — and thus as a possible experience of our own selves. But to open (our head and heart) to the inner life of the other we must orient ourselves to the other with care and love. Love is not blind but makes us see the other as other. So pedagogical sympathy attunes caringly to the inner life of the child, without confusing its own self in this inner life. In short, sympathy means pedagogically that the adult "understands" in a caring sense the situation of a child or young person. So pedagogical understanding is in this sense also engaged understanding.

A teacher who is judged sympathic by students tends to be described as warm, open, and understanding by them. There is little doubt that for most kids a sympathic orientation in their teachers is highly valued. This is a teacher who can pick up on the mood of the class, who can spot problems, to whom you can go if you have difficulties. In sympathic relations it is much easier to accept advice, encouragement, help, suggestions, and directions for learning. A teacher who has a general sympathic orientation to children tends to be seen as fair, helpful, and open-minded. The opposite to sympathy — antipathy — is characterized by aversion, coldness, indifference, unfriendliness, aloofness, hate, and contempt, all qualities that make the possibility of pedagogical influence far less likely and less deep.

The Relation between Reflection and Action

Generally we make a distinction between action and reflection. It is important to keep in mind the difference between being actively engaged in teaching children and being disengaged through reflecting on a past, present, or future situation. Reflection is possible in those moments when we are able to think about our experiences, about what we did or should have done, or about what we might do next.

Reflection is a fundamental concept in educational theory, and in some sense it is just another word for "thinking." To reflect is to think. But reflection in the field of education carries the connotation of deliberation, of making choices, of coming to decisions about alternative courses of action. It occurs in such phrases as "reflective teaching," "critical reflective practice," "reflection in action," and so forth. It is usually impressed on novice teachers by their professors that good teachers are reflective teachers; beginning teachers are taught how to adopt a reflective orientation to their practice. However, beginning teachers are not usually taught that the daily life of dealing with children is such that there seems little opportunity for reflection — and that this is not the fault of teachers or anyone else. Rather, it is a feature of living together in constant interaction which prevents teachers from critically reflecting on what they are doing while teaching. But more problematic is that there is little opportunity to reflect thoughtfully with colleagues about the practice and meaning of pedagogical experiences. One of the challenges of the teaching profession is to try to create those spaces and opportunities. This is partly a professional political issue.

These considerations lead us to make an immediate distinction between reflection on experiences and reflection on the conditions that shape our pedagogical experiences. It is safe to say that virtually all teachers (and parents too) experience in their lives constraints that frequently seem to make it difficult to be a significant influence on the children or young people for whom they feel pedagogically responsible. Many of these constraints have to do with institutional and political factors that operate in peoples' lives. For example, a common concern for teachers is that modern schools tend to be run like businesses, complete with measurement of "production performance," "output figures," "projected increased rates of success," "effectiveness of teachers," "students' standardized test outcomes." Consequently, the teachers' ability and inclination to reflect thoughtfully on the pedagogical nature of their lives with students are being atrophied by the objectifying and alienating conditions under which they work.

In the attempts by the educational bureaucracy to bring the processes of instruction under increasingly administrative and centralized control, the teachers' tasks have become "rationalized." The result is that the teacher as professional has become increasingly deskilled as the curriculum has become more and more prescriptive and dictated by centralized control, and as the pedagogical care of students has become highly fragmented ("streamlined") by referrals to resource teachers, psychologists, counsellors, school administrators — many of whom have too little contact with the students to be of much help to them in any sustained way. As the teacher is expected to treat the job of teaching more and more technically, the teacher is less and less able to reflect on the meaning, purpose, and significance of the educational experiences of students whom the school and the curriculum are supposed to serve.

Recently, educational theorists have argued that every situation in which we are to act pedagogically with children is theory-laden. By virtue of living in a scientifically advanced society our everyday experience is shot through with theoretic elements. Accordingly, we may distinguish among several levels or degrees of systematic reflection, some of which fuse into each other. First, there is everyday thinking and acting — partly habituated, partly routinized, partly composed of intuitive, pre-reflective, and semi-reflective rationality. This is the level of common sense thinking and acting in ordinary life. Second, we reflect in an incidental and limited way on our practical experiences in everyday life. At this level we put our experience into language and give accounts of our actions: We recount incidents, tell stories, formulate rules-of-thumb, practical principles, do's and don'ts, limited insights. Third, we reflect more systematically and in a more sustained way on our experience and others' experience with the aim of developing theoretical understandings and critical insights about our everyday action. At this level we may use existing theories to make further sense of these phenomena. Fourth, we reflect on the way we reflect, on the form of our theorizing, in order to come to a more self-reflective grasp of the nature of knowledge, how knowledge functions in action and how it can be applied to our active understanding of our practical action. It is important for educators, not only to act more thoughtfully and reflectively, but also to understand the nature and significance of reflective experiences and of the types of knowledge they use.

Naturally, reflection too is an experience. Some reflection is oriented to future action (anticipatory or preactive reflection); some of it is reflection on past experiences (recollective or retroactive reflection). But in either case, reflection is a form of human experience that distances itself from situations in order to consider the meanings and significance embedded in those experiences. By reflecting on an experience I have the experience of grasping and appropriating meanings embedded in that experience. Inevitably the reflective moments of life involve a temporary stepping back or stepping out of the immediate engagement we have with the world. "Where there is reflection, there is suspense," said Dewey.[43] As we reflect, we suspend our immediate involvements in favor of a more contemplative attitude. And, of course, some active or interactive reflection happens in the midst of life, as when we stop and think while we are doing something. All these forms of reflection regularly make up the life we live with children:

(1) Anticipatory reflection enables us to deliberate about possible alternatives, decide on courses of action, plan the kinds of things we need to do, and anticipate the experiences we and others may have as a result of expected events or of our planned actions. Anticipatory reflection helps us to approach situations and other people in an organized, decision-making, prepared way.

(2) Active or interactive reflection, sometimes called reflection-in-action, allows us to come to terms with the situation or problem with which we are immediately confronted. This stop-and-think type of reflection permits us to make decisions virtually on the spur of the moment.

(3) There is also a common experience composed of the interactive pedagogical moment itself, characterized by a different type of reflectivity: a certain mindfulness. It is this mindfulness that distinguishes the interaction of tactful pedagogues from the other forms of acting described above. While we are interacting (talking, gesturing, listening, working) with people, we usually do not have time or opportunity to reflect on our experience as it is happening. Most likely, much of our pedagogical interacting with children is made up of an ongoing rush of pedagogical situations and circumstances. In the immediacy of our actions, reflection does not occur in moments of interrupted stop-and-think action, neither does it occur parallel with our action. In other words, instant action is not usually produced by reflection. Yet this interactive experience or "rush" itself may be mindful.

(4) Recollective reflection helps us to make sense of past experiences and thus gain insights into the meaning of the experiences we have with children. As a result of recollective reflection we may become more experienced practitioners as teachers or parents because our lives have been enriched by the reflective experiences that offered us new or deeper understanding.

Reflection before action

There are at least two, albeit related, types of anticipatory reflection that teachers engage in. On the one hand, there is reflecting in anticipation of having to deal with pedagogical situations. For example, a student, Len, has been confronting the teacher in a manner that has become a recurring problem. The teacher is not quite sure what to make of these conflicts. She tries to gauge what the situation is like from Len's point of view. When she has a talk with Len after class they seem to come to an understanding. But in class Len seems to become a different person. He turns disruptive during the study activities and makes good group discussions almost impossible. The teacher talks to some of her colleagues in order to try to come to a better understanding of the boy. She also phones Len's mother to see if she can receive some further insights, and possibly support, to help Len become more cooperative and interested in school. The teacher has to decide on a course of action with Len that is appropriate. In other words, the teacher engages in anticipatory pedagogical reflection regarding the way she should act with Len the next day.

Here is another example: a mother had phoned last night that Dorothy feels sick and does not want to go to school. But she is not sure whether the sickness is real or imagined. She knows that Dorothy has been very unhappy the last few days because she feels that no one likes to play with her at school any more. Dorothy feels that some kids are behind this general ostracism. The teacher promises to look into the matter. The situation leaves open an array of alternative actions by the teacher. Does the teacher speak with Dorothy and suggest that the child try to speak openly about her hurt feelings to her best friends? (Would Dorothy be able to handle this? Are her friends open to such an approach?) Does he speak confidentially to Dorothy's best friends to let them understand Dorothy's unhappiness? (Would the kids understand? Do they have resentments that do not permit them to be sensitive to Dorothy?) Or does the teacher talk to the class as a whole and invite anyone who feels so inclined to make contact with Dorothy? (Is there a danger that this might place too much attention on Dorothy's case?) Would the teacher want to take a more indirect route with the class and read with the class a story about friendship and what it feels like to be rejected? (Would the children be able to see that this story applies to themselves?) Might the teacher draw Dorothy's name as "student of the week" about whom other children in class will write "nice" things? (Could this backfire if the other kids made fun of Dorothy?) Or should the teacher ask Dorothy herself if she knows a way that she could be reconciled with her classmates? (Would Dorothy be embarrassed about the teacher's intervention?) This kind of anticipatory reflection refers to those moments when we have to pull ourselves together and decide how we are going to deal pedagogically with a challenging, difficult, puzzling situation.

On the other hand, there is the more systematic task-oriented reflection of lesson planning. Planning is an exercise in systematic anticipatory thinking. In planning we may draw up columns showing how we intend to cover a subject. We imagine how we will traverse the landscape of learning: this first, that second, we will deal third with the more complex, and so forth. From past experience we have found that the planning is most successfully done for matters of fact: this reading assignment, those study questions, that review exercise, the scheduled tests. We try to imagine how the students may be responding to the itinerary of the course. Where do we need rest stops? Where do we need to stop to assess what we will have accomplished?

Looking ahead to plan lessons or decide how to act in pedagogical situations is a *sine qua non* for good teaching. Teachers who do not plan ahead will not be ready for teaching. Through planning and thinking things out beforehand we make ourselves pedagogically available to children in a meaningful way. It is impractical not to plan. But we need to see as well that curious consequences flow from planning when this planned instructional program becomes too fixed, too inflexible, too prescriptive for life with children. For one thing, inflexible planning may freeze the body of knowledge that is otherwise dynamic, vibrant, and alive.[44] Such planning tends to reduce to a scheme what is otherwise a rich, multifaceted subject matter.

It is a special characteristic of planning that, in a sense, it turns every subject into an object. Even the children for whom the planning is done become objects whose behavior and responses are thought about in more manipulative and predictive ways. Even the planner must become an objective element in the plan or program. As I plan deliberatively into the future I project myself. For example, I plan to tell a story as part of a science lesson and in this anticipatory thinking I become aware of myself as I am going to be, a story teller. And yet, as I script my behavior for the science project lesson and plan what to say and do, I strip myself of part of my own subjectivity and of my immediate and active relation with the world.

Once the plan or program has been drawn up I must sooner or later put it into practice. In a sense, my planning for a particular teaching situation becomes a commitment, an embodied tension, which orients me to this situation in a certain way. For example, if I plan to tell a story about a scientist, then I project a certain atmosphere into this future situation. In this way I ready myself for the situation in which I have to act in a teacherly way. If I can hold on to the quality of the intention and atmosphere of the plan, then I enable myself to be ready for almost anything — the mood of the students, their questions, and all the rest.

But there is a danger in the deliberative nature of planning. Planning that tries to fix totally the future situation robs me of the liberty necessary to remain open to the pedagogical moments of the situation as they arise. When planning becomes too fixed, the adult's interactions with children run the danger of losing the tentativeness and openness that characterize much of everyday human interaction. Planned action can thus turn into scripted action. Even though in real situations, plans are rarely followed to the letter, some teachers make a diligent attempt to stick to their plans as if they were iron rules.

We need to realize that when we carefully plan for a certain teaching situation we experience this planning as a choice and a commitment that take hold of us and that actualize themselves once we are in the situation for which the planning was intended. That may be why a planned lesson that we repeat later in the day sometimes turns out less animated, less inspired than the one we just did. For the lesson to go well we need to hold on to the atmosphere that the original planning generated in anticipatory imagination. Further, it should also be clear that when we teach somebody else's plan we may not have charged ourselves up as when we do our own planning. True planning always involves this experiential sense of commitment and orientation that takes hold of us and is released once we can act out the anticipated activity.[45] If we merely follow someone else's plans, we turn into mere executors or technicians of an externally determined set of behaviors.

Naturally there are degrees or levels of anticipatory reflection that may range from loose rehearsing to carefully planned structures and sequences. Moreover, there is a kind of anticipatory reflection that has more to do with a total philosophic outlook or a comprehensive educational program that one gradually adopts over the course of time. For example, when I adopt an individualized approach to teaching, then I am preparing pedagogical situations that will differ in certain important respects from a more group-based approach to teaching and learning.

Reflection in action

One answer to the criticism of the teacher as a mere executor of some prespecified plan or curriculum program has been the notion of the teacher as a "reflective practitioner." It posits that the interactive process of teaching is essentially a reflective practice. The idea of the reflective practitioner says that the teacher is a professional who operates within a domain (the educational or pedagogical enterprise) just as other professionals do in the domains of medical practice or engineering.

It has been argued that the reflective practitioner is the professional who reflects in action through constant decision making. In this decision making the professional is seen as guided by the theoretical and practical principles of his or her discipline — even though these principles may be operating in a more or less tacit fashion. Thus, some of the theories of the teacher as reflective practitioner try to be sensitive to the intuitive, dynamic, and nonrational features of the act of teaching. They stress that we should not reduce the act of teaching to a simple theory-into-practice model of human action. Teaching is not a technical production process, with inputs, treatments, and outputs. Yet most models eventually seem to offer a reconstructed logic of the interactive moment of teaching that looks surprisingly similar to the process of rational deliberation or decision making. How accurate is the image of the reflective practitioner in comparing, let us say, the family physician and the school teacher?

I explain my ailments to the medical doctor: I have experienced a paralyzing sensation in my right arm. Although the use of my arm has been restored over a number of weeks, I still suffer from strange and anxiety-producing symptoms — weakness, stiffness in muscles and joints, prickling sensations in the fingers, some pain. I still do not have the full use of my fingers, a nuisance when I try to write. The doctor listens and writes some things down. He asks more questions and examines my arm. Then he sits down again and while I am silent, awaiting his suggestions, I notice that the doctor is making columns on his paper. He has quickly drawn vertical lines and is filling in the columns with technical terms. I am sitting back now. Obviously the doctor is reflecting on what to make of my ailments and what possible action to take. I wait a bit longer, and then I clear my throat. I ask the doctor what he is drawing and writing on this little note pad. The doctor indicates that in the first column he has jotted down the various symptoms that I have indicated: arm weakness, heart palpitations, pain, loss of sensation. In the next column he has matched the different symptoms with possible diseases. In column three he has entered the tests which would check the likelihood of the various diagnostic possibilities. The doctor lists in column four the treatments to be suggested in case any of the tests turn out positive. The doctor explains to me that he is trying to decide which diagnostic speculation seems most plausible and thus with which tests he should start first. When the doctor makes out a referral form for some lab work, it occurs to me that this doctor has just shown me an active and concrete picture of the reflective practitioner at work. In the practice of this medical professional there are evidently moments of detached reflection, deliberating about possible alternatives, deciding on the best course of action, and then acting on this judgment. These are components of a reflective form of acting, which we may see as a kind of "deliberative on the spot decision making." Competent experienced doctors often develop a perceptive and intuitive eye for their patients' ailments. For these doctors the process of reflection is absorbed into a more tacit or intuitive competence[46] that shows itself in the immediacy of acting in the medical situation. But even the latter more tacit reflection-in-action process is conditioned by problem-solving behavior based on medical science.[47]

How does this image of the experience of the reflective practitioner, the physician involved with patients, compare with the teacher who is involved with students? In the example above the physician is a problem solver who uses his medical knowledge of the body and its diseases to help restore the patient to a healthy state. Is the teacher or parent a reflective practitioner and problem solver in the same sense? Sometimes yes. Obviously teachers are involved in a wide variety of practices. Sometimes the teacher deals with such problem-solving as how to share insufficient material resources with a large group of students. Sometimes the teacher prepares and plans lessons, assignments, or tests. At other times the teacher is involved in routine or habituated teaching sequences. Periodically the teacher meets with parents or with resource people to discuss the progress or special needs of selected students. There is little doubt that when a teacher (or a teaching specialist such as a reading consultant) does diagnostic work with a particular child who seems to have a specific difficulty, as with reading, this diagnostic process may show marked similarities with the practice of the family physician. In fact, the reading problem may sometimes appear to have a physiological base. Thus the reading specialist may typically engage in a process of (deliberative) reflective practice. However, here we do not want to address primarily those specialized diagnostic settings. Nor do we want to speak primarily of teaching only when routines and habits are governing the process. Rather, we are interested especially in the interactive reality of the pedagogical moment or situation. Indeed it is the immediate acting on the spot, in the ongoing flux of pedagogical moments, that is little understood in educational theories.

The situation that parallels best the reflective practice of the medical situation of doctor and patient is the pedagogical situation of teacher and student. But, unlike the medical doctor, the pedagogue seems less involved in problem-solving reflection than in reflecting on the pedagogical meaning or significance of certain experiences. Problems seek solutions, "correct" knowledge, effective procedures, solution strategies, productive techniques or methods that get results! When I consult the doctor with a physical ailment, I have a problem that the doctor can hopefully solve and rectify.

But problems of teaching are seldom "problems" in this sense. Rather, teachers deal with situations, predicaments, possibilities, and difficulties. Situations and predicaments must be handled the best we can, and possibilities and difficulties must be realized and worked through. Ultimately predicaments and difficulties constitute "problems of meaning," or rather questions of meaning. For example, when a child is "difficult" or when a child experiences "difficulty" (which often means different things), then this difficulty can rarely be "solved" and done away with. I must ask what the meaning of this difficulty is for the child, and what the pedagogical significance of this is for me as teacher. Meaning questions cannot be "solved" and done away with once and for all. Few pedagogical problems can ever be eradicated on the spot or overnight. Rather we must learn to get on and get along with these situations and with each other.

Pedagogical meaning questions are deeply normative;[48] questions that deal with the meaning of experiences must be better or more deeply understood, so that on the basis of this understanding I may be able to act more thoughtfully and tactfully in this and future situations. But pedagogical problems (questions, predicaments, difficulties) can never be closed down. They always remain the subject matter of conversation. They need to be appropriated, in a personal way, by anyone who hopes to benefit from such insights. In other words, "difficulty" is something we have to interpret, work at, and remain attentive to.

Thoughtful action in pedagogical situations

Earlier in this book I described the pedagogical moment as that situation when the pedagogue does something appropriate to learning in relation to a child or young person. But pedagogical situations usually do not permit the teacher to reflectively step back, analyze the situation, deliberate about possible alternatives, decide on the best course of action, and act on this decision. Some researchers have estimated that teachers on average make a decision once a minute. They mean that the teacher is constantly acting in ever-changing situations. Most often the pedagogical moment requires the teacher to act instantly. With the hindsight of rational observation this instant action may look like a kind of decision-making-on-the-spot, but it is not really decision making in the usual problem-solving and deliberative sense. It should be reiterated that all reflection always presumes a certain time element and taking distance from the experience that is the object of our reflection. In this distancing we always become aware of our actions in some more or less objectified manner. The ego mirrors (re-flects) the self in an I – me relation. For example *I* noticed *myself* getting confused or irritated.

In pedagogical interactions we do not commonly experience a splitting between two egos or selves, I and me: one who acts and one who reflects on the action. Of course, we can be thinkingly aware of what we are saying or doing while we interact with children or students. But this awareness is usually volatile and transient. There may even be elements of catching ourselves saying something we feel we should not have said, or catching ourselves and holding back before we do something that we might regret. But these are acts of "self"-consciousness, of embodied mindfulness or tact, that little resemble the decision-making practice of deliberative reflection. (It is significant that self-consciousness, meaning consciousness of one's own acts, easily turns into an overly tense awareness of oneself, making normal social interaction uncomfortable, artificial, or even impossible.) In our pedagogical lives with young people we are actively and immediately involved in a manner of consciousness (with mind and body, head and heart) that only later is open to true reflection. When we are confronted with a child in a situation that demands a response or an initiative from us, the common experience is that we have already acted before we really know that we have acted.

The experience of thoughtful pedagogical action in pedagogical situations has a peculiar structure. It is neither largely habitual nor problem solving, neither solely intellectual nor solely corporeal, neither purely reflective in a deliberative sense nor completely spontaneous or arbitrary. Living the pedagogical moment is a total personal response or thoughtful action in a particular situation. Thoughtful action differs from reflective action in that it is thinkingly attentive to what it does without reflectively distancing itself from the situation by considering or experimenting with possible alternatives and consequences of the action. So when we come to tactful action rather than say that it is "reflective" we should say that tactful action is thoughtful in the sense of "mindful."

Over the weekend I have read a thoughtful interpretation of Rilke's poem, "The Panther." Now it is Monday morning and I walk into the twelfth grade classroom totally stimulated and turned on in anticipation of the lesson on "The Panther." If I were an inexperienced or naive teacher then I might have thought that I can just walk in and "teach Rilke." As long as I knew it all and I expressed it all the task would be done. The measure of how well it would have been done would depend on how carefully I had thought through what I would need to say and do, and on the extent that the students caught on to what I was trying to do. But now I know that it is not enough to just walk in and expect the students to be ready for Rilke, even with an appropriate motivator. Yes, in part I am positively tense with excitement about this fascinating interpretation of Rilke's "The Panther."

But as I walk into the classroom I intuitively get a sense of where these students are coming from. I know that some of them have been working part-time during the weekend, others have had good or bad experiences on Saturday and Sunday, some have had late nights and are not necessarily looking forward to another week of school. Yet all these kids have managed to get on the bus or somehow arrive at school, and they have all managed to sit down in their seats at eight this morning. Right now they could not care less about Rilke or poetry. So as I walk into the classroom I am somehow sensitive to the atmosphere and dynamics of the group (even though I do not really make this awareness conscious). I happen to focus in on Darryl, whose loud shuffle and laughter somehow seems to flavor the mood of the class. He catches my eye and I smile at him. Somehow he seems to interpret this as an invitation to make a comment about the ice-hockey team that lost in the semi-finals. Hockey is not really my interest but I sympathetically nod, and I crack a joke about it. Some more impromptu comments are exchanged, other kids are tuning in, and the class seems to come together. This is superficial chitchat. But we need to connect somehow before we can really make a start at anything.

Monday morning classes are often not too hard to get started because quite literally the students are not yet fully woken up. Just as we slide out of bed on Monday morning and toothbrush our way groggily into the new week, so we ease into the Monday morning lessons at school by warming up our interest and stimulating our readiness to think. On other days of the week the students may show less willingness to slip into a language arts lesson about conjunctions, or metaphors, or a novel, play, or poem.

I had planned to start the Rilke lesson with a question on the board for the class to think and write about before we got started with group discussions about some themes from Rilke's poem. But somehow it does not seem the right starting point just yet, and so I begin with an appeal. "I like to read to you a poem by Rainer Maria Rilke, entitle 'The Panther.'" (As I am talking I have a feeling already that the mood is not quite right for this sort of thing and before I can help it I offer something that almost sounds like an apology:) "I realize that poetry may not be foremost on your mind this morning ... " (A couple of kids look at me askance and Martha rolls up her eyes as if to say, "you can say that again!" ... But now a feeling of self-righteousness emerges in me. I do not wish to be apologetic and I continue with a bit more zeal.) "Sometimes it is difficult to do things we set out to do and the Panther poem has a story connected with it that illustrates this point."

Rilke was a person who lived his life very intensely and his poetry reflects an incredible commitment to explore life as deeply as possible. To earn money, Rilke had become secretary to the famous French sculptor, Rodin, but working in Paris, Rilke got very frustrated with his inability to write. One day he confided in Rodin that he had been unable for several months to write any poetry. Rodin gave him advice that changed the course of Rilke's poetic development. Rodin suggested that he go to the zoo, select an animal, and look at the animal inside the cage until he could really see it. "Go and sit in front of a cage. A few weeks wouldn't be too long," said Rodin. Just imagine looking at an animal with that kind of patience and attentiveness! Rilke picked the panther and eventually he wrote the poem by that name. After the panther poem he wrote much more poetry based on that kind of careful observation. These were later called "the seeing poems." In each of the seeing poems it is clear that Rilke saw much more than we ordinarily see when we look at an animal. In the case of the panther, Rilke seems to have captured something of its wild soul.

As I am telling this story to the students I am constantly aware who is with me and who is fidgeting or seems preoccupied. This is a teacherly awareness of the contact that one is making with the students individually and as a group. But as the story progresses the whole class seems to come together. The attentiveness of the students prods me to turn a bit more dramatic in my relating of the Rilke anecdote. I ask if anyone has ever seen any sculptures by Rodin, and we talk a bit about the way that creative artists "see" things. Can they see things that we cannot see? I tell the students that the panther poem always makes a deep impression on me. "I have three translations of this poem, which was originally written in German, and before I give you the texts I would like to read them out loud to you. Afterwards we should try to determine which English translation you find the most evocative and poetically the strongest."

No matter how well I have planned my lesson or how enthusiastic I am about the subject matter, the interactive situation in the classroom is such that I must constantly remain aware of how it is for the kids. (In high school you only see the students so many minutes every day or two, and so it is easy to slip into a mode of teacher-centered, content-centered thinking and acting that completely ignores the students.) And yet this awareness is more a thoughtfulness than a calculating or deliberative reflectiveness, which would put one equally out of touch with the students, since that would create a distance that accompanies any manipulative interpersonal relation between teacher and students. So as I interact with the students I must maintain an authentic presence and personal relationship for them. What the example is meant to show is that life in classrooms is contingent, every moment is situation-specific. And the immediacy of the interactive pedagogical processes is very difficult to describe, since any description tends to place the experience at a reflective distance for our contemplation.

Here is another example, this time from a home situation: Mark is practising his violin. But he is weary, uninspired, and mostly going through the motions. The violin sounds tired, too. The grandmother who is over for a visit at Mark's house peeks into the room. She sees Mark and the sagging violin on his shoulder. Mark's face shows his disheartened mood. Unobtrusively Grandma slips into the room and sits down on a chair in the corner. She quietly continues her needle work. But Mark does notice her presence, for his posture straightens, the bow strikes the strings with new vigor, there is a sudden dynamism in the way he is playing the piece. Mark is no longer just practising. He is performing for Grandma. There is feeling in this music. And Grandma is listening with obvious delight.

It is marvelous how Grandma instantly knew what do. Yet if she were later asked to give an account of her action, she might even say that she did not really decide to try to inspire Mark. She just sat down because the moment seemed to call for it, and her mere presence animated Mark into a better effort in his violin practice. Grandma realized that her presence might stir Mark into a musical mood. But in what sense was reflection involved in her action? Did she think of this before she sat down? Maybe, in some vague sense. More likely, she was aware of the pedagogical benefits of her action just as she sat down. She would also want to say that it could have gone otherwise. Mark might have stopped playing altogether and complained to his Grandma that he just does not feel like practising. What would Grandma have done then? Would she have been able to convert that situation into a pedagogical moment too? Perhaps. In our pedagogical living with children nothing is ever completely foreseeable, predictable, plannable, manageable. And it is usually not until afterwards that we have the opportunity to think reflectively through the significance of the situation.

Just as there are degrees or levels of anticipatory reflection that may range from loose rehearsing to carefully plotted plans, so there are modes of immediate acting that range from the intuitive thoughtfulness of immediate improvisational acting on the one side to the more self-conscious thoughtfulness of mediated improvisational action on the other side. In the self-forgetful intuitive mode, the "thinking" is truly dialogic or conversational in nature, meaning that we interact in an open, direct, and sharing manner. In the more self-conscious mode of acting there comes into play a noticeable tension between the conversational I or self and the reflective I that holds the spontaneous conversational nature of intuitive acting at a distance. In some situations this may be due to the nature of the topic or participants in the conversation, which forces me into a more cautious thoughtful or thinking mood. This happens when I realize in the middle of a conversation that I am not sure of my own view or motive, which leads to an increased self-awareness and attentiveness to detail. In this case I become aware of myself acting while I am acting. In other situations the spontaneous dialogue of immediate acting is somewhat forced when I realize that I do not trust the other with whom I am interacting. And now I pick my way through the situation in the way that I pick my way through a hectic traffic rush hour. I change lanes to take advantage of the shorter line.

But I already know that I am running the risk of getting stuck behind left-turning traffic and thus lose the advantage of having chosen the shorter left lane over the right hand lane. In active on-the-spot judging of traffic situations I am already aware of possible consequences of certain kinds of configurations. I instantly know where something might lead. In rush hour traffic, too, there is no time for the deliberative process of reflection.

One more example may show the relation between immediate action and the reflective attitude. Father is busy with something, when out of the corner of his eye he notices that his six-year-old son Tony is hiding something behind a cupboard. "What are you doing there, Tony?" asks the father. "We don't put things behind the cupboard. Why don't you use the drawer to put things in?!" Tony stops in his tracks. He seems a bit embarrassed, guilty even, but says, "Oh no, it's nothing, Dad. Nothing important." His father persists. "But what were you doing there behind the cupboard, Tony? Will you show me?" Sheepishly Tony produces a small pocket knife. "This is Jeff's knife. He let me borrow it for today. I won't even take the blade out. I am just keeping it until tomorrow. It was okay with Jeff's mother." Tony's face is a bit red and drawn. He knows that his father does not like him to play with knives. And indeed his father says, "Well, Tony, you know that we do not play with knives in this house. Would you please take it back to Jeff?"

Tony leaves the house. But father now feels bothered. Why had he acted like that? Even while he was talking to Tony, he had started to feel uncomfortable about his response. Later he talks over the event with his wife. He says, "You know what bothers me most is not that Tony had this knife, but that he was trying to keep something from me. Maybe I felt that he was trying to be sneaky. And I was being excluded from something. It was as if there was something that had come between us. Tony and I are always so open and trusting with each other. Now I felt that this knife was like a secret that had created a distance between us. I could see from his face that he was embarrassed. It was as if he had this mask over his face rather than his usual openness." Mother and father talk a bit longer about knives and secrets. The next day the father takes Tony aside. He says, "Tony, I did not know that having a knife meant so much to you. I guess you should be old enough to own one." Then he hands Tony a real pocket knife. "Let me show you now how to handle this knife so that we won't have any accidents with it. Do you know how to open it and how to cut? Right, you are doing well ... . Always hold the knife like that and cut away from your body."

Tony's father gives his son the responsibility of owning a knife. But there was more at stake. Tony had been keeping a secret. The father responded directly to this new experience of his son's keeping something hidden from him. Upon reflection Tony's father has come to the recognition that keeping a secret is not necessarily a bad thing. So now Tony's father is more inclined to let Tony have his secrets. The father even sees the importance of it in the gradual growth of Tony's independence.

These anecdotes show two situations: one where an adult fulfills a pedagogic moment (Mark's grandmother); and another where an adult at first misses the pedagogical opportunity to act appropriately in the situation (Tony's father). But Tony's father learns something from the experience, and he is able to recover a pedagogical possibility that was initially lost. He reflects on the meaning for a young boy of possessing a knife, and he reflects on the meaning that the experience of secrecy may have for Tony. Thereafter the father adopts a more pedagogically thoughtful orientation. If or when, at a later time Tony may again be hiding something from his parents, his father may then be inclined to overlook it, because now the father has a more thoughtful understanding of a child's need for personal, private space. But when this happens, it is the result, not of thought-in-action but as reflection on action.

Reflection on action

So we may say that the pedagogical moment requires not so much reflection *in* action as reflection *on* action. But reflection on action is recollective; it always occurs after the situation has passed. Sometimes we reflect on what we did or did not do because something about the situation troubles us and prompts us to reflect. At other times we reflect on past actions simply because pedagogy requires a reflective orientation to life. When we are pedagogically involved with children or young people we tend to reflect also on the seemingly insignificant and trivial aspects of situations.

Generally speaking, pedagogical reflection tries to be mindful of whether the action in the pedagogical situation was appropriate (good, right, best under the circumstances). What was going on in this situation? What was it like for the child? What is the pedagogical significance of this? Did I say or do the right thing? In other words, recollective pedagogical reflection on action wonders "what one should have done." By thoughtfully reflecting on what I should have done, I decide in effect how I want to be. In other words, I infuse my being and my readiness to act with a certain thoughtfulness. And yet, how I am now as a teacher will not be clear until I have had further opportunity to act in more appropriate ways. How I am as a teacher depends on what I do, on my possibilities for acting thoughtfully. But my possible actions do not magically arise, they depend on the thoughtfulness that I have been able to acquire in recollective reflection.

Recollective reflection on action may, of course, be done through conversation with others. In fact, it is often in a conversation with another person that we are best able to reflect on the meaning of a particular situation (as Tony's father and mother did). But conversational reflection too can only be practised by distancing ourselves in time and space from the experience that becomes the subject of our reflection. In everyday life we tell each other stories about the experiences we have had with children. This telling and retelling of anecdotes can be seen as a form of practical theorizing in which parents and teachers spontaneously engage. As we tell others about our experiences with children we are already making sense of these experiences by bringing these experiences into speech. Often, when we feel frustrated about our actions, we say, "What I should have done is. ... " This is not just water under the bridge: As we reflect on our experiences we have an opportunity to become aware of the significance of these experiences.

Let us by way of example reflect on the meaning and significance of children keeping secrets from their parents. Very young children tend to respond freely and openly to their parents' questions and communications. But as children grow older it is not unusual that suddenly they may begin to feel resentful about the questions that parents ask in all sincerity. Suddenly the child experiences the questions as if the parents were prying. This is a new experience for the child: to know something that his or her father or mother does not even know, to possess something for oneself alone! There is even a certain sense of power associated with keeping a secret from the parents, who are for the young child so all-powerful and all-knowing. To have a secret gives the child a feeling of personal identity. In the experience of secrecy children discover inwardness, privacy, inner invisibility. When something is hidden or kept secret from someone else then the "self" is somehow concealed; that is why secrecy confers a certain value on that which is kept secret. (And that is why people will often go to great lengths to detect, unravel, or find out what is kept secret!)

The child's hiding of a secret is also a sign of growth toward autonomy, toward independence. Now a certain openness, mutuality, transparency is transgressed in the child's keeping a secret from the parent. By having a secret, by hiding something, the child separates self (the soul) from the family (community).[49] Thus, the experience of learning to keep a secret is a necessary part of childhood and of growing up. Significantly, many children's games have associated with them a quality of secrecy. At first, keeping a secret from the parents (and from siblings or friends) is an experience of emancipation for the child. It is a discovery of privacy and an assertion of selfhood. Later, sharing a secret with the same parent or with a trusted friend becomes another significant experience in the process of growing up toward independence. A person who cannot keep a secret lacks independence, but a person who cannot share a secret lacks independence, too.

These paragraphs show how pedagogical reflection considers the meaning of certain experiences and what one should have done in those situations. Thus, pedagogical reflection on action serves to make subsequent action more mindful and tactful. When some day Tony's father notices again that Tony seems secretive about something, he may be more tactfully inclined to let it pass. This is not because he is reflectively deliberating on the spot on the significance of his six-year-old's keeping another secret from him. Rather, he is already thoughtfully conciliated by his previous fatherly reflecting on his past interactions with Tony. In other words, Tony's father's actions are already attuned to past reflections. If Tony's father is demonstrating more tact in living with his child it is because his behavior consists of actions sensitized to the pedagogical significance of the child's desire to keep a secret. A tactful parent will want to respect the child's secrecy, since to pry into a child's secrets is to disrespect the child's individuality and the child's need for personal, private space.

In contrast to the physician who reflects *in* action on what he or she should do in a medical situation, the pedagogical moment calls for action that is both "thought-ful" and "thought-less." In other words, the pedagogical interactions of parents or teachers with children is not marked by reflection in the course of action but rather by tactful acting marked by thoughtfulness. Tactful action is thoughtful in that the educator shows appropriate sensitivity to what is good and required in a situation. But tactful action is "thoughtless" in that one cannot step back and reflect while one acts. Tactful action is an "instant thinking acting" that cannot be fully reflective — in other words, it is not really the outcome of a problem-solving process or a decision-making activity.

Pedagogical situations require our immediate response and participation. Because a teacher or a parent does not have time to reflect in order to deliberate and then decide what to do, it follows that one often may make mistakes by doing or saying things, or by not doing or saying things, that seem inappropriate in hindsight. In this, pedagogy differs fundamentally from medicine. When a doctor makes a mistake it can have serious consequences for the patient's health. When a dentist pulls the wrong tooth, the tooth can no longer be reinserted. But when a parent or teacher makes a mistake it can almost always be remedied or rectified. In fact, admitting to having made a mistake, and talking about it openly, can have positive consequences for personal growth and for the relationship between parent or teacher and child.

Can routinized and habitual acting be thoughtful?

At this point we should remind ourselves that in everyday life, at home as well as in the school, many of our actions and interactions with children are to a certain extent routinized. In addition, we have formed certain personal habits which have become part of our pedagogical lives. It is quite possible that in many cases the existence of routines and habits is a sign of the inflexibility and dreariness that often governs children's lives. We all know teachers who, we feel, should insert more reflectiveness and innovation into their daily practice. Sometimes teachers have irritating habits as they talk monotonously or they overuse a word like "okay": "Okay, settle down now, class! Okay, what I want you to do now is. ... " But the existence of routines and habits does not in itself signify that these practices are unreasonable or pedagogically reprehensible. In fact, good teachers probably demonstrate a well-established set of routines and habits that find their origin in careful reflection. For example, it may have become my "second nature" (habit) to refrain from speaking in front of a class of students unless I have the attention of all the students. I may habitually lower my voice and slow down my speaking when a class of students seems to become restless and agitated.

Let me give another example of good routines. In Teachers' College in the Netherlands I recall that, as novice teachers, we discussed the importance of always being aware that as teachers we should not be callously wasteful of children's time with poorly prepared lessons or with activities that should have been organized so that students could be more involved, rather than having to wait around for their turn, or until the teacher got the film-projector finally figured out. (One half hour of wasted classroom time in a class of thirty students is fifteen hours of children's lives!)

Related to this reminder of respect for children's time was the then-prevalent conviction that, as a rule, children in elementary schools should start every morning with learning and practising mathematics, since this subject requires a certain concentration and fresh energy. In contrast, "free reading time" was typically suggested for late morning or late afternoon when the children could use the quietness of the silent reading experience. Thus "math first thing in the morning" became pretty much the custom in many elementary school classes in the Netherlands. And this routine was grounded in a defensible pedagogical rationale.

In contrast, in Canada and the United States it is currently suggested that in elementary schools children start each morning with "uninterrupted sustained silent reading." We could examine how "math first thing in the morning" versus "silent reading first thing in the morning" is a beneficial routine for the child. But apart from the question of which routine makes more sense, routines and habits are not necessarily bad pedagogically speaking — even when these routines are not subjected daily to critical reflection. In fact, children not only need to be stimulated by new and challenging learning experiences, but also they benefit from the trust and security created by routines and habits grounded in past reflective pedagogical decisions. Habits, in their proper place and proportion, make life to a certain extent habitable, predictable, comfortable, and reliable.

Life might well become unlivable if all of our actions always needed to be the result of immediate critical, rational reflection. Teachers as well as children need to be able to rely on routines, habits, and customs that are, however, in principle pedagogically justifiable. When we teach children to be honest, friendly, and considerate, or routinely practise "uninterrupted sustained silent reading" in the morning, then these habits should be based on past pedagogical reflection. Of course, these habits are always open to review and further pedagogical reflection. Children can be taught habits while also learning to reflect critically on these routines.

Naturally, habits and routines may become blind, mechanistic behavior that no longer makes sense. For example, some schools have disciplinary policies that completely overlook that schools are meant to be pedagogical institutions and not criminal colonies or law courts whose main function is the "management of social order." The maintenance of discipline in schools should not be based primarily on juris-prudence but on pedagogical principles. The question should always be, "What can this child, and our whole community, learn from this?"

Routines, habits, and customs are not necessarily blind to the contingencies of life. In fact, they may be highly responsive and adaptive to ever-changing circumstances. Indeed tactfulness itself may turn into a habit, a way of relating to children. The teacher has the habit of being tactful to children, which means that the teacher has the tendency to act thoughtfully towards children in constantly changing situations. And even the routine of "math first thing in the morning" would mean that the teacher is sensitive to the requirements of the curriculum and the needs of the students.

There are certain habit-like features of teaching and relating to students that might best be described with the term *style*. And style is more than a habitual and idiosyncratic way of behaving or talking. Similarly, style should not be confused with teaching technique or method. Style is the outward embodiment of the person. In some sense, to have a style is being yourself, being who you really are. When someone says, "That is not my style," he or she is really saying, "That is not the way I am. That's not me."

Novice teachers must spend time discovering who they are, what belongs to them, what habits they can acquire. When a teacher settles down a rowdy class with a simple look of the eyes, or when the teacher motivates the students' interest with an enigmatic smile, these behaviors are not easily imitated. The reason for this is that they must be animated by the embodiment of this teacher. Teachers thus use certain habitual ways of behaving and presenting themselves with children or young people, of which they themselves are at best only dimly aware. Educational theory rarely addresses what these stylistic features of teaching consist of, since these features have more to do with what is unique and personal than with what is common and generalizable. Yet the essence of good teaching may have something to do with this phenomenon of personal style.

The very way we teach science, art, literature, or math is in large part a function of the way that we embody these subjects. A science teacher is more than just a person who happens to teach science. A real science teacher is a person who thinks science, who wonders about the nature of science and the science of nature — a real science teacher is a person who embodies science, who lives science, who in a strong sense is science. And so we can often tell whether a person is a real teacher by the way this person "stylizes" what he or she teaches.

Teachers who do not feel for kids, or do not have a feel for the subject they teach, may be incapable of forming a style for these subtle and often elusive habit-like features of pedagogy. There is a way of orienting oneself to science that is different from the way one orients oneself to poetry for example. A good teacher often demonstrates a way of questioning, of thinking through problems, of being animated by an interest that has to do with the way this teacher has come to embody the subject matter in his or her style. These stylistic and habitual ways of teaching may be quite significant and yet not easily be subject to reflective analysis.

Pedagogical fitness is the mind-body skill of tact

In the sections above the main effort has been to determine the nature of action in the thick of dealing with children in pedagogical situations. Of course, in everyday life some teachers may act in ways that are predominantly authoritarian, insensitive, thoughtless. Other teachers may deal with children in ways that students find artificial, affected, stuffy, stilted, inauthentic, or distant. But action that is more in keeping with the pedagogical relation itself is action that involves thoughtful reflection. We have seen that action characterizing concrete experiences between teachers and students in pedagogical situations may not be reflective (in a deliberative decision-making sense). Yet this action needs to be mindful and to benefit from reflection. This capacity for mindful action we have referred to as *tact*, pedagogical tact.

Tact is the practical language of the body — it is the language of acting in pedagogical moments. Tactful action is an immediate involvement in situations where I must instantaneously respond as a whole person to unexpected and unpredictable situations. Tact as we experience it in our active living with children is a sentient awareness of our subjective self as we act. In other words, while we are acting as teachers or as parents with children we do not objectify or take distance from our acting.

Tact as a form of human interaction means that we are immediately active in a situation: emotionally, responsively, mindfully. Even when as tactful pedagogues we are engaged sensitively, reflectively with a child—searching for the right thing to say or do, we nevertheless are only dimly aware of our actions, (unaware of ourselves in a self-reflective sense).[50] And, therefore, philosophically speaking, our thinking, feeling, acting is relatively attenuated, drawn in, limited, or restrained by the possibilities of our corporeal being — and therefore also blind to deeper and more far-reaching possibilities.

Of course, our actions are always governed by certain intentions — for example, we are busy restoring order, or we are involved explaining a difficult concept, or we are trying to rouse

the children's interest. Yet the reflective component in our immediate interaction with others is limited. When a child "misbe-
haves" in class the teacher usually does not have time to reflect on
what is the best thing to do. A teacher who paused and deliber-
ated at some length about alternative actions to take about a
difficult child's rude comment may be interpreted as hesitant,
wishy-washy, and spineless. As a teacher you simply have to do
something, even if it consists of ignoring or pretending you did
not notice the rude remark.

Similarly, when a child during a lesson asks a question that
shows the child does not understand, the teacher usually does
not have the luxury of consulting a text on teaching to deal with
this question in just the right way for this child (a textbook would
not be likely to provide such advice anyway). The same is true
for parents and other adults with pedagogical responsibilities.
When the child falls and hurts himself or herself, or protests the
parent's reminder that it is bedtime, there is no opportunity to sit
back to figure out what to do in this situation. Where tact is required, there is no chance to reflect in a deliberative, planning
manner. Tactful action is always immediate, situational, contingent, improvisational.[51]

Tactful action is always framed by the special orientation or
commitment that defines my relation to others: there is tact in
friendship, there is tact between lovers, there is tact in the way
that the parent or teacher is oriented to the child. The pedagogical orientation to children is conditioned by the intentionality of
our love, hopes, and responsibilities. Wherein does pedagogical
tact find its resourcefulness? First, we recall that pedagogical
tact is pedagogical understanding in being attentive to young
people, through what we notice about them, in the way we listen
to them. This is not a detached manner of observing behavior as
a behavioral psychologist might do. Pedagogical understanding,
as practised in everyday life, is more common in the natural attitude of everyday acting.

Our exploration of the notion of pedagogy thus far may suggest that pedagogical fitness presumes a sense of vocation, a love
and caring for children, a deep sense of responsibility and of active hope in the face of prevailing crises, a reflective maturity, a
pedagogical understanding based on a capacity to listen to and
"see" children, and a generally trustful, sympathetic attitude

toward young people. The next section will suggest that pedagogical fitness requires a tactful sensitivity toward the child's subjective states, an interpretive intelligence, a moral intuitiveness, an improvisational resoluteness in dealing with young people, a passion for knowing and learning the mysteries of the world, the moral fibre to stand up for one's beliefs, a certain understanding of the world, a deep sense of discipline, and not least a basic vitality and sense of humor.

6 THE NATURE OF TACT

The Relation between Tact in General and Pedagogical Tact

To live is to be touched.

In general, tact implies sensitivity, a mindful, aesthetic perception. Webster's Collegiate dictionary defines tact as "a keen sense of what to do or say in order to maintain good relations with others or avoid offense." But, as I will try to show, the essence of tact does not inhere in the simple desire or ability to get on well with others, to establish good social relations with them. Tact has interpersonal and normative properties that appear especially suited to our pedagogical interactions with children. We speak of tact as instantly knowing what to do, an improvisational skill and grace in dealing with others. Someone who shows tact seems to have the ability to act quickly, surely, confidently, and appropriately in complex or delicate circumstances. It is important to state at the outset that tact does not necessarily connote a soft, meek, acquiescent sensitivity. One can be sensitive and strong. A tactful person must be strong, since tact may require frankness, directness, and candor when the situation calls for it. Tact is always sincere and truthful, never deceitful or misleading.

Tact consists of a complex array of qualities, abilities and competencies: First, a tactful person has the sensitive ability to interpret inner thoughts, understandings, feelings, and desires from indirect clues such as gestures, demeanor, expression, and body language. Tact involves the ability to immediately see through motives or cause and effect relations. A tactful person is able as it were to read the inner life of the other person. Second, tact consists in the ability to interpret the psychological and social significance of the features of this inner life. Thus, tact knows

125

how to interpret, for example, the deeper significance of shyness, hostility, frustration, rudeness, joy, anger, tenderness, grief in concrete situations with particular persons. Third, a person with tact appears to have a fine sense of standards, limits, and balance that makes it possible to know almost automatically how far to enter into a situation and what distance to keep in individual circumstances. Finally, tact seems characterized by moral intuitiveness: A tactful person seems to sense what is the right thing to do.

The term *tact*, like *tactile*, refers to *touch*, which according to Webster's means to "handle or feel gently with the intent to appreciate or understand" it in more than merely an intellectual manner. We notice that *touch* can also imply violation or harm, as in the expression "I never touched the child"; we speak of "a touchy subject." As for "a touching scene," something is "touching" when it is capable of arousing emotions of tenderness.

We need to distinguish between *tact* and *tactic*. A *tactic* is a method for accomplishing an end. There is a calculating, planning meaning to *tactic*, while *tact* is essentially unplannable. In fact, *tactic* and *tact* are etymologically unrelated. *Tactic* is derived from early Greek, where it referred to military science, the strategic talents of a general in moving his troops in battle. Someone who approaches teaching by way of tactics thinks of maneuvers, stratagems, masterminding a program of directives and objectives. To be good at tactics means that one is good at getting an organization to execute some plan of action. Thus, tactics also connote superintendency, supervision. The tactics of teaching are strategies, methods, schema, ways and means that one draws up like a master plan, scenario, outline, blueprint, timetable, schedule, or design.

In contrast, *tact* derives etymologically from the Latin *tactus*, meaning touch, effect, from *tangere*, to touch. A related term is *intact:* untouched, uninjured. *Tactful* means fully in touch, and it also suggests being able to have an effect. Some of the synonyms of tact relate closely to what it means to be a good parent or educator: to be tactful is to be thoughtful, sensitive, perceptive, discreet, mindful, prudent, judicious, sagacious, perspicacious, gracious, considerate, cautious, careful. Would any of these speak badly of an educator? In contrast, someone who is *tactless* is considered to be hasty, rash, indiscreet, imprudent, unwise, inept, insensitive, mindless, ineffective, awkward. In general, to be tactless means to be disrespectful, ill-considered, blundering, clumsy, thoughtless, inconsiderate, stupid.

Finally, there is the term *contact*, from *contingere*, which, according to Klein's Etymological Dictionary, means "to touch closely," connectedness, being in-touch. The Latin preposition *con* often has the effect of augmenting the term to which it is attached. In other words, *con-tact* carries the same meaning as *tact* but in enhanced, intensified form. It refers to a close human relationship, intimacy, connectedness. A teacher "in touch," "in close contact" with students, implies that the teacher's actions are governed by tactful sensitivity.

Most of us have an appreciation for the value of tact in social life. Often the word *tact* is used in situations where we are in some way stuck. Someone then says to us "Well, yes, I guess this situation requires tact." Saying this, however, is as much to confess one is at one's wits' end as to what exactly to advise. In this context *tact* is sort of a magical term that promises a solution without giving insight into the solution.

Tactful action is thoughtful, mindful, heedful. But it helps to make a distinction between thoughtfulness and tact. We should see that thoughtfulness and tact go hand in hand. They complement each other. Without thoughtfulness there is no tact, and without tact, thoughtfulness is at best a merely internal state. Thoughtfulness is the product of self-reflective reflection on human experience. In a sense, tact is less a form of knowledge than it is a way of acting. It is the sensitive practice of heedfulness. Tact is the effect one has on another person even if the tact consists, as it often does, in holding back, waiting.

This image of tact as a special interaction between people may be most relevant for education or pedagogy. However, there is an outstanding distinction to be made between on the one hand general social tact in the interaction between adults and the more specific form of pedagogical tact in the interaction between adults and children, on the other. This distinction harkens back to the nature and structure of pedagogical relations. General tact in the lives of adults is symmetrical between them, while pedagogical tact is asymmetrical. Among adults we expect tactful behavior to be reciprocal, in keeping with the nature and circumstances of the situation, and we teach children to practice general social tact toward other children and adults. To be tactful in a general sense means that we respect the dignity and subjectivity of the other person and that we try to be open and sensitive to the intellectual and emotional life of other people, whether young or old.

But as adults we do not have a right to expect pedagogical tact from children. Pedagogical tact is an expression of the responsibility with which we are charged in protecting, educating, and helping children grow. Children are not charged with the pedagogical responsibility of protecting and helping their parents or teachers grow and develop. This does not mean of course that children do not teach us and do not show us new ways and possibilities of experiencing and being in the world. But children are not there primarily for us, we are there primarily for them.

It is perhaps surprising that the notion of tact has not been of any systematic interest and study for educational thinkers in the English-speaking world. The person who introduced the notion of tact and tactfulness into educational discourse is the German educator Johann Friedrich Herbart. In 1802, in his first lecture on education, Herbart told his audience that: "The real question as to whether someone is a good or a bad educator is simply this: Has this person developed a sense of tact?" Herbart posited that tact occupies a special place in practical educational action. The main points of his lecture pertaining to tact were that (a) "tact inserts itself between theory and practice"; (b) tact manifests itself in everyday life in the process of "making instant judgments and quick decisions"; (c) tact forms a way of acting which is "first of all dependent on *Gefühl* [feeling or sensitivity] and only more remotely on convictions" derived from theory and beliefs; (d) tact is sensitive to "the uniqueness of the situation"; and (e) tact is "the immediate ruler of practice."

However, in spite of this fluid early conceptualization, Herbart's later writings, and especially that of his followers, assumed a more instrumental relation between educational knowledge and practical action. Even in these phrases from Herbart, there is evident a somewhat mechanistic concept of the mediating role of tact between theory and practice. But rather than see tact as a device for converting theory into practice we may see tact as a concept that can help us to overcome the problematic separation of theory from practice. And rather than understand tact as a process of making instant "decisions," we may reconceive tact as a mindfulness that permits us to act thoughtfully with children and young people.[52]

In Germany the notion of tact occasionally surfaces in discourse on the nature of pedagogical praxis.[53] But in the English speaking world a more technological and pragmatic rationality has governed theories of education and educational competence. The notion of tact has never been systematically studied, and references to tact in English texts about teaching are rare and sporadic.

One, however, is by William James, in a lecture he gave in 1892. He mentions "tact" almost in the same breath as he speaks of Herbart. James discusses the relationship between psychology and pedagogy, which in the case of the great system builder, Herbart, were developed side by side. In no way, however, was Herbart's pedagogy derived from psychology, says James. Pedagogy cannot be derived from psychology. Knowing psychology is absolutely no guarantee that we shall be good teachers, argues James:[54]

> To advance to that result, we must have an additional endowment altogether, a happy tact and ingenuity to tell us what definite things to say and do when the pupil is before us. That ingenuity in meeting and pursuing the pupil, that tact for the concrete situation, though they are the alpha and omega of the teacher's art, are things to which psychology cannot help us in the least.

James provides one brief example of what he understands by tact. He suggests how a tactful teacher can foster an early sense of scholarship in young people by working into school learning the characteristic of almost every child: the desire to collect things. "Almost all children collect something," James says. "A tactful teacher may get them to take pleasure in collecting books; in keeping a neat and orderly collection of notes, in starting, when they are mature enough, a card catalogue; in preserving every drawing or map which they may make." James' example suggests that the teacher should be sensitive to the child's natural impulses and connect these inclinations to the school curriculum.

We should note that there is more involved here than the more commonly agreed-upon challenge for teachers to motivate their students and to make things relevant to them. But what exactly is involved in that tactfulness of which James speaks? He professes that this fundamental question lies outside the domain of the psychologist. After indicating that psychology has little or nothing directly to say to pedagogy, James, in the remainder of his *Talks to Teachers*, makes no further reference to tact.

The important point for us here is that James reminds us that it is tact that is the operative notion that defines what a teacher does in a pedagogical moment. Tact is the pedagogical ingenuity that makes it possible for the educator to transform an unproductive, unpromising, or even harmful situation into a pedagogically positive event.

Pedagogical thoughtfulness and tact do not of course describe everything teachers (educators or parents) know, are, or do. There are many routine and more technical aspects to teaching and parenting. Teachers must know how to plan lessons, how to fill out report cards, how to make effective use of media; parents must be able to change diapers, keep house, prepare nutritious meals. But the real stuff of teaching and of parenting happens in the thick of life itself when one must know with a certain confidence just what to say or do (or what not to say or do) in situations with children. Therefore, pedagogical thoughtfulness and tact may be seen to constitute the essence and excellence of pedagogy. We might say that thoughtfulness constitutes the internal aspect and tactfulness the external aspect of pedagogy. Pedagogy is structured like tact.

Historical notes on tact

Herbart was not the only one to use the notion of tact in referring to a special quality of human interaction.[55] Hans-Georg Gadamer refers to the work of a contemporary of Herbart, the physiologist Hermann Helmholtz, to bring out two aspects of tact: tact as one aspect of human interaction and tact as social science scholarship. In the first sense, tact is commonly understood as "a particular sensitivity and sensitiveness to situations, and how to behave in them," but for which "we cannot find any knowledge from general principles."[56]

In the second sense, tact is practised through scholarship — such as developing a sense of the aesthetic or the historical — that the social scientist uses to do his or her interpretive work. The scholar demonstrates the measure of his or her tact by the insights that he or she is able to produce with respect to the meaning of a text or a social phenomenon. In making this distinction Helmholtz had suggested that tact is not simply a feeling or unconscious inclination, but rather that tact is a certain "mode of knowing and of being" that encompasses the important human science notion of *Bildung* (forming or education).[57] There is an implication here that tact is not a simple affect or learnable habit, but that it can be fostered through the more profound process of humanistic growth, development, and education. In passing, we should note that the notion of "tact in scholarship" is exercised in a different modality than tact in human interaction. Tact in scholarship is usually practised while reading or writing texts. This is a highly reflective human activity. In contrast, tact in human interaction is usually practised in the spur of the moment where one is required to act in an instant or immediate fashion.

The philosopher Friedrich D. E. Schleiermacher too has written on the substantive aspects of tactful action.[58] Schleiermacher employed the notion of "tone" to describe that special quality in human interaction that allows a person to behave with sensitivity and flexibility toward others. In ordinary present-day language we still say of a tactful person that he or she is able to "strike a good tone," thus creating a warm social atmosphere. When we walk into different schools or classrooms we are often struck by the presence or absence of this tone or atmosphere that somehow hovers in the social environment. This is not just a matter of how teachers and students speak to each other. A "good tone" comprises more than linguistic intonation or tone of voice. It is accomplished through such communicative devices as a "meaningful" wink or word, glance or gesture, smile or silence, posture and presence.

Appropriately, the notion of "tone" refers also to music from where the concept of tact was originally derived. In music, *Takt* is German for the "beat," the unit of musical time. The German word for the conductor's baton is *Taktstock*, the stick that beats time. The Latin *tactus* is a 15th and 16th century term for "beat," both with temporal meaning and as in "conductor's beat." The musical notion of beat refers to the "pulse" underlying a musical work — beat or pulse are elemental in the rhythmic quality of a work. The rhythmic beat or pulse in music is the heart of music.

The musician knows that beat, pulse, or rhythm can exist without melody, as in percussion ensembles or in the drumbeats of African music, but melody cannot exist without rhythm.

Shifts occur periodically in the application of rhythm to music. Such shift took place between the Baroque and Rococo period on the one hand, and the Classical and Romantic music that followed them on the other hand. The already strict rhythmic modes of the 13th century and the oratorical speech chants of the Renaissance were followed by the strong body rhythms of Baroque musicians such as Bach, Vivaldi, and Handel. In this music the beat was more vigorous or even mechanical, not unlike the role of the rhythm section in jazz. So important was this strong, ever-present beat that the conductor of a musical group at the time of the Renaissance and the Baroque commonly would conduct a piece of music by banging his stick on the ground. Jean-Baptiste Lully, the French composer and conductor, died of blood poisoning in 1687 when he accidentally stabbed himself in the foot with his stick while banging the beat during a musical performance at the court of the French King Louis XIV. When later conductors stopped banging the beat with a stick, this may have had something to do with the changing function of *Takt* in music. With the Classical masters (such as Haydn, Mozart, the early Beethoven) and the Romantic masters (such as Chopin, Schuman, Liszt, and Brahms) the beat that organizes the music became more subtle, retreating somewhat and less everpresent to the ear. This shift of *Takt* from the regular, mechanical, vigorous mode to more subtle and restrained forms may have contributed to the application of the notion of tact to the social sphere, where it acquired the meaning of subtle sensitivity and of restraint or holding back in human relations and interaction.

It is thought that Voltaire was the one who around 1769 imported the notion of tact from the musical domain into the social sphere.[59] The Germans, Dutch, and English adopted this usage from the French. But only in German educational theory has there been an articulation and discussion of tact in a pedagogical sense. Moreover, the German *Taktgefühl* expresses a more subtle sentient quality than the English "tactfulness." The term *Gefühl* means feeling, sensitivity, sentiment: the sentient quality of having a "feel" for something. Thus, to be tactful with another person one must be able to "hear," "feel," "respect" the essence or uniqueness of this person. The English "tactful" means having the quality of tact and literally being full of tact; the German word *Taktgefühl* has the additional connotation of having a feeling for tactfulness. There is a hint here that the quality of tact is somewhat like talent. We often think of talent as a fortuitous gift — either you are or you are not blessed with a "feel" or talent for the violin, the canvas, or the stage. But, of course, talent must be recognized, developed, nurtured, and disciplined. Similarly, pedagogical tact, although a gift in some sense, needs to be prepared and practised as a special "feel" for acting tactfully.

Naturally, musical "tact" is at best a metaphoric referent or analogy for social tact. It is usually misleading to try and follow the many possible implications of metaphoric comparisons, but it is tempting to venture a few steps further with the musical metaphor. In music the basic chords, beat, pulse are the elements on which the melody can be improvisationally created. It should be realized that *takt* and melody are not mutually exclusive however — they need each other. Yet, *takt* (beat, pulse) needs to retreat to the background and loosen its grip on the total musical situation for the more subtle improvisations of melody to become possible. And rhythm can even become the organizing element in the performance of musical improvisation. So the existence of the musical metaphor of *takt* may prompt us to wonder: What are the organizing elements which make tact in social life possible?

In some sense the answer to this question has already been suggested in discussing the nature of the pedagogical experience in the first part of this book. The tact that adults are able to show with children is a function of the nature of pedagogy itself. In other words, pedagogical tact is made possible by the nature of the pedagogical moment, the values and orientation of pedagogical reflection, the conditions of pedagogy, the elements of pedagogical understanding, the structures of pedagogical situations and relations, and so forth. What needs to be elaborated, however, is how tactful pedagogical acting itself is structured: What is pedagogical tact? And what is false tact? How does it manifest itself? What does pedagogical tact do? How does pedagogical tact do what it does?

False tact

Tact cannot lie

To judge tact is to raise the question how the other person orients him- or herself to the good, to what is good for a child. It is sometimes easy to mistake as genuine tactfulness what is really manipulative influence motivated by self-interest or greed, characterized by dishonesty or hypocrisy. Sometimes a smile, an accommodating gesture, a friendly word, a warm physical touch can be supercilious rather than sincere. This happens when a person feigns for someone else a tactful concern that really serves another purpose. People are capable of fooling others and even themselves by giving the impression of being sensitive to the other person's feelings and of being interested in the other person's good. But tact that is not driven by a selfless and authentic orientation to otherness and goodness cannot be real tact.

The parents have always taught their daughter Audrey tolerance and respect for people who are different from themselves. Lately Audrey, who is a young white middle class woman, has made friends with a young man who is black. Now Audrey announces that she wants to get engaged to him. The parents are initially able to hide their shock and feelings of dismay. However, when Audrey's friend has left the house later in the evening, her parents "tactfully" advise Audrey to give up her relationship. Audrey reacts angrily, "Just admit that you are biased toward blacks." But her parents respond very gently and understandingly. "We do not mind that you have a black friend. In fact we are proud that we have brought you up without prejudices towards colored people. We do not mind if a person is black, white, yellow, orange, or purple. But you must realize, Audrey, that not everyone is as tolerant as we are. There are many people who feel uncomfortable about interracial marriages. You would make life too difficult for yourself and for your friends. Besides, you are too young to get engaged. First we would like you to finish college. We are thinking about your future. What happened to the other wonderful boys you dated earlier? Really, we only have your best interest at heart — married life with a black person would just be very difficult." Audrey is confused: Are her parents not really trying to hide their own intolerance and the difficulties of having their daughter live in a manner that is different from what they desired and expected?

It is false tact to exert influence colored by hypocrisy or other selfish concerns. False tact is not animated by love and an orientation to the other, rather false tact serves the self. "Tact" that serves the interests of the self is not tactfulness in the original sense. Tact does not go with hypocrisy, deceit, greed, possessiveness, egoism. When I try to manipulate someone else's behavior for my own end, I may manage to give the impression of being tactful. But this behavior is really false tactfulness, since it corrupts the immanent purpose of tact, to minister to the other.

People who have "too little tact" are generally insensitive and inconsiderate of the feelings of others. But people who seem to have "too much tact" are also insensitive — insensitive to the good of the other, and also insensitive to the artificial quality of the impression that their behavior makes on other people. "Too much tact" is another false tact that may give the impression of goodwill and considerateness. We recognize this in the workers who constantly try to please their superiors by using sugar-coated language and expressions, or in the zealous salespeople who seem to seek favor with their potential customer by flattery and overly friendly behavior. We see this in people who cringingly ingratiate themselves by a menial or subservient attitude, but who really have aspirations to dominate others or who hope to obtain special treatment, favors, or privileges. An extreme picture of "too much tact" may resemble Dickens' character, Uriah Heep, who, under the cloak of a fawning humility, manipulates other people for his own ends. Thus "too much tact" exemplified by servile flattery and exaggerated attention tries to control rather than serve people.

Next, there is a cunning kind of behavior that may be confused with tact. This cunning behavior depends on the ability to probe the inner thoughts, motives, feelings, desires of another person by inferring these inner states from the person's gestures, expressions, body language, demeanor. While true tact may also operate in a similar interpretive manner, it is not driven by selfish interests. Cunning "tact" is behavior that camouflages its real intentions, by treating delicate concerns in a roundabout, indirect manner, or by giving information that is diluted, distorted,

skewed, slanted, not really representing things in the best interest of the other person. And of course, it is sometimes astonishing how vulnerable people are and how forgiving and well-
disposed they are toward individuals who shamelessly flatter
them.

To the extent that hypocrisy, egoism, greed, and possessiveness are seemingly oriented to others, they really are actively
turning others into appendages of oneself. The more I possess
and increase my status, reputation, or wealth the more I feel my
"self" increased, the "better" I feel I have become. For some people their children are such "property." Their seemingly tactful
behavior is only meant to cover up their investment in their children. We recognize such false tact in the actions of parents or
teachers who live vicariously through their children — who must
make the honor roll — and who are thus refusing to let their
children be themselves, live their own lives, become their own
person.

True tact is not just a form of behavior that we appreciate in
others because it makes smooth social relations possible. Indeed,
people who too demonstratively "show" tact should be treated
with suspicion since demonstrative tactful behavior is rarely
driven by tactful intent. A person who really tries to be tactful
knows that to demonstrate so-called tactful behavior would defeat the intention to be sensitive and thoughtful about the other
person's inner life. Rather than being demonstrative, true tact is
subtle and hardly noticeable, even though we do recognize it as
a positive quality in people. Tact tends to be recognized as a
holistic quality, since any particular tactful action is often difficult to distinguish or describe.

Should a person ever lie while trying to be tactful? The answer to this question depends on what we mean by "lying."
Broadly speaking, lying is done to manipulate others for a selfish
or other ulterior motive. Lying is deceitful. (In contrast, lies that
are told to protect the other person from something bad are
sometimes called "white lies" or "innocent lies.") But tact does
not have a manipulative intent. In other words, tact does not have
the intention to deceive or to use the other person for one's own
ends. For example, when we praise a child for an accomplishment, in truth far from perfect in some evaluative sense, then we

are not lying to the child but "seeing with love" what is good and commendable in the accomplishment.

But pedagogically speaking, false tactfulness is driven by a desire to manipulate and control the child for some ulterior motive that lies outside of the sphere of interest of the child. Manipulative tact in this sense is tact that is false or feigned.

Aspects of Tact

Nothing is so unnoticed as that
which is self-evident.

Just as we can distinguish between false and true tact, so we can distinguish certain aspects or features that give tact its meaning and significance. As we have seen, pedagogical tact is a special case of general social tact. Tact is certainly not an esoteric theoretical phenomenon. We recognize it as a common feature of everyday social life. We know in a way what tact is, yet we rarely reflect on its meaning. More often we may become aware of tact only when we experience situations where tact was sorely missed.

"Just look at that! That's no way to treat a child!" Who has never said something like this? It is what we exclaim when we see or hear of cases of child abuse or neglect. And sadly enough, physical, psychological, and sexual abuse of children appears to occur all too commonly. We even feel disturbed or aghast when we observe an adult demonstrate insensitive behavior toward a child who is at play, in need, or somehow getting in the way of an adult's activity.

When one adult insults another adult or hurts the other's feelings, we may consider such person ill-mannered or boorish. But when an adult hurts a child's feelings we tend to become even more deeply upset. We realize that in certain respects children are more vulnerable than adults — they may experience fear or terror that is more terrible than it would be for adults. In short, most normal adults recognize that children require different treatment than adults. For example, babies seem fragile and seem to require tenderness; adults will even adjust their tone of voice to the child's size and produce motherese or parentese chatter for the benefit of the infant. (In fact, behavioral research has shown that very young children respond positively to motherese talk and seem to prefer it over normal talk). When we sense that a child is fearful or anxious about something, we may try to alleviate the fear or calm the child down. Some things we won't talk about in the child's presence because we feel that the child is not yet old or mature enough to deal with such matters.

In other words, we all know about tact and the need for it in our dealings with children. Yet we do not speak of it. Theories of education are surprisingly silent about the significance of the quality of tact and its behavioral manifestations. Is it because we assume that tact is merely an extra, something desirable perhaps, but in truth superfluous to the real business of educating children? Or is it because tact is so self-evidently part of everyday life that we do not tend to wonder about its meaning?

There is a meaning to tact that distinguishes it from associated behaviors, such as "diplomacy," "address," "poise," "savoir faire," or "finesse" — even though these are terms often provided as synonyms of tact. For example, a diplomat is "diplomatic" for the purpose of manipulating perceptions for political ends. This does not necessarily mean that a diplomatic person would lie or be deceitful, but while diplomacy may not involve telling untruths it may involve withholding truths that should actually be told. A diplomat is ultimately motivated by self-interest or by the interest of the party the diplomat is representing. Tact, in contrast, is always in the service of the person toward whom the tact is directed. Without pursuing these distinctions much further, we might briefly note that tact avoids the political motivation and conciliation of "diplomacy," it does not stress the idea of dexterity and preoccupation with success in trying circumstances as does "address," it lacks the calculating cleverness of "being savvy," tact is not self-conscious of its own social bearing and self-possession as is "poise," it does not emphasize worldly experience and a sure awareness of expediency as does "savoir faire," and tact is more concerned with what is appropriate or good than with refinement of approach like "finesse." In the following sections some aspects of the nature of tact are examined, with a particular focus on pedagogical tact.

Tact means the practice of being oriented to others

Tact is the practice of otherness.

To exercise tact one must be able to overcome an orientation to the world that seems to come natural to human beings, the attitude of seeing oneself at the center of all things. Every child, every adult experiences the taken-for-granted relation of self to the world: I live my life, this is my world in which I live. I am at home in my world. "I live here" means I exist here and I belong here. When I speak or interact with others, I am constantly the subject of my discourse and my actions: I think, I see, I feel, I hear, I understand, I love, I do, I play, I wonder about things. I am involved in projects in the world which define my relation to the world, and which show who I am in the world. I make a meal. I favor certain foods. I enjoy reading a book. I have an opinion about certain people or about what they do. I work at certain things. I am proud about my accomplishments or I feel dissatisfied or unhappy with what I have done or what others do to me. I may go to a movie, to the pub, or to church. The point is, I am the center of my universe. I am my world.

When things go well I may feel "on top of the world." Everything seems just right. The things in the world exist as if they are there just for me. This world is my home, my kingdom. I belong here. Sometimes this experience of the centrality of the "I" can turn existentially oppressive for the individual. I cannot help but feel that ultimately I am alone in the world. When I undergo a crisis or when I suddenly face a serious illness, then I feel forsaken, shaken. This will be my death. In the awareness of my mortality and of my impending end, my world can shrink into a small circle of despair.

This experience of the primacy of the "I" in my world is neither good nor bad. It is the way human beings may experience the world, know the world, recognize the world as theirs. But of course this is not the whole of human experience. The human being is not alone. Some people may prize aloneness, independence, separateness; others may suffer from loneliness and alienation from others. Yet in these experiences the felt absence or presence of others is already implicit. In the world we experience the other person. There are other people who live beside me. There are others whom I encounter in the world. The question is: How do the others appear to me? Are they there simply for me, as parts of my larger world? Are the others only important for me insofar that they add to or subtract from my world? Are the others just there as objects for the satisfaction of my wants and needs: to be used, manipulated, made available by me and to me?

I do not really experience the subjectivity of the other until I am able to overcome the centeredness of my self in the world. The fascinating fact is that my possibility of the experience of the otherness of other, resides in my experience of the vulnerability of the other.[60] It is when I see that the other is a person who can be hurt, distressed, pained, suffering, anguished, weak, in grief or in despair that I may be opened to the essential being of the other. The vulnerability of the other is the weak spot in the armor of the self-centered world. I see a child who is hurt or who is in agony and, temporarily at least, I forget my present preoccupations. No longer am I driven by my personal agenda. For the moment I am just there for this child, for this other person. With this recognition of the other comes the possibility of acting for the sake of the other. So when a child is hurt and I actually "see" this child in his or her vulnerability, then I am in a position to do something for this child. In fact, most likely the situation is such that I find myself oriented to the child before I even think about it.

A mother has just received a phone call from the doctor that the results of a medical test that seemed to indicate the presence of a terrible malignancy, upon retesting turned out to be benign. The relief of pent-up anxiety is so strong that the woman breaks down crying. When the six-year-old enters the room and sees his mother wipe away the tears he asks, "What is wrong, mom?" "It is nothing, dear," the mother smiles. "You know, sometimes I feel so lucky to have you that I cry from happiness. Come and let me give you a hug." The mother feels that she cannot tell the young child about her own fears and vulnerabilities. Rightly or wrongly she instantly senses that the thought of his mother's fear of dying is too much with which to burden this young child. But there is something else she now knows. She knows that she values life, but that she would sacrifice it for her child.

A young single mother of a three-year-old is interviewed on

television. She knows that she carries the AIDS virus and that she will probably die from the disease. One cannot help but feel deeply moved for this young woman. How terrible to be so young and to know oneself to be so near death. But the mother speaks with remarkable strength and hope. "All I hope for," she says, "is that I will live long enough, long enough to give my child a good start in life."

We are all vulnerable. And yet we know that children are vulnerable in ways that adults are not. Especially with very young children (and even with young animals) it is quite common for adults to experience this sense of disarming vulnerability. Naturally, this vulnerability on the part of the child can be abused by the adult who may feel self-important and powerful in the face of the child's need for protection or help. Yet the adult feels disarmed and mellowed when he or she sees the child making mistakes or doing things that seem awkward and so "typical of children." Think of the laughter that children get on the occasion of the "not always perfect show" during the Christmas performance in front of the parents and the community. It is not a mocking or derisive impulse that moves adults to laughter when children unintentionally behave drolly or comically. The good-natured laughter is indicative of the adults' knowledge of the difference between being an adult and being a child.

It is in the face of the child's defenselessness and vulnerability that adults find it easy to be generous and giving. But what happens when a child turns rightfully self-righteous and demanding? How well can the adult still see the child's vulnerability and the child's otherness when the adult is too self-possessed, too preoccupied with the projects and concerns of self?

Of course, in a real sense every human being is vulnerable; every human being is mortal and subject to fears and dangers. Every human being is my other. The other is actually or potentially weak and vulnerable, just as I know myself to be actually or potentially weak and vulnerable. However, the existence of the other does not merely manifest itself as my feelings of pity or compassion for the hurt or suffering of this other person. More pointedly I experience the other as a voice, as an appeal to me. And this is what we mean when we speak of our living with children as a vocation, a calling.

The experience of the other is the breaking of the silence of my world, which is centered in the "I." The voice of the other de-centers my universe. In this sense we may say that the new-born child de-centers the "self" of the world of the woman and the man. The child changes the world of woman or man into the world of mother or father, and thus the woman is transformed into mother and the man is transformed into father. Of course, not every man or woman experiences the coming of a child as a transformation into parenthood. Some have great difficulty ac-cepting responsibility by making room in their lives for their chil-dren. But luckily it is common that sooner or later the new mother or father experiences the birth of their child as an appeal. The new-born in its vulnerability calls upon me to care for it. And the experience of this appeal transforms me from woman into mother or from man into father. I now must act in thoughtful attunement to the other for the other. In this sense tact is the practice of being oriented to others.

To be tactful is to "touch" someone

A single touch can be more
meaningful than a thousand
words.

School is over for the day. But before going home a teacher strikes up a conversation with a colleague. She is talking about a child who is new in her room: "Here is a child who is physically obviously very unattractive to her classmates and even to the other teachers in the school. She is generally shunned by the chil-dren. At any rate, she was hit on her upper arm with a ruler by one of the boys. And instead of complaining or fighting back she just stood there! Her shoulders hunched, looking down and sob-bing softly, I put my arm around her and gently rubbed her arm. For quite awhile I kept her in my arm as I talked to her and then began to deal with students who were coming into class. What amazed me a bit was her total surrender to my embrace. She did not recoil in the slightest. I just felt that she needed my physical contact. That noon she put a note on my desk saying: 'I love my teacher.' And after school she asked shyly if she could help me with something. It was amazing how this withdrawn child re-sponded to a human touch. It occurred to me with great clarity how important physical contact can be for children — especially for those who may get very little of it at home."

Tact touches a person with a touch, with a word, with a gesture, with the eyes, with an action, with silence. Although tact etymologically implies physical touch, the noteworthy fact is that tact carries the ambiguous sense of a nonphysical influence or effect of one human being on another. Tact is neither intrusive nor aggressive. Often tact involves a holding back, a passing over something, which is nevertheless experienced as influence by the person toward whom the tactful action is directed. Yet tact does have a corporeal quality: thoughtfulness incarnates itself in tactful action.

Tact should not imply that one is overly sensitive to the feelings of others, as may sometimes be the way we understand tact in everyday life. A person may be too "soft" toward another person when resoluteness or directness is required. Tact can indeed be firm. Tact describes the appropriate thing to do in a particular situation. At times the appropriate action is to be direct, decisive, and open in a situation when that seems beneficial. Prescriptive theories and ideologies of education go through cycles; our present ideology favors terms such as "freedom," "empowerment," "critical reflection," "emancipatory action," while it disfavors yesterday's language of "obedience," "discipline," "authority," "vocation." Yet we should not assume that "discipline" and "authority" are necessarily negative in a pedagogical or educational sense.

Although "manipulation" in the sense of exploitative domination and control is obviously a negative pedagogical influence, nevertheless it would be hard to deny that even under the most enlightened practices benevolent forms of manipulation seem to exist. "Manipulation" contains the root word for "hand." To manipulate is to "handle" a situation in a certain manner. Manipulation is not necessarily anti-pedagogical, just as leading a person into walking into a surprise birthday party is not necessarily a negative form of manipulation. Teaching, too, may involve manipulating or handling learning situations so that students are brought to internalize positive values and important insights. In some sense, every teaching program, every textbook, every instructional approach may contain elements of manipulation. With respect to children, manipulation may be defensible if it is for the child's good.

Now, the problem is of course that this latter kind of statement may seem to give any self-righteous person the prerogative to impose his or her will on the child. So here again there are no technical rules to determine what is objectionable and what is pedagogically defensible. Sometimes manipulation and even force are appropriate when they are unavoidable, and when they are not used as self-justifying principles in the service of some dogma. Manipulation and force, if applied with the spirit of tact, do not necessarily contradict the child's requirement for freedom and self-responsibility.

Tact cannot be planned

Tact is unplannable.

It is generally impossible to plan a tactful action or response. We become aware of the unplannable nature of tact when, for example, we have the unpleasant task of breaking bad news to a person for whom we care. Beforehand, we may find ourselves rehearsing the kinds of things we feel we should say. We need to be gentle. We don't want to create unnecessary hurt by being too blunt or saying something insensitive. We want to do what is right for the other person. But then, when we find ourselves in the situation, we usually let go of our mental script, for fear of being artificial. We meet the other person and with our eyes we search the person's face for the right words — which usually come forth. Tactful action cannot be planned or charted out beforehand — it always realizes itself in concrete and unexpected or unforeseeable situations in which one finds oneself and in which one must serve, help, respond to another person. But even though tact is unplannable, one can prepare for it — one can prepare the heart and mind.

In teaching it is often the unsteady, unstable, inconstant, variable moment that requires tactful action of a sort that is essentially unplannable. And these unstable moments are not accidents in teaching but rather are essentially an integral part of teaching.

The teacher had assigned the students to read the poetry of Leonard Cohen in one of their readers. They were to select one of the poems and write what they liked about it. The teacher's overall intention was to help the students become readers of poetry by thoughtfully dwelling on one poem. "We had done this kind of thing before. This was generally a good class from which I could expect work of quality. But when I asked the students to share their thoughts I received only a lukewarm response. Their language was negative, uninspired, and reluctant. It was obvious that I had misjudged the students' interest and that the lesson as planned would not work. So I asked them about their general reaction to Cohen's poetry. I asked, "You weren't offended by it, were you?" It appeared that the girls were taken aback by what they perceived as Cohen's bitterness, his abusive attitude toward women, and his appearing oversexed. The boys were similarly negative about the undertones of Cohen's feeling about life. They wondered why his poetry could not be about good things and the blue sky. I felt the need to rescue Cohen's poetry from an unfortunate misapprehension. But rather than lecture or try to persuade them I played them the sound track of his "Sisters of Mercy" and "Annie." I told them simply what I knew of the first song: that it had been written and dedicated to his women friends one night right here in this city; the women had been asleep and Cohen, grateful for their friendship, had left the poem for them. The students began to see that more likely this poem was a homage to women. From there the discussion went on to personal existential, societal, and gender issues and to deeper Jewish and other religious symbolism in Cohen's work. The students brought up concerns that showed their personal engagement in the themes of Cohen's poetry. It was a great poetry lesson! But it was far from what I had originally conceived. The irony is that from the point of view of my initial plan the lesson had been a total flop."

Tact is governed by insight while relying on feeling

Truly enabling knowledge is
embodied knowledge.

We think of tactfulness as a caring orientation to others. On the one hand, caring is the willingness to take on burdens, trouble, or grief for others. On the other hand, to be caring is to be heedful, affectionate, loving, tender. The term *caring* connotes an attitude and feeling rather than an ability or skill. I may care about something or somebody but not know what to do, or be incapable of doing what I should do. By contrast, although it seems appropriate to say that "tact" also implies a sense of caring, yet tact is more complex than the notion of caring. To be tactful is to be able to take other people's feelings into account. Tact is sensitive to delicate situations and having a feel for what they require. But tact is not merely a feeling or a sentiment. So it would not be right to say that tact belongs to the affective rather than to the intellectual or cognitive domain, an artificial distinction commonly made in education. Rather, tact is the expression of a thoughtfulness that involves the total being of the person, an active sensitivity toward the subjectivity of the other, for what is unique and special about the other person.

Tact is a kind of practical normative intelligence that is governed by insight while relying on feelings. Tact is possible because human beings are capable of exercising the complex faculty composed of perceptiveness, sensitivity, insight, and being attuned to each other's experience. This is true for adults as well as for children. Children are often quite sensitive to the mood, disposition, or authentic spirit of the adults in their shared lives. Children are often capable of remarkable tactfulness in their interactions with other children or adults. But as they get hardened and dulled by the process of growing up, children may become increasingly insensitive to the subtleties of other people's experiences.

To exercise tact means to *see* a situation calling for sensitivity, to *understand* the meaning of what is seen, to *sense the significance* of this situation, to *know how and what to do*, and to actually *do* something right. To act tactfully may imply all these and yet tactful action is instantaneous. The perceptiveness needed, the understanding and insight required, the feeling for the right action are not necessarily separate stages in a sequential process. Somehow, insight and feeling are instantly realized in a mode of acting characterized by a certain thinking attentiveness.

Tact rules practice

Tact knows no rules, yet tact is
not unruly.

There are no rules to follow for being tactful. There are no theories or models that explain the principles for behaving tactfully.
It is impossible to reduce tact to a set of techniques or skills for
acting predictably and consistently in situations calling for tact.
In spite of this uncontrollable nature of tact, it must be said that
tact expresses itself in a positive and normative manner in practical situations. At the basis of tact is a certain thoughtfulness or
mindfulness that animates tactful behavior.

A comparison of tact with social custom or etiquette may
be instructive. Tact is not the same as etiquette. To know etiquette is to know what social rules or manners to use in particular circumstances (as with table manners, for example). On the
surface tact may look like etiquette, since etiquette is concerned
with what to say or how to behave in order to maintain good
social relations. But etiquette deals with prescribed conduct or
procedures required in social and official situations. Practising
etiquette may suggest a sign of good breeding. The rules of etiquette are laid down by tradition or authority. Etiquette is in the
end predictable, rule-governed behavior. Tact lacks such a set of
definite rules. Instead, tact is improvisational.

In certain areas of everyday life — such as in living with
children — tact may be the basic feature of human interaction. In
this sense, tact rules praxis (defined as "action full of thought,
thought full of action"). Tact rules practice, although tact cannot
be reduced to rules. Yet tact is not in itself unruly. In other words,
tact is not arbitrary, it does not operate randomly. Tact demands
a delicate discipline. Tact requires that one can "read" or interpret social situations for what actions or words are appropriate.
Tact requires that one know how a situation is experienced by
the other person.

7 PEDAGOGICAL TACT

How Does Pedagogical Tact Manifest Itself?

What does pedagogical tact look like? How and where can we see pedagogical tact at work? These are difficult questions. It may not always be easy to tell genuine tactful actions from artificial, feigned, false forms of behavior that do not seem motivated by an authentic interest in children's welfare. Children often can tell the difference quite accurately between teachers who are "real" and caring and those who are "fake" and not truly interested in them.

Pedagogical tact manifests itself primarily as a mindful orientation in our being and acting with children. This is much less a manifestation of certain observable behaviors than a way of actively standing in relationships. Nevertheless, there are ways of describing how tact manifests itself in our pedagogical being and acting. The following sections suggest that tact shows itself as a holding back, as an openness to the child's experience, as attunement to subjectivity, as subtle influence, as situational confidence, and as an improvisational gift.

Tact shows itself as holding back

Sometimes the best action is
non-action.

A couple of months ago Cornelia was absent from my English class. It is sometimes hard for a teacher to remain open and friendly to a student who one suspects is skipping class. Then I happened to see Cornelia with her friend Melanie in the hallway during a break and I asked her why she had not been in class that morning. She gave me an innocent look and said, "Melanie was not feeling very well and I decided that I should stay with her." As a teacher I just bristled with exasperation and I was about to retort with a snide remark and disciplinary action. But instead I turned to Melanie and asked, "Are you all right?" She said, "Yes," but it was obvious that something was bothering Melanie, so I put my arm around her and asked if she needed my help. Melanie said again that she would be all right, but I saw that she obviously was on the verge of tears. I had held back any remark to Cornelia, and at that moment the bell sounded for the next period.

Later in the day when I had almost forgotten the incident, the fourth period students entered my class. Melanie is in this group. As she passed me my first inclination was to ask her how she was. But there was something in her demeanor that made me hold back. I observed her indirectly to gauge her state. During the lesson that followed Melanie acted as if she would rather not acknowledge the incident of that morning. So on a hunch I let it pass and decided to pursue it no further. It is significant that since then Melanie has been a different student in my class. Before the incident her behavior used to be somewhat sour, uncooperative, and generally uncommunicative. But since my showing of concern for her, it appears as if there has grown up a new unspoken understanding between us. This new attitude has had a positive effect on her learning. So tact includes a sensitivity for knowing what to pass over, what to leave unsaid, when not to step in, when "not to notice" something.

A special form of holding back consists in patience, the ability to wait with equanimity. Indeed, patience has been described as a fundamental virtue that every teacher and every parent should possess.[61] Patience enables the educator to bring the child into harmony with the course of time required to grow or to learn something. When expectations and goals have been set at appropriate levels, patience allows us not to worry or to give up when they are not fulfilled, when more time is needed or when other approaches need to be tried.

In our western culture parents and teachers tend to be proud and happy when the child progresses beyond expectations and learns to do things much earlier, faster, or better than one would ordinarily anticipate. It is in the nature of childhood that the child wants to grow and become more independent. And it is in the nature of pedagogy that parents and teachers want the child to grow, to make progress, to learn. So rather than holding back, the adult is sometimes inclined to push and force things a little. It is very difficult to know when to hold back and to wait. For example, adults know that most children will learn to read quite readily by the time they reach school age. But the adult also knows that with a bit of pushing many children may be able to read sooner; and with a lot of pushing some children may even learn to read at a surprisingly early age. Much in a child's development cannot be forced, and requires patience of the adults. But, because it is possible to speed up to some extent the rate at which children learn and mature, it becomes very tempting to hurry things along that really ought to be given their own space and time.

It is often terribly trying for an adult to hold back when the child does not seem to know how to do something, when the young person does something wrong at first, or when the student does something so agonizingly slowly. The adult becomes exasperated and is inclined to intervene, to "help," when the child should or may want to deal with the situation himself or herself. Or the adult offers to do it for the child ("here, let me tie your shoelaces!") when the child really needs to figure it out, to learn and to practice. Of course, from the child's point of view the adult is always in a hurry. And the adult cannot understand how the child just seems to dawdle when there are other more important things that need attention. The same thing often happens in the classroom. Although quite a few children have not yet quite understood or mastered a new concept or skill, the teacher cannot wait, wants to move on, and imposes a test as a result of which many children will learn the meaning of failure, poor performance, and low self-esteem.

A tactful understanding of when to hold back, when to pass over things, when to wait, when "not to notice" something, when to step back, rather than to intervene, draw the attention, or interrupt, is a gift to the child's personal development. Of course, there are situations where the right and tactful thing to do is to act in a manner that is forthright and direct; for example, when a class is out of control or when there is too much risk and danger in a certain situation. Sometimes it would not be tactful to hold back, to pass over things, as when a child needs to face something directly, or when the child clearly is in need of help or feedback.

Moreover, it would be wrong to pass over everything, to refuse to step in when the adult's active involvement is necessary. Some teachers or parents are practically indifferent to what their children do. They may be inclined to hold back from direct involvement all the time, thereby stepping completely out of the pedagogical relation with young people. For example, there are teachers who pride themselves on letting the children make all decisions for themselves. Similarly there are "permissive" parents who simply refuse to recognize the need for any guidance, direction, involvement, constraints, demands, or commitment on their part in the daily experiences or life decisions of their children. They pride themselves on allowing their children total "freedom." But freedom that knows no boundaries or standards is not real freedom.

Tact shows itself as openness to the child's experience

Always ask first: What is this
experience like for the child?

During the day seven-year-old Willy is a wizard on the skateboard and he does daring tricks even though he already has suffered several bruises and stitches. Among his friends Willy is admired for his guts and ability. He clearly is a kid who is not overly fearful. But during the evening, when it gets dark, Willy is afraid to go up to his bedroom by himself to put on his pajamas. His parents have noticed this. Even though they wish he would conquer his fear of darkness, they remain patient and understanding. They are tactful parents who sense that Willy's fear of the dark is objectively ungrounded but that subjectively the experience is real for the child. The parents do not want to close themselves off from the possibility of understanding the child's experience for what it is. Moreover, they realize that for many adults, too, the dark has threatening qualities. So it is now up to the parents to decide upon a course of action for helping Willy face his fears and overcome the conflicts from them. For this they need to remain open to the meaning of Willy's experience for Willy.

It is not always easy to stay open toward young people. Lauri's language arts teacher is taken aback by the dark images, the rebelliousness, the deep hatred, and the blaming that pervade all of Lauri's creative writing assignments. Most ninth grade teachers have no use for Lauri, who dresses unconventionally and who defies the school policy of no smoking by smoking in the washroom. But the language arts teacher cannot help but feel that being judgmental toward Lauri is wrong. Somehow, Lauri seems to feel that her language arts teacher is on her side: One morning she approaches the teacher and asks if she would be willing to read her poetry. The teacher would be pleased to and takes the student's folder home. What she finds is writing that gives evidence of adolescent morbidity and conflict, but the poems are also exceptionally eloquent and powerful. Here is a girl who writes because she must write, both for personal and artistic reasons. Even though the teacher feels that she does not really understand Lauri, she nevertheless knows that she should remain open, supportive, and sympathetic to her.

Hank's parents have requested an interview with the teacher and the school principal. They are concerned that Hank, who is only ten years old, is more preoccupied with friends who are already into girls and street life than with his school work. They explain that Hank is very concerned with his "looks," that he is unhappy when his friends do not seem to consider him "cool" because his parents impose certain restrictions. And he wants to do things that seem inappropriate or premature for his age — such as roaming the streets during the evening, spending money in the arcade, hanging on the phone with girls, watching videos that contain violence and sexually explicit material. The teacher and principal know what Hank's parents are talking about. They see the pressures that peer groups put on children. It is very encouraging that Hank's father and mother are not simply rejecting Hank's behavior. The parents must try to maintain an open relationship with him. The teacher recommends that the parents talk frequently with Hank for them all to explore and remain in touch with each other's feelings. Hank is a sensitive boy who wants to hurt neither himself nor his parents. By remaining open to Hank's experience, rather than simply criticizing and censuring his behavior the parents can try to encourage positive friendships. It would also be helpful for the parents to involve Hank more with the family, to spend time together and to do things as a family.

To be open to the child's experience means that one tries to avoid treating situations in a standard and conventional manner. It means that one tries to see past the adult's — teacher's and parent's — perspectives on the child's experience.

Tact shows itself as attuned to subjectivity

Try to treat the other as a
subject rather than an object.

A teacher talks about the effect of enrollments on her ability to remain attuned to the subjectivity of each child: "I started in September with twenty-two students in my sixth grade class; now I have thirty-one students and I really notice the difference. Whereas before I could deal with the antics of Chrissy, one of the students with behavior and learning difficulties, I find that with the number of kids I have now I am much less tolerant of her. I am less inclined to consider her needs and in what way I can turn Chrissy around to more cooperative and productive relations in class. Instead, I know I show less tolerance. I tend to see and deal with Chrissy's behavior more in purely management terms. My concern becomes now: How can I keep her quiet?! For example, I know she was upset with something yesterday and I guess it has to do with stuff that happens at home. But rather than try to catch her and take her aside, all I can do now is discipline her. It makes me feel bad because I know that with some understanding she can do better and she would do good work. ... "

A student complains, "Why do I have to take this stuff? I want to go into engineering and I don't see any point in learning English grammar. I don't aspire to become a writer. This is just one big pain!" Another student gripes, "Why are we doing these math problems? I have absolutely no use for all these exercises. Even my father says that he has forgotten how to do high school mathematics." For teachers it may be frustrating to deal with

"Why do we have to learn this?" questions. Some teachers say: "We have to do this because it is required by the curriculum." Or, "You have to know this because it may be on the exam." Or, "You need it to get into college." These are ready responses. But they are also weak responses since they merely defer to the authority of the curriculum, the exam committee, or the university entrance committee. These answers are not sensitive to the fact that for these students some of their learning experience still remains meaningless and even frustrating. Some teachers may try to justify grammar rules or math questions by appealing to their application or to their relevance to the ideal of becoming an educated person. But even pragmatic or idealistic answers may not satisfy reluctant students. In a sense all these responses are insensitive to the students' subjective experience of the curriculum. In contrast, pedagogical tact would aim to help the students develop an intrinsic interest in all aspects of language or mathematics. But if that is not possible, then a tactful response to the question, "Why do we have to take this stuff?" would at least try to be responsive the student's subjective experience of the learning itself.

An underlying metaphor for teaching suggests that, in order to come to school and learn new things, students need to cross barriers (for example, a street) to get over to the teacher's side (the school). But a teacher who is closed to the child's experience may not be aware that the student is still trying to understand things "from the other side of the street." Many teachers simply expect the students to come over to where the teacher stands. These are teachers who stand in front of the class explaining things; their attitude is that it is up to the students to "get" the explanations. If they do not get it, then tough! However, students may have difficulties, lack interest, or simply not know how to cross over to the teacher's side. The teacher seems to have a certain view, passion, conception of the subject matter, and seems to expect that the student has the same experience of the subject as the teacher does. But what the teacher forgets is that learning is always an individual affair.

A tactful educator realizes that it is not the child but the teacher who has to cross the street in order to go to the child's side. The teacher has to know "where the child is," "how the child sees things," how it is that this student has difficulty crossing the street to enter the domains of learning. The teacher has to stand beside the child and help the child locate places to cross over and find means for the child to successfully get to the other side, to these other worlds. In this gesture lies indeed the meaning of *educare*, "to lead into" the world, the world of increased awareness, responsibility, growth, and understanding.

Tact shows itself as subtle influence

We are always under the
influence.

Jason is a big fellow. When he walks into class he seems out of place, as if the classroom should be a bar or pool hall. His swaggering gait and his muscular physique suggest a maturity beyond his age. There is no denying that Jason nurtures a "cool" image of himself. The English teacher likes Jason, although she wonders sometimes how this tough kid puts up with the poetry lessons and the sometimes emotionally stirring discussion that follows. The teacher pulls Jason into the lesson, but cautiously so as not to force him to act out of character. Usually Jason sits rather quietly in his undersized desk, not very communicative, but not disruptive either. On account of his spaced-out behavior at times, the English teacher had first suspected that Jason was doing drugs. But when she had a talk with him recently Jason explained that he had been working late hours as a short-order cook in a local restaurant. They talked a bit more and Jason indicated that he needed this part-time job to save for a motorcycle. According to other teachers, Jason is just sitting out his time in school. He rarely does any homework. As soon as he can he will be quitting school to become a truckdriver.

One day before class, Jason walks in early, stomps a bit awkwardly around the teacher. Obviously he has something on his mind. "Uh, look, I wrote this," he says, pushing a piece of paper on her desk. It is a poem. The teacher is surprised at its quality. "This is very good Jason, I like the imagery." "Well, I like writing poetry," says Jason, "I've been doing it for a while ... since I started taking your class." And then he adds, sort of casually, "Maybe you can put it up." The teacher has been posting selected student work in the hallway on a large board. As a former elementary school teacher she has been pleased to see how keen high school students are to find their work displayed. It is not only in elementary school that kids like to see their work. For Jason to suggest that she display his poem surprises her. She is surprised that Jason cares about things like that. But she is happy to comply. Later in the day she notices Jason with a friend. He's pointing to the wall: "That poem over there, it's mine."

Sometimes teachers do not realize how they do influence students, even those from whom they least expect it. The influence may be so subtle that in the thick of everyday life we teachers do not ourselves notice it, until it is brought home to us by a surprising incident or recognition. What accounted for the subtle influence? Was it the special attention in the one-to-one talk that the teacher had with Jason? Was it her sensitivity and her careful treatment of Jason in the conduct of the poetry classes? Was it the climate she created with the students' work on the walls? Perhaps it was all of these or perhaps something else. We see tact in this teacher's style and in her response to Jason. Even when Jason gives her the poem the teacher seems to realize that when a poem comes unexpectedly like this you need to accept it happily. This is not the time to say: "Oh well, Jason, you made some spelling mistakes here." Or, "Jason, the ending is not quite right, you should change the last lines." The teacher knows that there will be opportunity later to help Jason improve his poetry. Initially, she may try to give him some insight in a roundabout way into ending poems, by treating it as a general topic in class. In this way again she may be able to influence Jason subtly to develop his skill and understanding of poetry writing without prematurely singling his work out and criticizing it. Jason also shows us how easy it is to misjudge a child or young person. There are ways to "touch" students even when others may have given up on them.

Tact shows itself as situational confidence

There is a good tone
for every situation.

"How envious I am of her," says one teacher about another, "somehow she always finds the right tone with every student or class." This remark betrays as much a feeling of insecurity as of incompetence. No matter how well teachers may have planned for a class or a situation, it seems that there is always an element of uncertainty about any teaching situation.

The class is involved in a variety of projects in the science lab. The teacher is moving amongst the students, raising a question here, giving encouragement there, and providing assistance where requested. There is a pleasant hum of productive activity in the room. The teacher feels joyful ... until Jack noisily walks into the room. He's late but he makes no attempt to be unobtrusive. Before too long he has disrupted several groups of kids. "Here, Kathy, I brought you your homework," he calls as he flings a condom in her lap, "I'll help you with sex if you help me with math." Kathy shrieks at him and the rubber thing ends up in the middle of another group of kids. There is laughter and the object is airborne again, propelled like a deflating balloon. It is amazing how rapidly a positive learning situation can deteriorate into chaos. The teacher calls, "Quiet, class. Order. Order!" but to no avail.

This kind of situation is probably the terror of many a beginning teacher (and some experienced ones as well). It is a challenge to meet unpredictable situations with confidence. The possibilities are numerous: a student who talks back in a taunting and disrepectful manner; a whole class out of control; students who refuse to do what they are asked; a child who overreacts to something with a bout of hysteria. It is in situations like these that the teacher needs to be able to demonstrate confidence and tact.

A teacher who is generally tactful has learned to trust himself or herself in ever-changing situations and circumstances. And, most important, such a teacher communicates this confidence to the students. Of course, there are teachers who seem to show a lot of confidence in their ability to deal with situations, but the students somehow know that this confidence is fake or false. Fake confidence is fragile and easily torn by conflict or serious resistance. False confidence is unfounded since it claims substance where there is emptiness. It is very difficult for a teacher to fake confidence or to keep coasting on false confidence for any length of time. In either case the substance that is missing is a thoughtful tact that grants a teacher trust in self, and the trust of the students.

Of course, there are ways of handling social situations

through intimidation, domination, and the authoritarian exercise of power. Teachers who deal with situations on the basis of these may have trust in self, but they do not receive trust from their students. And relations between adults and young people not built on trust have thereby forsaken their pedagogical legitimation.

Tact shows itself as improvisational gift

To teach is to improvise.

"This is what I will do to him if I see my father again," says Martin, and he throws some ugly punches with his fists. "I hate my father." When Martin came to kindergarten in September he was an angry and uptight little boy. The teacher learns by the grapevine that Martin's father has left wife and family for another woman, and soon after that Martin's mother had sought refuge for her feelings of loneliness in a close-knit religious group. However, her new-found faith no longer allows her to practise birthday celebrations, special festivities, and Christmas ceremonies. And life at home has become difficult economically and draining emotionally. Martin seems to blame his father for all that has gone wrong in his young life. Even in school Martin quickly turns resentful when things do not go his way. The teacher feels that Martin is vulnerable and she goes out of her way to make life at school supportive and relevant to Martin's interests.

In a few days it will be Father's Day and children are making special cards and gifts for their daddies. Celebrations like this pose difficulties for teachers since various children live without their fathers. However, Martin seems to be determined to make a Father's Day card for someone. Later in the day the teacher is surprised by a stranger identifying himself as Martin's father. Would he be allowed to spend the afternoon with Martin at school? The teacher says that the school values parental involvement and she walks the man into the playroom where Martin is busy. Inwardly the teacher is worried about Martin's reaction to an encounter with his father. But she senses that the experience may be good for him. When Martin sees his father he stands up abruptly, then he freezes and turns very pale. The father stands there too, awkward, uncertain now about his presence. "Hi, Martin," he murmurs softly. "I wanted to see you." But Martin stands immobile. The tension seems unbreakable. Then the teacher whispers into Martin's ear, "What about your beautiful Father's Day card?" Martin turns around, picks up the card and reaches it over to his father. The latter takes Martin's hand. And the next moment Martin clutches his father's big frame. There are lots of mixed emotions. But all the anger seems to have dissipated from his small body.

Of course, the teacher is not kidding herself. This is not just a simple story with a happy ending. How will Martin's mother react when she hears about the visit? And will the father prove dependable for his son? But the teacher has made a resolve to take the mother aside and talk with her about Martin's need. Maybe the father can become a continuous presence again in Martin's life. To attempt to help bring that about is the teacher's intention. Maybe she can invite the father to visit Martin regularly at school. Much may depend on the way her discussion with the mother turns out. For that the teacher will again have to demonstrate improvisational ability about what to say, how to say it, what to do.

Teaching children or young people is difficult, not merely because teachers are constantly busy and they have to act; it is difficult because teachers continually have to act in ways that are pedagogically tactful. A teacher who is more than a mere instructor is constantly required to know instantly what is pedagogically the right thing to say or do. In other words, like the jazz-musician who knows how to improvise in playing a musical composition (and thus charm the audience), so the teacher knows how to improvise the curriculum pedagogically (for the good of the students). The jazz musician's criteria of goodness are aesthetic, while the educator's standards of goodness are pedagogical. And, of course, another difference between jazz and education is that music is an artistic performance, while teaching is a pedagogical activity.[62]

What Does Pedagogical Tact Do?

Pedagogical tact is a form of acting educationally. It refers to the ways mothers and fathers can act with their children. It describes the ways that educators can act in teaching/learning relations.

Pedagogical tact portrays the ways any adult can act pedagogically with young people. In acting pedagogically the student is influenced, but if this influence is mediated by tact then it is not authoritarian, controlling, dominating, or manipulative in exploiting the child or making the young person dependent and powerless. *Tact* is not a value-neutral term. And *pedagogical tact* too is governed by normative sensitivities. Whatever we do as parents or educators, our pedagogical actions are always informed by normative intentions: We always intend to act in ways that are good for those children or young people for whom we bear some responsibility.

What does pedagogical tact do? Pedagogical tact does what is right or good for the child. But how do we know what is the right or good thing to do? If one cannot go up to the abstract level of moral or critical theory to answer this question in a general manner then one needs to go down to the concrete level of everyday experience to observe what tact does in specific situations or particular circumstances. We know from our experience of living with children what kinds of actions lie in the sphere of pedagogical tact. In the subsequent sections it is suggested that pedagogical tact does the following: preserve a child's space, protect what is vulnerable, prevent hurt, make whole what is broken, strengthen what is good, enhance what is unique, and sponsor personal growth.

Tact preserves a child's space

Growth and learning
require space.

Corey completely lost his cool and confidence while presenting the results of a tenth grade science experiment in front of the other students. Now he feels so embarrassed that he wants to sink into the ground so that he will never have to face his classmates again. The kids have noticed his inner struggle and some have started snickering while others feel so embarrassed for Corey that they pretend not to notice. This makes the situation even more difficult. Corey stands there frozen. His face twitches. The silence turns unbearable. But then the teacher breaks the awkwardness by handing Corey a piece of chalk and asks if he would capture the main findings with two or three points. Corey has a chance to turn to the blackboard and collect himself while not facing the other kids. Meanwhile the teacher makes some comments to the class, which help Corey get back on track. Corey ends up doing a decent presentation and the teacher says finally: "Thank you, Corey, you had a difficult moment. But we all have moments like that. You handled it well."

What Corey's teacher had done is to make an awkward and embarrassing experience livable. By her tactful intervention she has made Corey's experience lighter, bearable, just an awkward moment that Corey may not feel proud of, but that he can come to terms with nevertheless. The teacher stepped in to rescue the situation, but rather than making Corey's position as presentor impossible (for example, by suggesting that he sit down), she helped save his space, as it were, by enabling him to regain control over the situation. After stepping into the situation she as quickly stepped out of it again to turn it back to Corey.

Tact means to step back whenever possible, but remaining available when things turn problematic. By stepping back, the adult creates the space in which the young person is enabled to make decisions and act in his or her own way. However, there is a difference between tactfully stepping back and stepping out altogether, thus simply leaving a child to his or her own devices. The latter laissez-faire approach in education is often mistaken for child-centered democratic progressivism. A child should be allowed the freedom to make mistakes and learn from them. But it is false tactfulness to step out of the pedagogical relation altogether and leave the child "free" to make decisions and choices for which he or she may not be quite ready yet.

In many families adults may be too preoccupied with their own affairs to be very aware of what goes on in the inner life of the child. Good communication maintains a level of intimacy without suffocating the child's need for personal space. In most families adults probably communicate too little with their children, but on the positive side this allows an inner life to develop. Overprotective or overly snoopy parents communicate too much with their child in prying into the child's thoughts, dreams, imagination, feelings, fears, and so on. A balanced communicative relation promotes greater opportunity for self-knowledge while the human satisfaction of closeness and intimacy promotes sensitivity. But undercommunication is probably more common than overcommunication in most families. Prying parents tend to be suspicious of their children and, therefore, such children may have a greater need to keep certain things secret from their parents. Thus a silent struggle develops between the child's need for autonomy and the parent's desire to keep control of the child's affairs. Of course, one way to find out someone's secret is to look for evidence of supression which will sometimes tell us the nature or location of the secret (for example, the preadolescent suddenly avoids undressing in sight of his or her parents).

Teachers not only should be aware of the child's need for tactful support as well as for personal space, they also need to be aware of both under- and overcommunication at home. The way the child communicates at home may affect the child's preparedness to share thoughts and feelings and willingness to take risks at school.

Tact protects what is vulnerable

The child's vulnerability
weakens the adult.

The Physical Education teacher has taken his class swimming. Most children are enjoying themselves, and some he helps to improve their stroke. He sees Stephen, a good swimmer, on the diving board. Stephen stands there for a long time, estimating the distance down to the surface of the pool. He wants so much to follow the example of some of his friends and take a brave leap. But he simply cannot get over his fear. Friends call him to jump and come and play water tag. But Stephen shakes his head and pretends that he likes it up there on the board. "Later!" he shouts back. "I'm taking a rest." Finally, when no one is looking at him Stephen clambers down the side of the board and jumps in the water to join in the game. The teacher who has witnessed his struggle realizes that it would have been wrong to step in to openly encourage Stephen to conquer his fear and thus draw the attention of Stephen's classmates. Later he finds an unobtrusive opportunity to give Stephen a pointer or two, helping him to take the first jump. Before the swimming is over Stephen once more ventures up on the board and finally takes a leap down. After that he tries a few more jumps. Stephen is obviously overjoyed in his new-found courage and skill. The teacher notices this and praises him: "Good for you, Stephen! I like the way you straighten out your arms and legs while jumping."

A tactful educator is able to discern qualities in a child that are positive but that may at first seem to be weaknesses. Rather than riding roughshod over such situations, tact requires that one can bypass or pass over situations by treating them as "seen-but-not-taken-notice-of" or as "shared secrets." Adults often have difficulty with this. For example, teachers who go back to school to work for additional qualifications or for an advanced degree often experience extreme vulnerability when taking tests or having to perform in front of their peers in university classes. Yet these same adult teachers can be quite insensitive to their own students' vulnerabilities.

Generally, however, adults tend to feel responsive and compassionate when they notice how vulnerable children are. The child's helplessness and relative weakness makes the adult feel tender, softhearted. We might say that the child's weakness and vulnerability weakens the adult, and calls him or her demandingly to feel responsible for the child. Few adults fail to feel the power of the appeal the young child makes on them. Exactly to the extent that the child is vulnerable the adult experiences an immediate appeal that issues from the child's defenselessness and vulnerability. Not with power and might but from within this vulnerability the child is able to transform adult brusqueness and thoughtlessness into gentleness and considerateness. In a way the child's powerlessness and unprotectedness make him or her peculiarly independent of the adult. The child makes a claim on the adult which prevents the latter from arbitrary and willful abuse of power. The adult who abuses his or her power against the child thereby suffers a moral defeat.

Tact prevents hurt

Hurt must be made forgettable.

As Sheila walks home from school, her boyfriend, Tom, passes by on his new motorcycle. They wave to each other. "Don't forget tomorrow!" he calls. She gestures, smiles in anticipation of their date. He roars off. The smile is still on Sheila's face when suddenly a car appears on the road. The motorcycle veers, spins through the air. Like a thrown doll, the rider tumbles, hits another car, then lies still on the road. That night Sheila wakes up screaming. She had a terrifying dream. Her mother comes into the bedroom. Mother knows that it makes no sense to tell Sheila that she must try to forget the accident. "I keep seeing it, Mom. Over and over. How can I stop seeing it?" Her mother sits down beside her, just holds her, the way she used to do when Sheila was still a little girl. "Aren't we lucky that Tom is still alive," she says to Sheila. "He will need your friendship now, while he is recovering. You may have to help him with his homework." Together they sit like that, mother and daughter, in the stillness of the night.

Sheila's mother tries to help to make the memory of the experience forgettable. Not forgettable in an absolute sense, because one cannot erase what happens to us. But one can try to make them bearable, and thus forgettable in the sense that the trauma is erased from the memory of the experience. A forgettable experience is an experience that does not become discontinuous with our other experiences and thus not discontinuous with our sense of self-identity.

Discontinuous experiences are experiences that have left deep injuries and hurt in one's personal history. A child loses a parent through death or divorce, and this loss may become a traumatic memory that needs to be repressed for the person to be able to go on living. Yet repressed injurious memories are only seemingly forgotten. Though not conscious, they are not forgettable since they have not been dealt with. They turn into discontinuities in our being which express themselves as fears, dependencies, obsessions, distortions that stand in the way of healthy relations with the world and to others.

Ordinary experiences at school can turn into such scarred memories that we later recognize as "fear of failing at things that seem difficult," "fear of math," "hatred of science," "revulsion at poetry," and so on. To the extent that some of us have not developed such discontinuities, we may well owe this to the thoughtful tact of significant teachers.

Tact makes whole what is broken

Tact heals.

A child is sad because he feels betrayed by all his classroom friends. A student is frustrated because a series of low marks makes her feel like a failure. A pupil acts defeated because he thinks that he has lost the respect of a favorite teacher. In people's lives, and especially in children's, things constantly break or threaten to break. It is especially in this context that tact does what it does. Tact tries to prevent things from being broken, and tries to restore what is broken. A child who feels betrayed, frustrated, or hurt not only thinks that something is broken in his or her life; more important, the feelings of frustration, betrayal, and hurt reflect broken relations in the child's life. When one feels betrayed or disappointed with someone, one's relation to this person is no longer whole.

Tact has to deal with the objective and subjective aspects of the child's experience. Teachers may want to ignore such seemingly trivial happenings as conflicts among school children, but an observant teacher knows how these "small" matters may be experienced as giant obstacles in the child's daily school life. Feelings of acceptance or rejection are likely to be more consequential for the child than the math or science lesson that the teacher had prepared for this morning.

There are many trends in education in conflict with the deeper interests of pedagogical tact: curriculum policy that is predominantly concerned with measurable learning outcomes, teachers who feel compelled to teach toward the exam, schools whose policies do not help kids experience a sense of community — these all tend to lose sight of the fact that all education is ultimately education of the whole person. Many teachers intuitively understand that for all students their education is a life project. Each subject, each course, each accomplishment must make sense in terms of this larger life-project of the young person. Many teachers find themselves fighting silent battles and personal crusades against the blind forces of bureaucratic, administrative, and political structures in order to preserve a wholesome quality to their students' educational experiences.

Tact strengthens what is good

To believe in a child
is to strengthen that child.

What does it mean to strengthen what is good? Almost two hundred years ago, in his Stanser letter, Pestalozzi expressed it like this:

> The adult desires what is good and the child is willing to be open to it. But the child does not want the good for the sake of you, teacher — the child wants the good for *itself*. Moreover, the good to which you are to orient the child should not be subject to any of your whims or passions; rather, it must be good in itself, it must be good in the nature of things, and it must strike the child as good. And then the child must feel the necessity for your wanting this good according to *its* situation, and according to *its* needs, before the child desires the same *itself*. The child wants all that *it* likes. The child wants all that brings *it* credit. The child wants all that arouses great expectations in *it*. The child wants all that gives *it* strength and that can make it say, "I can do it." But this desire is produced, not by words, but by care for the child in every way and by the feelings and forces that are aroused in the child by this all-round care. Words do not produce the thing itself, but only a clear insight, the awareness of it.[63]

An educator needs to believe in children. Specifically he or she needs to believe in the possibilities and goodness of the particular children for whom he or she has responsibility. My belief in a child strengthens that child — provided of course that the child experiences my trust as something real and as something positive. An adult who says, "Let me do it for you," may simply want to be helpful. But the child may consider it an affront to his or her ability and self-sufficiency. "I'll do it myself!" he or she may say. Another child who interprets the "Let me do it for you" as a lack of confidence may react more passively. He or she may grow uncertain and distrustful of his or her own abilities. Mistrust or suspicion makes real pedagogy quite impossible. Adults who are unable to have and show trust in children are unable to be real teachers or parents as pedagogues. This may be the condition of adults who themselves are injured in their trust in the world and in others. If I mistrust others, if I am suspicious and cannot stand up in life with confidence and hope, then I may be unable to cherish trust for the sake of a child.

Suspicion calls forth negativity, badness, wickedness, even evil. It tends to produce suspicion and distrust in children: "Why did you have to do that again!" "Can you never do it right?" "Why should I believe you this time?" "I know you won't be able to do that!" "I know I cannot count on you!" "What did you do now?" A child who hears or feels an adult say, "I knew I couldn't count on you!" is captured in a relational sphere in which it is difficult to find the right tone. This may produce in the child stealthy glances, a stammer, awkward pauses, a downcast look, or a propensity to be apologetic and to say things the adult supposedly wants to hear. And the adult will find his or her suspicions confirmed. Soon the pedagogical relation turns into one of power and manipulation — a relation in which learning becomes a farce.

Tact enhances what is unique

Always be attentive to the
uniqueness of the child.

The other day I thought of Henry again. Henry may have seemed an unremarkable child. At least that is what the comments of the various teachers reflected in their entries in Henry's cumulative record. He was the kind of child you do not notice, even though he sat right up front in my fifth grade class. Physically Henry already looked like a small bespectacled middle-aged person. He was somewhat pudgy, walked with a waddle, and was awkward in gym class. However, Henry sported a cheery disposition and an oddly mature way of talking, emphasized by a British-Jewish accent. In almost all subjects Henry performed at a low average level. His math skills were definitely problematic. But I had been struck with Henry's uncanny feel for poetic thought and language. Strange that a child who appeared so mediocre in virtually all school subjects could write such fine and carefully crafted poems. In fact, other teachers in Henry's elementary school had been surprised when they heard of the hidden skill of this boy, who was no favorite amongst his peers either.

But fifth grade had become a year of unimagined productivity for Henry. He felt so special! With some encouragement and coaching, Henry wrote poems on significant events of his young life. He even published in a regional literary magazine. His parents were ambivalent about Henry's newly discovered talent. They would have been more pleased had he been able to get higher marks in math. Henry was doing his best, but could never quite satisfy their ambitions for him. When Henry went on to sixth grade and then to junior high school his parents were no doubt relieved that his enchantment with poetic language abruptly halted.

It was in ninth grade that I unexpectedly ran into Henry. I was visiting his school for the day. "Well, Henry," I said to him, "it's so nice to see you again. I have often wondered what has become of the poet." Henry admitted shyly that for the last four years his activities as a poet had come to an end. And that was that! He shrugged and smiled apologetically. "Too busy, you know!" Besides, writing poetry wasn't really his forte anymore. I think that I gave him a wondering glance and then we shook hands and parted. But before the day was over the principal of the school delivered an envelope to me. "From Henry!" Inside were three poems. They sang with unmistakable promise. They did this, despite their somewhat unoriginal title: "Odes to a Teacher." I was overcome. "A poet after all," I thought.

Tact discerns what is unique and different about a child and attempts to enhance this uniqueness. In contrast, a tactless teacher fails to see differences among children. A tactless teacher treats all children the same way in the mistaken belief that such an approach serves the principle of equal justice and consistency. Of course, all children are not the same in temperament, ability, nor background. Being concerned about equality among children still can mean that one is able to see uniqueness and difference among them. Pedagogical tact knows how to discern and evaluate uniqueness. Pedagogical tact aims to enhance the difference that "difference" makes in a child's personal growth and development. Every pedagogue should constantly ask him- or herself these questions: In what respect does this child differ from me and from others? How can this child be different? How does this child want to be different? What can I do to assist the child in realizing his or her uniqueness?

Tact sponsors personal growth and learning

Personal growth is deep
learning.

In an eleventh grade English class, each student has been assigned a short story to discuss and interpret. The teacher impressed upon all the students how important it is to read all the stories: "You don't want to have to discuss a story that nobody else has read. Read them because they are interesting. Read them also out of respect for your friends in class." This all the kids understood. (They seem taken aback for a moment when the teacher mentions in passing how often teachers have to prepare and discuss something the students have not bothered reading.)

Now each story has been read by all, and many times over by the student responsible for presenting it. The discussions are often animated, the interpretations, thoughtful and personal. Like every reader, students tend to interpret the stories in the context of their own experience. When Stefan gropes for words to explain that the story presented by Laurie, though entertaining, "did not do anything" for him, the teacher asks permission to paraphrase Stefan's opinion. Using Stefan's words, she skillfully brings out the distinction between "escapist literature" that mostly entertains and "interpretive literature" that deepens our understanding. Both forms of literature are valuable. And, of course, it sometimes happens that what is interpretive literature for one person is escapist literature for someone else who is amused but not touched by it.

As a result of the teacher's mediation, both Stefan and Laurie find their personal response to this piece of literature confirmed by the literary concepts that the teacher employs. The teacher is pleased because, in order to help clarify the very different reactions to the text by Stefan and Laurie, she is able to anchor their learning in a way that neither will likely forget. They will understand that interpretive literature is the kind that captures one person although it may leave someone else indifferent. We have all read a book at times that, like a stubborn melody, does not let go of us. We must make sense of it, interpret it. We recommend the text to friends in hopes of being able to talk about it with them. Interpretive literature is literature that lets me interpret the text while in a way the text interprets me. Escapist literature, in contrast, may be valued for the experience or thrill it provides me. But the experience of reading escapist literature is fleeting, soon forgotten, like a needed cup of coffee on a Sunday afternoon.

In a next-door twelfth grade class, another teacher dictates a definition of "interpretive literature." All the students are writing it down in their notebook. They are not personally engaged by these terms. There is no time in this class to use the "student discussion method" because the teacher feels the pressure to teach for the final exams. She hopes the students will respond properly to a multiple-choice question about the concept of interpretive literature. Yet, it is not likely that this concept will help them to make sense of their experience in reading literature. In the eleventh grade class the students possess their learning experience in a different way from the twelfth grade students. In fact, the latter do not really "own" the stories and concepts they are cramming for their exams; they do not turn this learning into something that is their own. Obviously, the more indirect method of teaching English literature through student discussion seems much less time-efficient while the more efficient approach of dictating notes and cramming for the exam saves a lot of time for the inclusion of even more content in the curriculum. Yet the more efficient approach ultimately fails since the students only gain shallow knowledge that is more easily forgotten.

The contrast illustrates several points. The method of teaching/learning a particular subject has consequences for the way the content is learned. Not just efficiency or effectiveness is at stake. The relations between teacher and students too have an altered pedagogical quality: more control-oriented in the grade 12 class, more dialogical in the grade 11 class. In the twelfth grade class the teacher is guided by considerations of time-efficiency. In the eleventh grade class the teacher is guided by considerations of relevance to students' lives. All education is normative. The question is whether the teacher will or is able to opt for pedagogical as opposed to non-pedagogical norms.

Learning is a process of increasingly developed explication and clarification of experiences initially more or less prereflective. Children and young people learn to live in the world and to interact with significant aspects of the world, such as reading or literature. Next, they learn to reflect on the world, and specifically on their experiences of the world, for example, by being able to distinguish between literature that is mostly enjoyed as recreation and literature that is enjoyed for the insights it provides.

We need to look past the superficial qualities of a classroom lesson toward the way that the teacher is present to the students. We will see that both the selection of subject matter content and the teacher's tactful approach to teaching this content almost always has consequences for growth and learning that may affect the child's character and ability to reflect and make critical sense of the world. Pedagogical tact sponsors personal responsibility in young people for studying and learning.

How Does Pedagogical Tact Do What It Does?

Pedagogical tact does what it does by exercising a certain perceptive sensitivity as well as by practising an active and expressively caring concern for the child. On the one hand, pedagogical tact relies on our ability to sense what the needs are of a child and also the possibilities for this particular child. This means that pedagogical tact can only work when the pedagogue's eyes and ears search in a caring and receptive manner for the potential of a child, what this child can become. This requires a perceiving and listening oriented to the uniqueness of the child, using a multiplicity of perspectives, considerations, and vantage points to try to gain a vision and pedagogical understanding of a child. It is important to contrast the openness of this sensitive capacity of tact to the inclination to see and hear only what one wants to see and hear about a child. The latter orientation leads to inflexible judgments, stereotyping, classifying — seeing only the external behavior of children and not their inner lives and their individual intentions and projects.

On the other hand, the sensitive eye of tact mirrors back its caring glance. Tact does what it does by using the eyes, speech, silence, gestures as resources to mediate its caring work. We can compare the analytical and detached glance which coolly observes and judges from above, as it were, with the sympathic glance that establishes contact and searches for pedagogical understanding in a dialogue with children. The eye that only observes the behavior of children objectifies, whereas the tactful eye subjectifies: The tactful eye makes contact, makes personal relationship possible.

We know the difference in these two types of glances when we think about occasions when in interacting with another person we feel that the other person is not really conversing with us but studying us. In the latter case the other person is not looking at me but at my body, my hands, my face, my legs — the other is "looking me over" and thus "overlooking me," who *is* my body. The objective glance cannot mediate my tactful action, and similarly the objective ear cannot ask my mouth to mediate the thoughtful response of the hearing in tactful speech. If I cannot hear the undertones of the inner life in the child's speaking then I cannot produce tactful speech myself. In the following sections I will make some suggestions about how tact can be mediated through speech, through silence, through the eyes, through gesture, through setting atmosphere, and through example.

Tact is mediated through speech

Tact creates a positive speech
climate.

The teacher says: "Now I want you to take out your book. ... Turn to page 87. I don't want to hear any talking! You shall first read the directions to Lesson Fourteen and then complete the questions based on the reading. ... "

Another teacher says: "Kathy seems ready for a change of pace. Do we all feel like Kathy, would this be a good time to discuss the poetry that looked so intriguing yesterday? Let's turn to page 87 and see. ... "

Both kinds of talk we meet frequently in classrooms. What

are some of the implications of the way that these teachers address their students? The difference between the first teacher and the second is that the first teacher places herself at the center ("I want you to turn to page 87"), the second teacher starts from the situation of the students while drawing herself into the relation that the students have with the text of the curriculum ("Let's turn to page 87"). Even though we do not know anything else about these two teachers, we do sense a difference in tone with which each teacher addresses the children. In the case of the first teacher there exists a certain distance between teacher and students; the teacher's speech seems to reflect a management attitude toward the class of "do this, do that." In contrast, the second teacher seems to establish contact with the children; her way of talking reflects engagement, connections, relationship. While the first teacher speaks with heavy use of the first-person pronoun, "I," the irony is that it is the second teacher who, while avoiding frequent first-person pronouns in her talk, creates a speech climate of personal in-touchness.

The kinds of speech that govern a classroom or a school may prevent or contribute to a sense of being in touch between teachers and children. This climate is a function of the relative presence or absence of a certain tactfulness in the manner in which, for example, the teacher calls upon a student, gives directions, makes suggestions, offers explanations, and so forth. We all sense the difference in the climate created by a teacher who addresses students by their first names as opposed to teachers who use only students' last names; a teacher who says, "Can't you hold your pen properly?" in contrast to a teacher who asks, "Can you hold your pen like I do?"; a teacher who commands "Practise!" versus a teacher who asks, "Are we ready to practise this?"; a teacher who commands, "All right, you may sit down now!" and a teacher who says, "Thank you for making this contribution!"

Rightly or wrongly much school time is filled by the teacher's voice. And, of course, the voice is a primary means of contact between human beings. That is why it is so important to realize what miraculous variety of inflections, timbres, and tonal qualities of which the voice is capable. A voice can be harsh or gentle, arrogant or modest, demeaning or encouraging, indifferent or caring, depressing or uplifting, sour or joyful, agitating or calming. After many years we may still remember the special quality that a significant tactful remark of mother, father, a teacher, a friend, a lover left us with — even if we can no longer recall the exact words that were spoken. It is the tonality that touched us, and it is the special atmosphere created by the voice that we remember. We all have been in situations where we became irritated by a discontented, grating, or whining voice. Such a voice stimulates us to rebel and resist. In contrast, a gentle or tactful remark can stir us to become more agreeable and suddenly see things in a new light. In both cases it is not just the words themselves that have such effect. It is also the climate created by the voice that makes the difference. The same words spoken differently can have an opposite effect.

A good teacher knows how children who are agitated or hyperactive may be quieted by a calming voice. People have a tendency to raise their voice when they want to discipline a child or a group of children. But a tactful teacher has learned the subtle effectiveness of the minor inflection of the tone of voice through which a sense of regret, disappointment, admonishment, or sadness, or, conversely, a sense of surprise, satisfaction, or joy resonates. The tactful voice establishes contact. When there is genuine contact between adult and child (and I do not mean of course the kind of goody-goody, namby-pamby, mealymouthed voice), there is usually little room for negativity and little need for "discipline and punishment." It is hard to overestimate the relevance of voice and speech climate for pedagogical relations as in the classroom. If living with children is to be a tactful affair, we need to take account of the tone of our voice, the way in which we speak.

On first reflection it would seem rather simple to substitute tactful for tactless speech. It would not seem too difficult to learn to use the kinds of expressions, speech formulations, tones of voice, and ways of talking that foster a relation of being in touch. But more likely the learnable speech formulations that superficially seem to reflect tactful behavior have little in common with the speech that is generated by thoughtfulness itself. The tactic of the specially trained salesperson is a good example. The salesperson has been trained to use certain gestures (e.g., the handshake) and verbal techniques (e.g., addressing customers by their first names) in order to create an instant relation of "closeness," "cordiality," and "friendship." But many people quickly sense that this instant relationship is a false, inauthentic one. Establishing a feeling of connectedness cannot be achieved through a trained set of speech practices because tactful speech is situation-specific and cannot be captured by a fixed set of patterns and formulations.

Tact is mediated through silence

Silence speaks.

Kenny is all worked up. He has hurriedly finished his writing assignment, but the teacher points out that he is not really finished. He has skipped several parts, failed to check his spelling, and his handwriting is abominable. The teacher tries to appeal to Kenny to be reasonable. "Do you agree that you can do much better?" the teacher asks. But Kenny refuses to agree. He probably experiences the teacher's demand that he be reasonable as unreasonable. "I won't do it all over again," says Kenny emphatically. But his teacher insists that she cannot accept work that is below his standard and therefore not really finished. She says to Kenny: "Look, if you could not do much better than this work suggests, then I would accept it from you. But I know you, Kenny. I respect your intelligence and your ability. In my estimation you are a very good student." Kenny angrily returns to his desk and very ostentatiously refuses to resume his work. He sits there, defiantly, arms folded, his books closed, looking straight ahead, muttering that he has had enough of this! Some children look at him curiously. Kenny is making a display of confrontation and resistance. Surely he is going to get in trouble with the teacher. But the teacher seems oblivious to Kenny. She has turned her attention to other children. She knows Kenny. He has a sense of pride and strong feelings of self-worth. Kenny does not like to be told what to do. Yet for the teacher to accept his challenge to a confrontation would benefit neither Kenny nor the atmosphere in class.

She knows something of Kenny's fragmented family life. She wants to fully encourage Kenny and she is asking Kenny, in a sense, to engage himself fully — by demonstrating fully his abilities in a positive way. She refuses to play into Kenny's confrontational reaction. The teacher remains silent and ignores Kenny's posturing. It takes a while for Kenny to cool off. But then the teacher notices, out of the corner of her eye, that Kenny has finally reopened his books and settled back into work. Kenny is stubborn; he is also quite bright. He is learning what it means for an assignment to be "really finished," and that standards have something to do with what he means to his teacher. Chances are that his work will be greatly improved when he shows it to her the next time.

Jim approaches his twelfth grade teacher after class. "Would you have some time for me this noon? I have a real problem with my English assignment you set for us yesterday and I wonder if you can give me some suggestions on how to deal with it." The teacher says, "Sure Jim, why don't you sit down with your lunch right here. We can eat and talk at the same time." While they start eating, Jim is soon talking a mile a minute. He is unsure about some things, but he has quite a few ideas. The teacher mostly listens, nods encouragingly and only rarely asks a question. Jim does most of the talking. Finally, Jim seems satisfied. He carefully rounds out the idea for his projects, then he leans back. The teacher smiles and both are quiet for a while, until the teacher rises, "Come on, it is time to get ready for the next class." "Thanks a lot, you are always so helpful," says Jim. But the teacher knows that, much more than ideas and suggestions, what he gave Jim was his silent attention.

Silence is certainly one of the most powerful mediators of tact. In tactful interaction silence can function in different ways. For example, there is the silence that "speaks." This is the tact of the "silent conversation" where chatter would be misplaced, or where intrusive questions may only disturb or hurt. The etymological root of "conversation" has the meaning of "living together, association, company, acquaintance." The noise of words can make it difficult to "hear" the things that the mere conversation of companionship can bring out. In good conversation the silences are as important as the words spoken. Tact knows the power of stillness, how to remain silent.

Further, there is the granting of silence that leaves space for the child to come to him- or herself. This kind of silence is not just marked by the absence of speech. Rather, it is the silence of patiently waiting, being there, while sustaining an expectant, open, and trusting atmosphere. It may involve a quiet trustful acceptance (while not interrogating or probing the child's mood), or a resolute turning away (while not really leaving), or a quietly passing over (while not in any way neglecting), or an unobtrusive lingering presence (while not being demonstrative or purposive about being there for the child). Of course, tactful silence should not be confused with the negative silence of giving someone the silent treatment as in the punishing silence of the adult or the defiant, revengeful silence of the child.

Finally, there is the silence of the listening ear. This is a wholehearted attentiveness to what occupies the thoughts and feelings of the young person. Tactful silence does not mean that one systematically refuses to speak, but that one realizes that there are moments when it is more important to hold back opinions, personal views, advice, and any other comments.

Tact is mediated through the eyes

When mouth and eyes
contradict each other, the child
tends to believe the eyes.

It is diary-writing time. Three times a week the children and the teacher in grade four spend about twenty minutes in the morning writing in their diaries. Although most children share their diary with the teacher, they are not compelled to do so. Nevertheless, many of them regularly put their diaries on the teacher's desk, who reads and returns them with a verbal comment. Both the children and teacher have come to value this time for reflection and the opportunity it creates for saying things and expressing feelings that are otherwise more difficult to express. Through the diaries the teacher has learned much about the children's lives outside of this inner-city school. She knows which of the children are likely to come to school in the morning on their own steam, without a decent breakfast or a nutritious lunch. She knows about the incidences of abuse and neglect, of the lifestyle of alcoholism in various homes, of the effects of physical conflict, parental absence, divorce, unemployment, homelessness, and the welfare cycle. Each child's life is a story against which this child's school performance must be measured. As the teacher is writing in her own diary about her own two children at home, she looks up momentarily and her eyes come to rest on Nicole. Nicole has a special relationship with this teacher (as in fact many of the children do). The teacher knows that it is difficult for Nicole to talk about her feelings about the problems she experiences at home. Nicole's mom and dad cannot get along. Both mother and daughter live in fear of an abusive husband and father. As Nicole walked into the class this morning the teacher asked, "Are things all right, Nicole?" and Nicole answered, "Yes." But from Nicole's face the teacher knew that things were not all right. But what Nicole cannot talk about directly she has learned to write about in her diary. In one sense the teacher should be pleased. Here is an inner-city child, a fourth grade student, who only four months ago could hardly write a full sentence. Now this student is actually writing to express herself. But the content of Nicole's writing is too serious for the teacher to feel simply victorious. Nicole looks up from her paper and her eyes meet the teacher's. "Are things all right, Nicole?" the teacher's eyes seem to ask again. In this understanding look, in these knowing eyes, Nicole finds the possibility to express her need: "He will kill us if he finds out that we are going to move," she writes. And she adds, "But I will miss my father. And I will miss my teacher. She means so much to me."

From moment to moment, teachers and children read from each other's face and eyes what is important, interesting, disturbing, moving, boring, stirring, disquieting. Through their eyes the adult and the child are immediately known to each other. When face and voice contradict each other, children are more likely to believe the eyes than the mouth. Why? Because children know intuitively that the eyes have a more direct connection to the soul than the words which flow from the mouth. Good teachers in this respect are like children. Unlike many adults, who have forgotten this truth, they cannot be fooled by mere words. A good teacher can read a child's face, just as the attentive parent can read the face of his or her child.

There is little doubt that we experience the presence of the other person most strikingly by way of the eyes. Through the eyes we may sense the innermost being of the other person, his or her soul. They literally provide me a "glance" of the other person's essence. And through the eyes the other person also has access to my being. Eye-to-eye contact is being-to-being contact. And through the eyes we are able to speak to each other about things that words may not adequately convey. It matters not so much what is said than how: the openness or vulnerability that makes it possible for eye-to-eye contact to be a genuine encounter — an encounter in which I know myself addressed at the heart of my existence.

We know how the eyes are capable of expressing mixed moods of the soul. Are these the eyes of love or hate? enthusiasm or dejection? honesty or deception? trust or fear? hope or despair? caring or indifference? The look of the eyes can express all these and more. We can see this in the children with whom we live. And what do the children see? What do our own eyes speak of? Do we know when the look of our eyes contradicts what our mouth is trying to say?

It is important to be able to read moods in children's faces, to be attentive to children. The eyes can only mediate tact when there is eye-to-eye contact. Here again we become aware that to speak of "tact" is to speak of "contact," of "in-touchness." Ultimately, to be able to be attentive to what is expressed in the face, the eyes of the other is to be able to see and interpret the soul of the other — to see through the look, through the eyes, to what gives expression to their particular look. In this way, the tactful wink, the warm glance, the look of appeal may be able to disarm the angry glare, melt the despondent gloom, or sway the critical scowl. The understanding glance the knowing look realizes that in the very depth of the eyes, in the constant volatility of the face lies the vulnerability of each person.

How does tact do what it does? Tact knows how to play the eyes. On the one hand it means that one must know how to interpret what goes on in others' eyes, and on the other hand that one must learn to express oneself through one's own eyes. This sounds strange. Don't we live through our eyes naturally? Yes, of course. But just as a great actor learns how to play the language of the face by more authentically letting the face speak for the whole body, so many of us can get in closer touch by way of the eyes. To be able to act thoughtfully with children we need to be animated by the love and care for children that makes a pedagogical relationship possible. I may want to praise and prompt a difficult child who acts up out of a need for attention and encouragement. I may say the right supportive words. But my eyes betray my true feelings of dislike. Only if I can see past the child's difficulty to his or her vulnerability can I bring my eyes in authentic alignment with my pedagogical intentions for this child.

So it is important to realize that the look of the eyes normally cannot be as easily shaped and manipulated as the words we utter. An encouraging nod, an understanding look, a meaningful wink, an inviting and open face — these are not simply a set of behavioral skills that one can learn in a workshop on classroom management. A teacher who tactfully encourages a child with a warm and supportive look must feel warmly towards the child. The teacher must *be* the glance that he or she exchanges.[64]

Tact is mediated through gesture

We meet each other first through
body and gesture.

In a third grade classroom the children are all silently at work on their math. Mark sits slumped on the edge of his seat. He is intently involved in his work. He is only partially aware that the teacher is walking nearby through the aisles. Then there is a confusing flush. The startling rush of adrenaline through his body is overtaken by the laughter of the children. The teacher has all of a sudden pulled the chair from under Mark; he finds himself on the floor. "That will teach you to sit properly in your chair," the teacher says amusedly. But Mark hardly hears these words. Red-faced, he sheepishly climbs back in his chair. It takes a while before he is able to ignore kids' continued snickering and get back into his math work.

Another third grade classroom: The children are all silently at work on their math. Michael sits slumped on his chair. He is intently involved in his math problems. He is only partially aware that the teacher is walking nearby through the aisles. Suddenly the teacher's face is next to his, looking at his work. "Nice work Michael!" she says. "I like the way you line up your numbers so neatly. I can't see a single mistake." Michael can almost feel the warmth of the teacher's face as she whispers these words to him. It feels like a caress and Michael proudly straightens up and adjusts his position on the seat. He had hardly noticed that the teacher's hand on his slumped back was in part an encouraging pat and simultaneously an effective gesture to straighten his posture and pull up his chair.

On the one hand, bodily gesture is symptomatic of a person's mood, so that a perceptive teacher may be alerted to the psychological or emotional state of a student by the manner in which the student carries him- or herself. For example, a student who slouches in his seat may feel tired, bored, or lazy. Another student who sits on the edge of her seat may be totally absorbed in her work. On the other hand, a teacher's gesture may create atmosphere, relationship, understanding, a mood. In both senses bodily gesture is like a language that can powerfully infuse a situation with meaning or significance.

From the moment human beings meet and interact they are first of all present to each other through their bodies and their bodily behavior. For example, I approach Mr. Brown with a question or a comment and as we talk I feel somehow strengthened and confirmed in my attempt to express my thoughts. Later I get involved with Mr. Smith in a similar conversation but this time I feel self-conscious, hesitant, and my speech turns awkward and halting. What is the difference? It seemed to lie in the difference in gestural receptiveness of the two people. I felt strong in the company of Mr. Brown, whose whole body and face was intently and supportively listening to me. I felt weak with Mr. Smith, who was fiddling while I was talking and who seemed to look away from me impatiently. The difference was in the entire gestural make-up of the conversations. Some of these differences had to do with obvious gestural demeanors: the way the hands were held, whether there was a friendly nodding, a smiling expression; other differences may have been more subtle: a thoughtful or disinterested gaze in the eyes, a listening or rigid tilt of the head and the entire body.

The science teacher is demonstrating a physics experiment. The English teacher is introducing a poem. The art teacher is discussing the significance of Greek architecture. If we were present in these situations, unless we paid special attention we might not even notice how gestures and words fuse in the interpersonal space between teacher and student. Word is gesture, gesture is word. And it is through this gestural language that a shared reality is shaped. In a way the gestural quality functions to let the students enter naturally the meaningful reality of physics, literature, art. Through gestures the students dwell bodily in the realm of significances that the gesturing brings into being.

This does not mean, of course, that teachers must be wildly flailing their arms and moving their bodies. In fact, the English teacher hardly moves at all. Reading the poem she is merely standing there — straight, still, quietly concentrating on the words on the page in front of her. Her whole being resonates this stillness which the words of the poem tear in startling rips and tatters. Yet almost invisibly this strangely tensed body of the reader of the poem seems to shiver. Or is it the listener who shivers, now intently gazing upon this poetizing body? Maybe it is the original voice, the primal speaking of the poetizing language itself that deeply shakes both reader and listeners.

What can we learn from the gestural nature of teaching? We can learn from this that language is like gesture and gesture is like language. And that tactful teaching knows how to create the gestural openings into the realities of nature, literature, art, mathematics, and so forth, so that students can enter them naturally.

Tact is mediated through atmosphere

For human beings
everything has atmosphere.

A teacher has just finished with the last chapter of a book she reads daily to her class. She quietly closes the covers; some children sigh. There is a certain pain, a feeling of loss, when a fine book is finished. You wish the story could go on; you don't want it to be over. The teacher knows this feeling and she subtly cultivates the power of this atmosphere: "Some of you may want to borrow this book to read yourself." Several hands shoot up. "Meanwhile," says the teacher, "we could find out what other books this same author has written. Now, how shall we go about this ... ?"

The teacher who reads a story to the class in the right tone creates a sense of community as well as an experience of shared narrative. Some teachers feel that reading to a class is something that one only does in elementary school. But in high school too a special mood or atmosphere can be created by reading to the students which may contribute to a heightened appreciation of the power of story and literature, including its communal value.

Teachers create an atmosphere not only by what they say or do but also in the way that they are present to their students. They produce a certain atmosphere by the way they work with the spatial and temporal dimensions of their classroom. Atmosphere is created by the arrangement of furniture and by the treatment of the walls and the hallways. Every teacher's classroom and every school is characterized by a certain mood. The question is not whether there should be an atmosphere, but what kind of atmosphere is most conducive to pedagogical relations.

Children are quite sensitive to the atmosphere in which experiences are shared. A teacher who reads to children out of obligation, or to keep the kids quiet until it is dismissal time, or a parent who reads until it is bedtime, or merely to keep a promise to a child — such a teacher and such a parent are not likely to enjoy what they read. They create no true narrative climate. How different is the reading experience where both adult and child are engrossed in the story, and where the child feels that there is shared feeling in the experience. Not only do both adult and child enjoy the story, they also enjoy the pleasure they give each other.

A junior high school teacher tells her eighth grade class: "I have a wonderful story entitled 'One Thousand Paper Cranes' that I would like to share with you to commemorate Remembrance Day, when we remember those who lost their lives as a result of human conflict and war." The teacher quickly provides a context for the story. It is the aftermath of World War II. The atomic bomb has forced Japan to end the war, but people are still dying. The teacher starts reading. The class settles in. But as the story unfolds it becomes obvious to the students that the teacher has difficulty with her own reaction to the story. Her voice quavers — not artificially to create a sense of drama. This teacher is truly moved. What the students sense is the teacher's vulnerability to the power of narrative. But they also recognize the teacher's reaction to the story in themselves. And it is interesting that none of these junior high kids takes advantage of the situation to make the teacher look foolish. Why not? It would be so easy to poke fun at sentimentalism. But maybe these feelings were not just sentimental. The story opens up human truths. The students are all touched by it.

The teacher feels that it is better to stop, and she says to one of the students, "Could you read on from here? I guess this story always overwhelms me a bit." When the reading is over the teacher is aware that quite a few of the kids are touched by the story. Some quickly rub an eye with a finger and others keep their heads down to not betray how they have been stirred. No one talks. The silence that follows is not the silence of attention, of waiting, or of obedience. It is a stillness that allows the story to linger on to invite reflection, reckoning, coming to terms with something that is deep and powerful.

Tact is mediated through example

We cannot help but be examples
to the younger generation.

The English teacher is unhappy about the quality of the handwriting of her eleventh grade class. She has great difficulty reading some of the essays because of illegible penmanship. She makes sure her own handwriting is impeccable in her written responses to the essays. In class she makes an extra attempt to produce perfect script on the blackboard. She strives to let the students know tactfully, that is, by showing the difference herself, that clear handwriting makes a text pleasant and personable. Aren't we pleasantly surprised when we receive a letter from a friend and recognize the characteristically nice printing? It is like recognizing the pleasant voice of a person we know. Many educators feel that teaching by setting an example, or better by living the example that students should emulate, may be subtle in the short haul but is effective in the end.

The English teacher we have just described is showing an example without drawing special attention to it. Of course, sometimes one may want to be more explicit. But even at such times the teacher can maintain a tactful approach: The English teacher has just written on the board in nicely flowing letters. It is obvious to the students that she is not just scribbling something down. Then she steps back from the board, and while eyeing her writing from the vantage point of the students she says, "I hope you noticed that I am trying to change my life — from now on I hope that you will be able to read what I write for you." She adds, "You know, presenting text to others is like going on a date and making yourself presentable and pleasant to be with. I'm afraid that my writing sometimes suffers from 'bad breath.' Now I am determined to change my life."

Naturally not every class, not every student can be influenced by way of example and subtle prodding. But it is definitely tactless to throw a paper back at a student while groaning disgustedly. It is better to say, for example, "I like the thinking you put into this essay, but the handwriting suggests that you tried to work too hurriedly."

Some teachers seem to want to teach by negative example, such as those who insist on decent handwriting from their students but whose own script is simply abominable. Or teachers who strongly advise their students against the bad habits of smoking but who cannot quit smoking themselves. Of course, good teachers are not afraid to show that they too have difficulty with certain things. But they show by example what it means to make a genuine effort. Acting tactfully by using one's positive example as a way of teaching moves the negative focus away from the child.

It is important to realize that, whether they like it or not, adults cannot help but be examples to the younger generation. We show children and youths what we make of the world, how we live in this world, and what this world means to us. In this sense we are all teachers even if some of us have no desire to be educators. We are all teachers to the extent that we offer children and young people through us, through our cultural life forms, and through our individual personal lives images of how life is to be lived.

8   *TACT AND TEACHING*

The Significance of Tact in Teaching

The study of tact enables us to focus on certain elements of the teaching/learning situation which most theories, models, and methods of teaching have been unwilling or unable to address: the animating element of pedagogy that grants a special quality to the world of parent and child or of teachers and students; the element of the person of the teacher without whom the pedagogical situation cannot exist; and the element of contingency pervasively present in all pedagogical situations. How do pedagogues best prepare for their task of educating children and young people? The answer to this question has been: cultivating or developing a measure of pedagogical thoughtfulness and pedagogical tact in their living with children.

Pedagogical thoughtfulness and tact are the mindful skills that enable a teacher to act improvisationally in always-changing educational situations. Educational situations are always changing because the students are never the same, the teacher is never the same, the atmosphere is never the same, the time is never the same. In other words, the teacher is constantly challenged to give positive shape to unanticipated situations. It is this ability to see pedagogical possibilities in ordinary incidents, and to convert seemingly unimportant incidents into pedagogical significance that is the promise of tact for teaching. Indeed it should be the hope of every teacher that the tact of teaching does not leave the student untouched in his or her fundamental being.

Tact gives new and unexpected shape to unanticipated situations

Tact converts incidence into significance.

We may hear a teacher say that "the lesson this morning worked out well, even though it went differently than I originally planned." This shows that course and lesson planning is not irreconcilable with the possibilities for tactful acting. There is little doubt that careful and detailed lesson planning contributes to good teaching. This is in contrast to those who feel that planning creates inflexibility in a teacher's approach to the lesson and to the students. The latter view is grounded on an inappropriate interpretation of the significance of planning. To plan is not just to program an inflexible script. To plan is to think through, to anticipate, to imagine how things might go, how these children might experience or see things. As the teacher thinks through the things he or she wants to say and do with students during the minutes of a lesson, the teacher prepares an intentional structure for the pedagogical situation. The more carefully an educator thinks through anticipated interactions with the children, the more likely that he or she will be able to improvise on the planned script in order to be more responsive to the contingencies of a situation. A good teacher thoroughly plans lessons in order to be able to teach extemporaneously on the basis of this planning.

In unanticipated situations the teacher has to know instantly what to say or do in order to tactfully modify or reorient the lesson in a pedagogically responsive and responsible way. But teachers may view the improvisational moment as a disruption or deviation from what should have happened. A teacher may have planned a carefully sequenced language or math lesson, but discover during the first phase that the children are just not able to get involved in the way that was expected. A poor teacher will ignore the tell-tale signs of students' poor response to the lesson and simply attempt to force through the prestructured sequence, or give up on the lesson and substitute a filler to kill the remaining time. A good teacher realizes that the students' experience of the lesson determines the ultimate significance of what is being learned. Maybe some prerequisite skills were not as well established as the teacher had supposed; maybe the preceding lesson created a level of agitation or a focus of interest which tended to distract from the subject at hand; maybe the general classroom climate was just not conducive to the attention span required for the lesson as planned; maybe the children have a very different conception or understanding of the subject than the teacher expected.

Thus, tact enables one to discern the significant element of a pedagogical moment. A teacher who has a full sense of what is pedagogically worthwhile about a particular math or poetry lesson — because he or she has carefully thought through the essence and the structure of the lesson — is more likely to tactfully adjust the plan to suit the disposition or the circumstances of the students. A teacher who is poorly prepared, or for whom the lesson is only externally planned, is not in touch with the fundamental purpose and significance of the lesson. Such a teacher can only flounder.

The touch of tact leaves a mark on the child

A touch may work wonders.

The phone rings. A young man asks, "Are you Mrs. Walker, the teacher who taught English at Central High School? I am Peter Lemarsh. You taught me almost ten years ago and you had a poem of mine published in a magazine ... . You probably don't realize this, but that single poem changed my entire attitude towards school and learning. I used to think of myself as stupid and a loser. I had given up on school. Your teaching gave me pride and the courage to think that maybe I could do better. Since high school I have been taking English and some other courses at a local college in the evenings, which I have enjoyed immensely. And since I have now graduated I need your advice. I would like to do graduate work at a university, to become a teacher. ... Do you think I can do it? I need to know what it takes. You are the only person I feel I could ask for advice."

Obviously it is not only parents, teachers, and other educators who leave their mark, their influence on a child. Many experiences of a growing person contribute positively or negatively to character and selfhood. But only those adults who stand in a pedagogical relation to young people and who approach them with pedagogical intentions make the formation of character the project of their actions. Real learning is never merely intellectual growth: Real learning happens when the knowledge, values, and skills we acquire have something to do with the person we are becoming. Character is the distinctive identity that marks the individual person.

The Greek word *kharakter* referred to an instrument for making a distinctive scratch or impression on an object. Of a person we say that he or she "has character": We mean that there is an essential unity and consistency in that person's way of being, acting, and speaking. This is not to be confused with "personality." A person may "have personality," which means that he or she can dazzle others by the way this person behaves or carries himself or herself. To have "lots of personality" may not necessarily speak of a good character. Personality is what one is concerned about when one needs to act in front of people. A personality mostly made up of artificial manners is often irritating to other people. But a personality grounded authentically in a person's character has a desirable quality. Children often appreciate and admire a teacher who has "style" or "personality," as long as this presentation of self is genuine.

Sometimes young people adopt behavior from a favorite teacher they respect. In this sense a teacher may influence a child's personality. But pedagogically speaking personality remains largely outside the influence of the educator. Formation of character by contrast, is central to the task of education. "Education that really deserves to be called that is in essence character education," said Bollnow.[65] And many who have thought more deeply about education see that it cannot be limited to the instilling in children of certain knowledge and skills. Pedagogy always concerns the unique person: who the child is and who the child is becoming.

On the one hand, one may be skeptical that teachers can significantly affect a child's character. To be sure, the guidelines of many teacher handbooks, issued by Departments and Boards of Education, contain lofty statements: "The educator must teach children positive values, such as honesty, sincerity, respect for person and property, willingness to cooperate with others, responsibility, love of learning, tolerance, critical and open-mindedness," and so forth. In contrast, there are skeptics and minimalists who maintain that schools cannot be expected to do all these things. They feel that schools should keep to the basics: reading, writing, math and not a lot more — in high school some basic history, science, geography, and possibly a second language. Reasonably speaking, that is all that can be accomplished in school, so the skeptics argue.

But the skeptics and minimalists are being "realistic" at a terrible cost: the essence of their pedagogical relation to children. When pedagogy is no longer concerned with the unique person, then education is reduced to an enterprise in which the school has become "the market," the children and their parents its "customers" and "consumers," the teachers its "classroom managers," and the principal "the school executive." This is sometimes the language of modern educational theory. It allows a school principal to say that he really considers himself "an executive manager of a plant, not unlike the manager of a supermarket foodstore." In this scheme teaching is equated with "delivery" and curriculum with the "delivery systems" of educational "goods." What happens in this approach is that the discipline of education is reduced to something modelled on the transactions of the marketplace. Education is turned into an economic equation to make schools ever more "efficient" and "effective" places of production. Pedagogy does not fit such a scheme, for pedagogy always first asks the question, "Where to?" and soon after that, "Why is this important?" It is often the case that the most "efficient" modes of learning are pedagogically the least desirable.

The Primacy of Practice

Pedagogical theory is ultimately a practical affair. Whatever pedagogical knowledge we acquire, whatever insights into teaching, parenting, or child care we achieve, this knowledge must have consequences for our living with our children. We may turn this around and say, our daily living with children, our practice, is the starting point for our reflecting and theorizing about pedagogy. However, it would be wrong to assume that what is essential to good teaching is necessarily to be found in our practice. Just as theory is often completely cut off from and inconsequential for the practice of good teaching, so practice is frequently alienated from and forgetful of what is essential to the demands of good teaching.

In our daily lives with children at home or at school we often forget essential things. For example, as parents we are sometimes so busy that we do not have time for our children. Or we may have been so frustrated by our work or our personal problems that we have difficulty listening to our kids at home. Here, what is essential to good parenting — to have time to listen to our kids — is forgotten in practice. In schools, too, practice often tends to prevent us from seeing what is essential to good teaching.

The way that essential things can be remembered and restored to the activity of daily life in schools and classrooms is by a special process of reflection. To some extent we naturally engage in such reflection in everyday life. As we live and deal with children we are increasingly prompted to reflect on our lives and actions: "Should I have done that?" We sometimes feel guilty about the way we have treated children. And as we reflect on our successes and failures we are confused about what is expected of us, and what we should expect of ourselves.

In the world of teaching and learning there are some themes that recur in our daily experiences. These are themes such as difficulty, interest, discipline, and humor. In the following sections we will examine the significance of some of these themes with reference to pedagogical thoughtfulness and tact.

Tactful teachers find difficulty easy

Teachers need to be able to understand what it is like not to understand something, or to misunderstand something, or to understand it differently. For this, do teachers need to be smart? Or is it an advantage for teachers to have been poor students themselves so that they can identify with their own students who have difficulty? It would seem absurd to argue (although some do) that being very intelligent and being very knowledgeable about what one teaches is a handicap in good teaching. But smartness in itself does not guarantee that one will make an excellent teacher. Nor, of course, do those who have themselves experienced difficulty in school necessarily make good teachers, just as having been a failure at the violin does not make one a good violin teacher. More likely, excellent teachers are those who are both smart and yet who find difficulty easy to understand.

Teachers need to be experts at alternative points-of-view, perspectives, outlooks, biases, orientations. They need to be able to see things from the child's viewpoint. And children often perceive things very differently than an adult. In addition, one child may look at something quite differently from another child. Yet when there is misunderstanding, miscommunication, misinterpretation, it is usually not the teacher who is considered to be experiencing difficulty, but the child.

Children may have difficulty seeing something in the way the teacher sees it, or how the textbook explains it. It is not always easy to make clear distinctions in learning difficulties between those associated with psychological and with logical structures of subject matter. Educational researchers frequently employ the term "cognitive processes" or "cognitive strategies" to refer to the ways in which children think through questions or problems. We need to realize that such terms often represent highly inferential, abstracted, and generalized notions of how children actually do think. When it comes to concrete situations, the methodological advice pertaining to, for example, "cognitive instructional teaching strategies" may be of only limited value.

It is not always even very helpful to say that "these students need to have more 'concrete' experiences before doing the more 'formal' or 'abstract' exercises." In concrete situations it is important to sense what specific difficulties a particular student has with, for example, the concept and operation of place value in mathematics. Does this student grasp the meaning of the decimal point? What image does the child have of a decimal number? Is the idea fuzzy and fleeting? What kind of understanding is the child forming? Mathematics textbooks often try carefully to simplify and sequence the logical structures of mathematics into teachable psychological structures. But the psychological processes and the examples and exercises provided by the textbook author sometimes make mathematical concepts even more difficult to understand for the child. Experienced mathematics teachers know this and try to remain sensitive to the emerging meanings that children themselves form about mathematical notions and operations. So in classroom situations teachers have to know how to connect with the child's existing understanding, when to press for understanding, when to teach the mere skill to solve the math problems, or when to teach the short-cut method. Tact means being sensitive to the child's understanding, the child's state of mind. Only when a teacher has a grasp of a child's understanding can the teacher know how to get the new concepts to the child, rather than leaving it up to the child to somehow figure out the teacher's meaning and how to scramble to reach it. Only when the teacher stands beside the child, as it were, can he or she know where together they should go and how to get there.

Whatever the difficulty of learning is for a student, the teacher needs to try to sense the meaning and significance of the student's experience of difficulty. A good teacher finds difficulty easy to comprehend. Or, to say it differently, a smart teacher understands what smarts when a child experiences difficulty. Smartness in teaching is not sheer intellectual cleverness, smartness in teaching is thoughtful sensitivity. A teacher is smart when he or she is sensitive to what prevents a child from being smart.

Sometimes learning is painful. In fact, it could be argued that all consequential learning may involve a certain amount of anxiety, stress, or difficulty. Yes, to live at all is in some sense to live in difficulty. Rather than make everything in life easy, we may need to restore some of life's difficulty to provide for positive challenge, risk, adventure, encounter, and for coming to terms with consequential questions and human issues. But much anxiety, difficulty, and stress that children experience in school has negative rather than positive value. Teachers know, for example, that a certain amount of anxiety may help students to do better at a learning task or test, provided that this anxiety contains at the core a sense of personal confidence about one's fundamental ability.

Negative anxiety is anxiety that does not make the child stronger but that saps the child of vital strength. Negative difficulty is difficulty that does not make learning more meaningful but that makes it trite in what it demands of the child. Negative stress is stress that does not deepen one's sense of self but that simply wears down the child's resourcefulness. Negative anxiety, difficulty, or stress hurts the child rather than strengthening, building, and contributing to the child's growth and maturity.

A tactful pedagogy, therefore, tries to prevent the circumstances and factors that make an experience injurious and hurtful to children. This means, however, when an educator poses challenges and creates learning tasks for children, he or she has to have an understanding of the meaning of anxiety, difficulty, and stress in students' lives. Some forms of anxiety (such as those created by tests) are stimulating and challenging for certain students, while the same sources of anxiety can paralyze other students into poor performance and even physical distress.

On the one hand, teachers and teacher educators often seem to assume that it is the mission of education to make learning and the curriculum easy for all children. How to make math, writing, second languages, science easy? That is the question at the base of much educational research. On the other hand, teachers at times give poorly prepared assignments or adopt a hard line on being unavailable to their students on the mistaken assumption that they are forcing their students to take more responsibility for their own learning. Obviously, a "difficult teacher" is not necessarily a good teacher. Neither is an "easy teacher" always pedagogically desirable.

A good teacher knows how and when a particular learning experience is too difficult or too easy and whether this difficulty, or lack of it, is pedagogically positive. Moreover, a good teacher knows that any learning situation is experienced differently by different students. What is negative for one student may be a positive challenge to another. So when two students, on separate occasions, ask a teacher for assistance in explaining a similar assignment or problem, the teacher may quietly help one to think through it properly while equally quietly encouraging the other to stick with it and try to work through it independently.

Of course it would be wrong to conclude from the discussion above that teaching is not difficult. Good teaching is difficult, especially because there are no technical solutions or ready-made remedies for the predicaments that pedagogical situations pose to educators.

Tact is interested in the child's interest

"Show interest!" teachers say to students who seem to lack motivation or willingness to participate in the lessons. Report cards commonly carry the message to parent and child: "Should show more interest in schoolwork!" From their side, students complain in turn that the teacher should "make things more interesting," the teacher should "help us to get interested." Few teachers would disagree that interest is a fundamental requirement for learning, especially learning in that somewhat artificial environment of the school.

But interest is not a state of mind that can be requisitioned or produced upon request. "Interest" is rather a word that describes a person's way of being in the world. To be interested in something is to stand in the midst *(inter esse)* of something, to take part in, to maintain a caring relation to something. To be interested is to be intensely present to something or somebody. By being intensely present to something I experience the subject matter of my interest in a focussed way. I experience my personal orientedness in a more defined way, as well. As I focus on a subject of interest, my focus allows me to concentrate and to be attentive. Thus, in being intensely with something or somebody I gain an awareness of the possibilities, the indefinability, the openness of the subject. A subject that interests me is a subject that matters to me.

Unfortunately, disinterest, boredom, indifference may be prevailing conditions among many school children and youth, especially those who have left the primary grades. Yet what could be more fundamental and essential for the child's preparedness to learn than interest, even animated rapture, in the subject that the teacher teaches? Interest is one of the most fundamental aspects of the relation between person and knowledge, reflection and life. Without interest, genuine interest, everything that happens in school is in danger of turning into empty pretence, illusion, sham, and feigned importance. The teacher's command to "show interest!" may really be a request to the student to fake it, to cooperate in a game of illusion.[66] When the teacher asks for a show of interest, students may feel that they are required to simulate, to feign a certain behavior — to put on a show, a front that covers their real feelings. The problem is that neither the educator nor the students are willing to admit to the grand illusion in the show of interest. Yet to the students school is often experienced as "boring!"

The experience of boredom or ennui spells dullness, tedium, sleepiness, lethargy, passivity. No deep, meaningful learning can take place in such atmosphere. In contrast, interest is accompanied by attentiveness, effort, striving, discipline, concentration, achievement — all values that teachers recognize as essential to learning. But attentiveness, effort, striving, discipline, concentration, achievement must stand in a direct, primordial relation to interest.

Attentiveness that is coerced, and not prompted by the impulse of interest, is only fleeting attention. Effort extorted, and not energized by the thrust of interest, is only half-hearted effort. Striving that is the effect of someone's pushing, and not lured by the fascination stimulated by interest, is inauthentic striving. Discipline that is imposed by threats, and not taken on in the desire to follow systematically the paths of interest, is mutiny-raising discipline. Concentration compelled from without, and not an internal response to the inner interest, is likely to be an absent-minded concentration. Achievement purchased at the cost of tedium, not the outcome of engaged interest, is likely to be shallow, short-lived achievement.

What happens when we fail to understand that there exists a primordial connection between learning and interest? In schools and classrooms where learning now must be pushed in the absence of interest, one replaces the intrinsic power of desire and interest with the extrinsic motivation of hidden seduction or coercive compulsion. This means that we come to expect and demand from the child industriousness, diligence, good work habits, a willingness to apply oneself obediently to lesson assignments and activities that students tend to experience as dreary, dry, tedious, and tryingly boring. Of course there seems much to recommend in the positive moral values of diligence and hard work. When children no longer relate to a subject matter with interest, there may be little alternative for teachers than to stress forced effort, industriousness, work habits, diligence, and artificially generated goodwill. Yet it seems wrong to assume that we must routinely substitute the instrumental value of work for the natural value of desire that accompanies real interest in learning.

There is a sense in which the notion of interest signifies that one has a stake in something. This is the more materialistic and financial meaning of "interest" as having a legal claim to something. "To have an interest" in something in this sense means that one has a lien on it, that one has some control over it. But what does it mean to have a hold on something if it does not have a hold on us? There is also a deeper sense in which to have an interest in something means that one has a stake in it. For example, something that is of general interest should serve the common good. Interest defines our relation to the world in which we live, and to become interested in something is to be drawn into that aspect of the world. A teacher may draw my attention to something and thus spark my interest. The teacher knows that it is interesting to us when it has power to attract, to draw attention, to concern us.

It would be hard to think of a child who has lost all interest in things. I see a child at the ocean beach completely captured by the treasures that the receding waters have left among the rocks and in the sand. Would a child still be a child if he or she were totally jaded among all these "treasures," as some adults may have become? To be a child is to live with interest. The active term of interest is "wonder," which is the opposite of dullness, ennui, boredom, the taken-for-granted. A tactful educator will keep alive and strengthen the wonder that produced the child's activity.

Tactful discipline produces self-discipline

Discipline, especially classroom discipline, is not just the order adults are able to manage with respect to the behavior of children. A person's attitude toward discipline is the measure of that person's own orientation to order. It has often been noted that when asked what they value in teachers, young people in the middle school years frequently mention a sense of order, clarity and fairness. Especially early adolescents favor teachers who are knowledgeable, who know how to organize subject matter, how to approach learning situations, how to handle assignments, and how to test in a manner that is confident, clear, and resolute.

Teachers who are poorly prepared, fuzzy, indecisive, insecure, and inconsistent unwittingly create situations in which young people may turn disorderly, disruptive, inattentive, and unwilling to learn. Here we have therefore the cause for a teacher's having a discipline problem. When discipline becomes a concern over rules, the question of discipline turns into a management problem — how to control the disorderly behavior of students and manage daily classroom routines.

The term *discipline* is related to the notion of *disciple* (someone who follows a great teacher or a great example), and also to the notion of *docere* (meaning to teach), and to the term *doctor* (a learned person). A disciplined person is prepared to learn and to be influenced toward order. To create discipline in students or in oneself is to create conditions for real learning. Of course, teachers are frequently in situations where there are some students who seem to be totally disorderly and completely unwilling to get seriously involved in learning. For whatever reason, such students seem to use every opportunity to disrupt or otherwise spoil a lesson or a discussion.

A teacher has just read a short story and she asks the students to reflect on the reason why the main character in the story acted in the way he did. Immediately Rodney speaks up. "This is just a stupid story. Nobody in his right mind would do a stupid thing like that. I do not see why we have to deal with this stupid stuff." The teacher feels annoyed because in a previous class this story had generated thoughtful and animated discussions, but now Rodney's quick condemnation seems to have created an instant atmosphere of effrontery. Students who would otherwise have been inquisitive now seem disinterested or infected by the same mocking attitude. The teacher regards Rodney with a scowling glare. "I have no intention of debating with you the worth of this lesson since I very much resent your negative attitude to whatever we do in this class. It is unfortunate that you cannot be more positive to language arts, but since you seem to be failing this subject anyway, why don't you get yourself a job collecting garbage!"

The teacher may feel understandably resentful toward this student who seems to let no opportunity pass to criticize, disturb, and agitate. But to meet defiance with vengeful ridicule and threat of failure does not contribute to the atmosphere of the lesson, and it does not prompt Rodney to turn more positively to language arts. Of course, if the teacher manages to rule the class with an iron hand, she might intimidate Rodney into submission. Kids are sensitive to being ridiculed or humiliated in front of their peers. In the face of the tight rule of formal discipline Rodney might actually feel challenged to practice more subtle subversive techniques.

However, if the teacher has come to expect this kind of uncalled-for response from Rodney, she might more tactfully try to prevent him from speaking before his turn and first give the floor to other students who would help set the discussion on a productive course. For example, she might say to the class: "Please take a moment to reflect on the theme of the story .... Write down for yourself what you consider the important points, and in a moment I will call on some of you to read your response aloud."

So there is a formal kind of discipline that is largely maintained through the rule of fear: fear of failure, fear of punishment, fear of public ridicule, fear of sarcasm, fear of rejection, fear of humiliation.[67] This kind of "management of order" in the classroom is a false discipline. The typical reaction, especially of the growing adolescent, to this type of discipline in middle school is either conflict and rebellion or surrender and conformism.

The teacher who relies on formal discipline tends to fail to be personally present for the youngsters he or she teaches. Such a teacher is experienced by the students as a mere "instructor," a taskmaster — someone who may have excellent knowledge of the subject matter and who may teach this subject matter with praiseworthy clarity and effective and efficient procedures. But the teacher who needs the discipline of fear (like certain animal trainers) is a mere instructor of subject matter, not an educator of children. Ultimately the child or youth experiences the knowledge learned in such a setting as external and unrelated to his or her own life.

Only when a teacher's presence embodies the subject matter in a personal way, and when he or she is able to show that there is a living relationship between this subject and his or her own life, only then can the atmosphere of the classroom change from the authoritarian discipline of formal coercion to living vibrancy and spirited animation. But order that is not personal, order that is imposed and equated with rigid rules, will ultimately defeat learning. Thus, pedagogically significant discipline comes from a strong personal orientation to order — an orientation that arises as disciplined passion, or passionate discipline, from within the self. There is no better discipline for a child than this sense of self-discipline.

The tact of humor creates new possibilities

School has reopened after the summer vacation. The grade 10 class is assembled in their homeroom and the teacher is putting directions on the board. There are some tensions and "first day" anxieties in the room. Larry asks his new teacher a question: Should the word 'occuring' have a double r?" He points at the word on the board. The teacher looks confused for a moment, then says, "You are right." And she adds with a crooked smile, "Just testing!" But Larry is not gracious, "And are yòu going to teach us spelling this year?" as if to say "What kind of language-arts teacher are you anyway?!" Then he looks sort of shocked by his own cockiness. Several kids have started snickering. However, the teacher takes the swipe in her stride, "Well, I was hoping to keep it a secret a little longer, but now the truth is out: I am nòt perfect! But of course that won't stop me expecting perfection from all of you."

Humor often manifests itself in a person who finds himself or herself confronted by his or her own shortcoming, fault, failing, weakness, or inadequacy.[68] Humor is especially effective where relations of power may be experienced as unequal, as between students and teacher. One's reaction to an awkward moment is typically comical, droll, foolish, or funny as one realizes what the situation really is all about, what was expected, or what should have been one's proper behavior. In such situations humor may erupt from the person because of the surprising turn, startling moment, or unexpected happening catching the person off guard. Sometimes, instead, the reaction is anger, annoyance, embarrassment, or irritation. Then the situation usually becomes even more awkward or sour. But if the reaction comes as a humorous response then the tension is typically broken.

Humor can open new possibilities where things otherwise get edgy, messy, stuffy, stodgy, dreary, or stuck. Our everyday lives with children are filled with moments when the atmosphere is too stifling, when things have gotten bogged down, when events take an embarrassing turn, when a predicament proves too immutable, when a situation is so complex that it is no longer comprehensible, when a relationship has generated tension that is no longer comfortable or safe. Humor can take the edge off such situations. Humor is a humane means at our disposal to loosen, dissolve, free, or restore situations that have become pedagogically unproductive. Moreover, in such situations humor may also help us to keep our composure. An extreme example is Sir Thomas More, who on the way up to the block is purported to have said to his executioner: "Will you please help me up? I'll be able to get down by myself."

Ten-year-old Jason is obviously not diligent about brushing his teeth in the evening. As he is about to skip toothbrushing before bed, his father remarks, "Only brush the ones you want to keep." Humor is a tactful way of telling a child the truth without making it less truthful. The child does not experience the truth served up through humor as a judgment that crushes, denigrates, or condemns. Tactful humor disarms, where derisive humor or the brutal truth might have driven the person into estrangement, hostility, a loss of face, alienation.

For the child, humor may be the means of redefining relations with the adult. For the adult, the child's humor may mean that the adult has been offered a new perspective. Actually, humor is a marvelous device for maintaining a relaxed, friendly, open, sympathic atmosphere between teacher and students. Humor is good when the laughter comes from warmth, from empathy, from love. When the whole group laughs together, then the laughter seems to warm the shared space with a sense of community, togetherness. Good humor brings people closer together as it relaxes the atomosphere among them.

A good comedian says, "I never make jokes about those who are vulnerable, or about a downtrodden minority. But it is okay to laugh at ourselves or at those who have power and who should be reminded of the relativity of their power." Of course, teachers, by virtue of their position, can be figures of power to students. The students' telling jokes about teachers or poking fun of situations in class may be their way to diminish or equalize a power that has more to do with bureaucracy or autocracy than with pedagogy. Teachers need to see that becoming objects of children's humor is not really a threat to their personhood or to their true pedagogical authority. Humor can be a beneficial force to restore and balance good relations between teachers and students.

Of course, humor is not necessarily the same as joking or making people laugh. Rather, humor is the ability to make things lighter and more bearable where they might otherwise weigh us down. Generally we may distinguish between two kinds of humor: There is tactful humor that is positive and that creates openness and possibilities. And there is derisive humor that is largely negative and nihilistic. Derisive humor mocks and laughs at those made the object of ridicule. Derisive humor may express itself as cold cynicism, hateful scorn, biting sarcasm, bitter irony, hostile jeering, or confrontational taunting. Like positive humor, derisive humor exposes things, but it leaves them broken.

There is also a humor that does not know what to do with itself and turns into silly cleverness. This is exemplified in the person who constantly tries to be facetious, witty, whimsical. We know the effect of this humor when we try to have a conversation with a person who treats everything we say or do as a joke. A real conversation is not possible. We finally feel awry, exasperated, and disappointed. Similarly, a teacher "who always tries to crack dumb jokes," as students say, is a teacher who tends to make deep learning, serious involvement in subject matter difficult.

Humor is important for the educator who feels strained and assaulted by the daily pressures of expectations that seem to lead from one disillusionment to another. Positive humor prompts our pedagogical orientation to our vocation and our children, to see the relativity of practical problems while not losing our sense of values and commitment. The latter is important because sometimes our tendency to see the relativity of situations leads us to the false belief that therefore all values are of equal value, or worse, that our values ultimately are not of any value at all. Positive humor knows how to instill in us all a certain humbleness, which has the strength of helping us to bend rather than break under life's daily difficulties and disappointments. Positive humor means that, as educators, we know how to come to terms with the modest role we play in educating our children while seeing our influence as essentially indispensable in the child's life.

For teachers it is sometimes a challenge, especially for the new teacher, to resist getting infected with the negative humor of disillusionment that is found in the staff room of some schools. In some inner city schools the daily struggle to prepare children for a constructive and healthy life may seem hopeless in the face of the societal forces of evil and destruction. In some schools, teachers may experience a lack of administrative support, or may get worn down by constant harping and criticism from parents, or by a high incidence of parental disinterest, neglect, or abuse.

Children themselves may be cynical about the worthwhileness of life and ideals that try to improve things for themselves and for the world. In the face of so much negativity, the power of humor is a miraculous resource. Children need teachers and parents who have not lost the faith that miracles do indeed happen in life and in education and are not rare. Learning itself is such a miracle. Maybe it is a miracle that for every child and for every adult there is or once was a mother, a father, or a teacher who took it upon himself or herself to dedicate many years of his or her life to the child, so that the child may grow into the adult.

Every educator should have a sense of humor. Humor is more likely an acquired disposition, the fruit of reflective wisdom, and less a genetic endowment or gift. We learn to look at life with a sense of humor when we are able to ignore the imperfections and frictions that accompany the events of daily existence. Our confidence and faith in children and in the goodness of life make it possible to preserve a sense of humor about the things that are in the end less important. This does not mean that humor consists of being tolerant of matters that are wrong or bad, or that humor should make light of affairs that require serious attention. But humor allows us to deal tactfully with children in situations that require our guidance.

Children need us even (or especially) when they do not seem to need us, as when they rebel or reject us. Tactful adults may hope to have an effect on children or young people even when the effort at first seems wasted. Humor that playfully uses the pedagogue's deep trust in his or her value for children's lives benefits both the pedagogue and the child. It helps the educator and the young person feel the depth of their mutual investment in each other, and the scope of their relation to the larger world.

The tactful structure of thoughtful action

Many teachers are forever telling anecdotes and stories about their daily experiences with children.[69] We might say that telling anecdotes is a form of everyday theorizing that enables the teller to bring experience into language. In this way we can come to terms, as teachers, with something significant, something worth telling, something important in the anecdote. Parents, too, tend to tell each other stories and anecdotes about their children's lives. Some of them are told with pride, others with curiosity, others with a sense of doubt or puzzlement. (Indeed for people who do not have kids it may sometimes be most aggravating to be caught amid a bunch of parents trading stories about their offspring.) Telling anecdotes is helpful because it gives people a sense of how to look at an experience or event, how to construct interpretations about what is pedagogically significant in those situations, and possibly what to do about it. One mother who is single mentioned that this is the most difficult aspect of being a single parent: You do not have someone to tell stories to, someone who cares as much about your children as you do.

Earlier I suggested that the pedagogical moment is that moment of the pedagogical situation when the educator or parent does something right in his or her interactive relation to a child. I also suggested that facts, values, and a knowledge of teaching methods and educational philosophies themselves cannot tell us precisely what to do in any particular situation with a child or with a group of children. Various sets of facts, values, methods, philosophies can orient our actions in a planning or preparatory manner, but in any particular situation they cannot inform our actions in an instrumental way. It is wrong to suppose that we can thus provide a sure ground for our pedagogical action. In our living with children an action occurs rarely if ever that can be technically or mechanistically performed. Rather, in everyday social and pedagogical living with children we first of all act — and we hope we act thoughtfully!

Everyday practical action is carried by our orientation to life rather than determined by a particular set of technical skills or competencies.[70] In acting tactfully I demonstrate unwittingly what I can do as a pedagogue with children. In thoughtful reflection I later discover what I have done, what tactful action I am capable of demonstrating. As I reflect pedagogically on my daily living with children I discover my pedagogical nature, its present limits and possibilities.

Thoughtful reflection discovers where unreflective action was "thoughtless," without tact. Thus the experience of reflecting on past pedagogical experience enables me to enrich, to make more thoughtful, my future pedagogical experience. This is not just an intellectual exercise, but a matter of pedagogical fitness of the whole person. What we might call "pedagogical fitness" is a cog-

nitive and emotional and moral and sympathic and physical preparedness. Indeed, as I proposed above, acting tactfully is very
much an affair of the whole embodied person: heart, mind, and
body.

We can speak of pedagogical thoughtfulness as a form of
knowledge; and yet pedagogical thoughtfulness is less a body of
knowledge than a mindfulness oriented toward children. To
think of thoughtfulness as an oriented mindfulness may remind
us of the etymological connection between *thought* and *mind;*
the word *mind* shares roots with the term *man, human.* Originally *man* did not refer only to the male half of the human spe-
cies. It meant "human being" as in the German term *Mensch* and
the Dutch *mens. Klein's Etymological Dictionary* suggests that
the roots of both *mind* and *man* stood for the "one who thinks,"
"who remembers."

The term *mind* is also related to *minne,* which originally
meant "loving memory," while the Greek etymology of the term
includes "desire, ardor, spirit, passion." Now, if thoughtfulness
has a spiritual quality of "minding," then tactfulness is its concrete equivalent. As we saw earlier, the term *tact* carries this
physical reference to "touch," "body," "tactile." To be tactful is to
be physically mindful of the person toward whom one is oriented; to be tactful is to incarnate one's reflective thoughtfulness
in concrete situations. If we were to epistemologize the relation
between reflective thoughtfulness and tactfulness, we might say
that tact is the embodiment, the body work of thoughtfulness.

By stressing the embodied quality of tact I do not mean to
suggest that the mind is less involved in this knowledge but
rather that tact is a more than intellectual knowing. Often there
exists a wide gap between what we know intellectually or theoretically and our practical actions. For example, I may know intellectually that smoking is bad for me but I continue to smoke. I
may know theoretically that children learn best if provided encouragements but I continue to criticize. In contrast, tact inte-
grates in more intimate ways mind and body, intellect and heart,
reason and emotion. For example, a teacher spontaneously raises
her voice enough so that her praise of a student who had not
experienced much success is overheard by others — the student
glows with pride. A parent automatically draws a child's attention away from a situation that could be emotionally disturbing.

A teacher immediately glances with admonishment at a student who is about to ridicule another student in class.

These tactful gestures of encouraging, shielding, and admonishing children are thoughtful even though the gestures were sudden, unanticipated, impulsive, spontaneous. This shows that thoughtfulness is a quality that can characterize immediate action as well as meditative reflection. We can become more thoughtfully tactful through thoughtful reflection on the pedagogical significance of children's experience. There is a difference between artificial thoughtfulness that is created by the mechanical application of an external technique or skill and the authentic thoughtfulness of true tact. Tact is not a skill we use, it is something we are. Thus, when we speak of the embodied thoughtfulness, mindfulness, heedfulness of tact we point at the way a person is in mind and body.

Tact is a kind of embodied-knowledge that resembles bodily skills and habits. We all know that the human body acquires or learns certain bodily skills and habits which become like second nature in our living. When I am thirsty I take a cup from the usual place, I turn the tap on and then "thoughtlessly" tighten the faucet. In a way I leave this routine behavior almost blindly to my skilled and habituated body. This does not mean that I am not aware of what I am doing, but that I can do habituated bodily things without having to do them attentively and consciously. Only when the tap won't open or when the water smells unusually bad would we probably break our routinized behavior.

For many things in life we rely on our bodies' knowledge to perform certain tasks. Where is the light-switch? How do you tie a knot? Which way does the tap turn to open? We may have to simulate the gesture to discover what our body already knows. A variety of intellectual tasks, too, relies on this kind of body skill: how do you spell "lieutenant"? Sometimes we may have to write the word on paper to discover what our fingers already know. Our body skills also permit us to perform actions that require flexibility and spontaneity, as when we drive a car or a bike across town. Once at our point of destination we may remember little of all the stops we made — our skilled body guided us through the hectic traffic.

Thoughtfulness and tact are not identical to skills and habits, yet they are like this constellation of embodied skills and habits that have become second nature and determine to an extent who we are, who we have become, what we are able to perceive, understand, and do. According to Klein's the word *skill* is related to the term *skilja*, the ability to discriminate, to distinguish, to separate between things that make a difference. Etymologically *skill* means "to have understanding," "to make a difference." So the notion of bodily skill is an unexpected ally in our exploration of the nature of thoughtful pedagogical perceptiveness.

When I teach a group of children and I notice that some children experience shyness, exuberance, frustration, animation, boredom, wonderment, curiosity, puzzlement, confusion, or insight, then what I see is less given by a technical instructional skill that I may have learned in a teacher-effectiveness workshop than by a more embodied orientational pedagogical skill that I have acquired in a more experiential and reflective manner.[71] However, this skill of perceptiveness (of sensing, for example, what a situation means for a child) is something I cannot practise to do in the same way that I may be able to practise a skill such as lesson planning, classroom management, or even storytelling.

Pedagogical perceptiveness relies in part on a tacit, intuitive knowledge that the teacher may learn from personal experience, or through apprenticeship with a more experienced teacher. Most human activities that depend on knowledge and skills involve tacit or intuitive complexes. For example, medical doctors confronted with certain symptoms may intuitively sense what is wrong with a patient on the basis of such tacit understandings — even though the symptoms may not be that easy to pinpoint or articulate.[72] Just so, a teacher who senses that a child has certain difficulties in dealing with a problem may not be able to identify exactly on what clues the perceptive understanding was based. The tacit or intuitive nature of our bodily skill and bodily knowledge is learned in subtle ways by attuning ourselves to the concrete particulars of situations.

The skill of pedagogical perceptiveness inheres in the thoughtfulness and tact we learn through the practice of teaching, but not simply by teaching itself. We come to embody tact by means of past experiences coupled with thoughtful reflection on these past experiences. We reflectively acquire sensitivities and insights in various ways — as through literature, film, stories by children, stories about children, and childhood reminiscences.

Thoughtful reflection is itself an experience. Thoughtful reflection is an experience that gives significance to or perceives it in the experience upon which it reflects. So the significance that we attribute through thoughtful reflection to past experience leaves a living memory that is no less embodied knowledge than are the physical skills and habits we learn and acquire in a less reflective manner. However, this thought-engaged body knowledge of acting tactfully attaches a mindful, thinking quality to our ordinary awareness of our everyday actions and experiences.

9 CONCLUSION

The Relation between Pedagogy and Politics

In many ways, parents and teachers are the mediators between the present and the future of the children or students for whom they have responsibility. Whereas adults must be careful not to strike from the hands of young people the opportunity to make their own future, educators need to be on guard that they do not condemn young people to a future of which they are victims rather than the makers.

There are ways of standing in life or viewing life that are inherently anti-pedagogical.[73] First, a view of life that sees the future essentially as hopeless defeats the possibility of establishing a pedagogical relation with children, since any relation between a parent or teacher with a child is always founded on hope. Second, an orientation to life that refuses to take an active responsibility for the world into which the child has been brought also is pedagogically to be rejected since we cannot be pedagogically responsible to children if we refuse to acknowledge that we are co-responsible for the world in which we live. Third, a view of society that denies any of its citizens the opportunity to develop their fullest potential in relation to the rest of society is pedagogically corrupt. The same is as true for philosophies of human nature as for political philosophies or programs. If human beings, and especially children, are merely seen as resources to serve the economy or the social collective, and if the individual is denied his or her uniqueness and individuality, then this view, too, is pedagogically reprehensible. Conversely, a political or philosophical view is anti-pedagogical if it has an eye only for the individual and if it does not acknowledge that humans can only realize themselves as social beings, because they always stand in relations of influence to others. Finally, it is anti-pedagogical to assume that by some criterion or other (of birth, nationality, skin color, ethnicity, religion, gender, genetic endowment,

economic status, etc.) some individual or group is somehow superior or inferior to others. Differences among people can never
justify children's being denied pedagogical care and full member-
ship in the human community.

It follows that various political, economic, and philosophical
views are incompatible with pedagogy — however, it does not
follow from this that pedagogy (our responsibility to protect and
help any child grow up in a child-friendly world) itself should be
turned into a political theory. The "pedagogical" is not identical
to the "political," and cannot be reduced to any particular political program or theory. At times parents or educators may even
have to protect children from forces that are political. Yet pedagogy, our care for our children, often requires of us active political involvement to create the space, conditions, and possibilities
for children to grow up and create a world of their own making.

Becoming a parent or a teacher often radically affects a person's view of life, political awareness, and moral outlook. People
who in the past have been fairly blasé about politics now may
become politically motivated as a result of a newly felt responsibility to their children. Even individuals who seldom reflect on the
fate of oppressed people in other places now feel compelled to
take up the cause of other children and other people as a direct
result of their sense of responsibility. After all, we desire that the
world be and remain a good place for our children to live. We
become concerned about political philosophies, social programs,
economic policies, and environmental practices which threaten
the health of the world that we leave to our children. For the sake
of our children we want to make this world a better place to live.

We see, then, that as fathers, mothers, or teachers our pedagogical concerns and intentions for children carry political implications. The social norms and moral values that we may desire
to instill in our children cannot contradict the social good of society and endanger the health of the earth on which we live. If
we teach our children group hatred, intolerance, prejudice, violence, greed, ecological indifference, then we are not only teaching our children immorality, we are also making them victims of
the social consequences of the negative values directed at others
or directed back to them. We should not, by means of our children, produce a world that we would not wish upon them.

Pedagogy may thus become the impetus for political thought
and action. Moreover, political views and programs should be

evaluated on the basis of their pedagogical acceptability. For example, a policy which puts profit above environmental concerns can be thoroughly unacceptable on pedagogical grounds, since from a pedagogical point of view our children's legacy and welfare have higher priority than our present adult life and economic interests. Thus, pedagogical tact requires of us a certain worldliness, and the moral fibre to stand up for political views in which we believe.

Finally, the institutionalized culture of the school and of the larger educational system also may be characterized by structures, expectations, and policies that are pedagogically questionable. Rather than surrender and conform to processes that are anti-pedagogical, teachers often feel compelled, covertly or openly, to take a political stance vis-à-vis the "educational" bureaucracy that surrounds them. It is ironic that the administrative practices of schools increasingly are so geared to the philosophy of corporate-style management and business organization theory that it has become increasingly difficult for many teachers to maintain pedagogical relationships with the students they teach.

Ongoing policy changes with regard to various curriculum areas are also a source of frustration for many teachers, who are essentially robbed of their authority as subject matter experts by the never-ending pressures to "implement" or teach new or modified curricula mandated by the local, state, or federal authorities. Especially in Canada and the United States, curriculum changes are frequent and often drastic as a result of new opinions and priorities about the nature of math, science, reading, writing, language, social studies, history, geography, art, health, business, computers, and about the ways in which these subjects are to be taught and learned. Rather than think of themselves as pedagogue-scholars and intellectuals, teachers are encouraged to see themselves mainly as instructional disseminators, knowledge retailers, technicians of externally determined curricula.

Pedagogy and Culture

To ask questions about the nature of pedagogy, what it means to educate and bring up children and young people, there are two essentially different starting points. On the one hand, we can start by developing a theory of education and then let our actions be informed by this theory. Or, on the other hand, we can start with life itself and let our reflections about our living with children and young people help us to better understand pedagogical life. Much educational theory follows the first route. Here we have tried as much as possible to start with life itself.

But to start with life as it is lived means that we must always situate our reflections about education and child rearing in the particular society and culture in which we live this life. It goes without saying that our grasp of our social-cultural situation is always inflected by the memories of the past and anticipations of the future. As I consider my ten-year-old son's request to see a particular movie, I cannot forget the things my parents and their generation found appropriate for me when I was a ten-year-old. Thus my childhood memories affect my feeling for what is good and not good for my children.

At the same time I cannot help notice that my child already lives in a world of the future — a world in which the question of what is good for a child is less clearly anchored than the way my parents viewed it, or from the way it was viewed by my parents' parents. While the family values of yesteryear were grounded and stabilized in some manner by the church, the community, or secular philosophies, present-day norms and values are much less circumscribed and less clearly actualized in daily life. In these contrasting values, and in the increasingly ambiguous nature of modern values, we sense the difference that culture and history makes.

But there are observations about modern life that are more profoundly unsettling than the contrasts and conflicts between the norms of the old and new. For example, there is the blurring of the distinctions between adulthood and childhood. It is important to realize that the very notion of educating and bringing up children is rooted in the idea of the relative maturity, wisdom, and experience of adults in contrast with the relative immaturity and lack of experience and knowledge of the child. Yet, as we move through the last decade of the twentieth century, the distinctions between older and younger generations seem to fade and fuse.

In a strange sense, the tendency to approach children

through pedagogy may to some extent have turned into a generalized tendency in society at large. Under the pressure of modern social forces, adults seem to feel more vulnerable than before, more like children themselves, and thus in need of continued education and personal growth. Children, in contrast, seem to adults to be "wiser" so much sooner. They seem to be exposed to so much and at such early age. The ever-present images of the mass media leave few secrets for children to discover as they grow psychologically and physically more mature. Yet this early "wizening" or pre-mature maturing of children comes at a price. If anything, children often seem to suffer from the same vulnerabilities as their caretakers.

No longer do parents and teachers seem to feel confident, as to some degree the older generation did a few decades ago, that they possess a certain common sense, sense in common, and a set of values that gives them guidance in the rearing and teaching of children. As it gets more difficult to distinguish between what it is to be a child and what it is to be an adult, it becomes more problematic for adults to exert influence over the children in their care. Is there a tendency among adults to want to *be* and *do* like children? Or do adults simply feel that they have less time available to be real parents or teachers to the children for whom they carry pedagogical responsibility? As the adults become more hesitant in providing direction to their children, the pressures and effects of peer influence, and the commercial culture become increasingly dominant in young people's lives.

We cannot presume that in modern society the everyday relations between adults and children are still generally governed by pedagogical qualities. Many parents no longer feel capable or want to get involved in parenting. Many teachers are just there to "teach" what they are told to teach and nothing more. In various spheres of North American society there is a loss of common assumptions as to how we should and should not deal with children.

Yet we may not assume that we have completely forgotten that we are invested with a great responsibility for our children. To the extent that, in our daily lives, we are actually forsaking our pedagogical responsibility as parents and/or as professional educators, we leave our children in the lurch, and rob ourselves of the occasion to act and reflect on the pedagogical impulse that gives meaning to the lives of our children as well as to our own lives.

From the point of view of living with children, the surrender to theorizing and ways of viewing the world that are nihilistic and that lack moral intuition is profoundly anti-pedagogical. Besides a pedagogy based on the notion of *in loco parentis*, as in this text, we may need to develop a theory of cultural pedagogy.

Cultural pedagogy can be studied from various perspectives. First, cultural pedagogy can be the cultural historical study of childhood and child rearing practices in culturally different worlds or in different historical phases of a particular culture. Thus cultural pedagogy helps us appreciate the variety of ways in which we can "see" and approach children. Cultural historical studies can enrich our understanding of what children have meant in the past and what they could or should mean to us at present. Second, cultural pedagogy can be interpreted as the pedagogy of culture as it was conceived in Germany around the turn of the last century. Pedagogy always deals with educational concerns at the level of the individual and of society. To ask what it means to be an educated person implies the question of what kind of society we educate our children for. So cultural pedagogy shifts the focus from the world of the child to the world of the culture in attempting to bring about a morally higher social order, in terms of justice, freedom, equality, community. A modern form of cultural pedagogy is represented by various forms of critical social theory.[74] A relevant cultural pedagogy may need to search for cultural political forms: political democratic structures, social assistance agencies, peace movements, environmental policies, fair gender laws, and global agencies that can make this earth livable for all children of our world.

Pedagogy is Self-reflective

Whatever educational book or magazine we happen to open we cannot help but notice that every new approach to teaching or education is always presented as an attack on an excess of uncritical attitudes. In itself this is quite understandable. We always want to advance our own reasonableness by pushing against the unreasonableness of those who surround us, including those who participate in the curricular discourse of our educational culture.

It is not difficult to sketch the unreasonableness of educational and curricular writing: The standard reasoning of traditionalists is criticized as being unreflective and oppressive, the self-righteous reasoning of fundamentalists is dogmatic and uncritical, the policy-oriented reasoning of the bureaucrats is mindless and dominating, the radical reasoning of the critical theorists is impractical and inconsequential, the rigorous reasoning of the scientific rationalists is intellectualistic and deliberately value-free, the accusatory reasoning of educational critics is irresponsible and self-serving, the playful reasoning of the postmodernists is nihilistic and amoral, the attention-getting reasoning of the feminists is accusing and unpredictable. The discourse on "what is reasonable and acceptable" uses a rationality that, applied to the work of others, always finds them too narrow or too broad, too subjective or too objective, too rigorous or too soft, too political or not political enough.

Critical reason that tries to unmask the irrationality of others as unreasonable is a struggle for power. But to criticize the unreasonableness of other educational approaches not only serves to combat the influence of other ways of seeing and doing things, it also serves the search for appropriate criteria for what is pedagogically accountable and defensible. In this text I have tried to locate appropriate criteria in living examples of pedagogy, since the notion of "example" offers a pedagogically relevant structure of self-reflection.

The logic of the example not only pays attention to what is being said or written, but also and especially to what one does and what the source is from whence one acts.

It is more pedagogical to give a good example than to criticize the examples of others; it is more positive to orient students to reasonableness than to unreasonableness. But how do we know what is reasonable? How do we know what is good for children or for this particular child? Pedagogically we know that there exists no closed rationality or moral system that will always tell us what is the right thing to say or do with children. However, what we do have are examples of experiences of living with children in a manner that was thoughtful and tactful. Whether we succeeded in being thoughtful is a matter of reflecting on the pedagogical significance of children's experiences and of the experiences we have with children. These experiential examples allow us to stand in a self-reflective relation to the normative meanings of pedagogical thoughtfulness and tact to which we can orient ourselves.

So we must always remain reflective about the deeper meanings and consequences of the experiences of children who are touched by us. This also means that we should not be afraid to make mistakes, since our examples may be well-intended but sometimes poorly realized. We might even say that it is impossible not to make mistakes and sometimes to do things that one later regrets and wished that one had done otherwise. The important difference lies in the constant striving that is animated by the pedagogical intent.

Exemplary influence is therefore an agogical[75] form of influence that does not mainly criticize others from the sidelines, as it were, but rather is an influence that shows us how to live by offering examples of living. Pedagogical theorizing involves the study of good examples, of the goodness of examples of pedagogical action. In other words, pedagogical influence is *eudaimonic:* aimed at what is good for our children. Therefore, pedagogical reflection must also be mindful of its origin *in loco parentis.* After all, the pedagogical influence of the mother or the father is, one hopes, not an influence that preaches, seduces, ridicules, or criticizes, but wants to strengthen the child by showing how one can live in an exemplary manner — even though in life we know that our experience of living with young people is such that we often seem unable to do just the right thing or to hold back at the right moment from doing wrong.

Notes

1. One might object that, in global terms, many children have very little possibility and openness in life. And this is no doubt true, especially of children who live in the desperate circumstances created by exploitive economic structures and repressive social-political systems. I am reminded of a remark once made to me by Paulo Freire, the Brazilian political educator. He said, "Yes, some adults and children live a life of poverty in North America. But the situation for many South American children is different. 'Poverty' is a luxury term for them; they live a life of misery and desperation. There is a difference between poverty and misery."

2. I am not taking an existentialist philosophical position here. There are obvious limits to human freedom in our social and political culture. However, it would appear to me that more so than in the recent past young people live in contexts punctuated by conflicting worldviews, competing norms for living, contrasting interpretive frameworks, antinomous values, discordant local and larger philosophies, and other influences that tend to have decentering, fragmenting, rupturing, and discrepant effects. Thus, young people stand in more uncertain, ambivalent, reflective and critical relations to their own traditions at the familial, social, ethnic, and cultural levels.

3. See, for example, E. Shorter (1977), *The making of the modern family.* New York: Basic Books.

Demographers predict that in Canada 40% of new marriages will end in divorce. In the United States 50% of all children born will spend all or part of their lives in a single-parent family. In Canada 13% of all families, at present, are single-parent families, less than 15% are traditional families in which one parent works outside of the home while the other is at home with the children. In the rest of the families, both parents work outside of the home; therefore, child care is now a business that is figured into national budget policies and the gross national product.

4. See M. van Manen (1990), *"In loco parentis."* Lecture at the University of Utrecht in memory of M. J. Langeveld. April 26, 1990.

5. See, for example, H. Arendt (1978), *Between past and future.* Harmondsworth: Penguin Books, pp. 173–196.

6. See, for example, J. Bruner (1982), Schooling children in a nasty climate. *Psychology Today*, January 1982, pp. 57–63.

7. In my native Dutch language, the term *opvoeding* is such a general concept that equally describes the efforts of teaching (education, including schooling) and of parenting (family child rearing).

8. The term "science" usually stands for that research and theoretical activity that tries to discover lawlike or invariant features of human behavior and learning. The object of science is to arrive at objective explanations, predictions, and possible control of certain phenomena. Such a concept of science is found in fields such as physics, genetics, engineering, and also in the behavioral social sciences. However, we can also speak of "human science," which implies a different mode of inquiry, focussing on understanding by means of description and interpretation the meanings of human experiences and expressions. In other words, human science studies the subjectivities rather than just the external behaviors in human life.

9. By "normative" is meant that parenting and teaching always are concerned with questions of value, preference, morality. We might say that education is fundamentally a moral activity, but the term "moral" is often associated with ethical theory and certain forms of practical judgment and moral reasoning. Interestingly, the term "normative" derives from the Latin *norma*, meaning the carpenter's square. To say that our pedagogical living with children is normative implies that we accept that as educators and parents we must have a sense of standards, that we orient ourselves to the good (whatever this good may mean in particular circumstances).

10. See John Dewey (1902), The relation of theory to practice in education. In *The relation of theory to practice in the education of teachers*, Third Yearbook of the National Society for the Scientific Study of Education (pp. 9–30). Bloomington, IN: Public School Publishing Company.

11. This may be due in part to negative connotations associated with the term "pedagogy." The dictionary defines "pedagogue" as, "A man whose occupation is the instruction of children or youths; a schoolmaster, teacher, preceptor. Now usually in a more or less contemptuous or hostile sense, with implication of pedantry, dogmatism, or severity." See *The Compact Edition of the Oxford English Dictionary* (1971), s.v. "Pedagogy."

12. "Agogy" is a rootword of pedagogy (leading or teaching of children). The agogical sciences are practical disciplines concerned with providing education, help, support, care for people (such as continuing education, psychotherapy, counselling, nursing, health care). The terms "agogy" and "agogical" have some currency in Dutch applied human science fields.

13. In these sections dealing with the notion of "influence" I am especially indebted to the work of M. J. Langeveld (1965), *Beknopte theoretische pedagogiek.* Groningen: Wolters. Also helpful has been the more recent work of J. D. Imelman (1977), *Inleiding in de pedagogiek.* Groningen: Wolters-Noordhoff.

14. There is a pedagogical optimism that expects too much of parents and teachers, and too little of the child in how and what the child contributes to his or her own growth and development. There is also a pedagogical pessimism that has no faith in the potential influence of educators and that expects too much of the child. We need to realize, however, that pedagogy is neither omnipotent nor impotent but that good parents, teachers, and schools can make a significant difference in children's positive development. For an interesting discussion along these lines, see Bas Levering (1988), *Waarden in opvoeding en opvoedingswetenschap: Pleidooi voor een uitdagende pedagogiek.* Leuven: Acco.

15. *The Oxford Dictionary of English Etymology* (1979), s.v. "influence."

16. Agogical relations deal with "good influence" (eupraxis) not only between parents or teachers and children but between people in general.

17. For example, see Alice Miller (1983), *For your own good: Hidden cruelty in child-rearing and the roots of violence.* New York: New American Library; and (1984), *Thou shalt not be aware: society's betrayal of the child.* New York: New American Library.

18. For example, I am thinking of those who, from a critical-theoretical or psycho-analytical perspective, see pedagogical influence mainly as a form of domination or power. Mollenhauer therefore proposes a communicatively oriented concept of pedagogical interaction. See M's discussion of "education as communicative action," in K. Mollenhauer (1974), *Het kind en zijn kansen: Over de plaats van individu en maatschappij in het opvoedingsproces.* Meppel: Boom, pp. 27–94.

19. M. Ondaatje (1979), *There's a trick with a knife I'm learning to do.* Toronto: McClelland and Stewart, p. 104.

20. See, for example, the fascinating text by Stephen W. Hawking (1988). *A brief history of time: From the big bang to black holes.* New York: Bantam Books. It is interesting how Hawking tells the story of the physics of time, space, and black holes by carefully narrating his personal curiosities, discoveries, and interests as researcher. The apparently self-indulgent interest of the scientist in his or her object of study may ultimately consist in a deep caring for nature. I have described this orientation earlier as follows:

In a beautiful story called "The Star Thrower," the late Loren Eiseley, professor of anthropology and of the history of science, recounts an experience that shows what it means to know something in a deep and disciplined manner: Eiseley is walking at an ocean beach. There are people collecting shells and starfish which the receding waters have strewn along the shoreline. As he walks past the boiling pots of the shell collectors and the starfish gatherers, Eiseley notices a lone figure in the far distance. A man is gazing fixedly at something in the sand. Eventually he stoops and flings an object beyond the breaking surf.

When Eiseley finally gets near, he sees the man stoop again. In a pool of sand and silt a starfish has thrust its arms stiffly and is holding its body away from the stifling mud. With a quick yet gentle movement the man picks it up and spins it far out into the sea. "It may live," he says to Eiseley. Eiseley is a bit embarrassed. He notices that no other people have ventured so far down the beach. "Do you collect?" he asks. And while gesturing at the threatened life lying on the shore, the man says softly, "Only like this. And only for the living."

What Eiseley points out with this story is that the essence of the discipline of science is not simply collecting and classifying nature for the worldly uses of the humans. To be truly disciplined is the be a "thrower." The one who saves and restores. The one who labors to understand the nature of nature, for the sake of the natural, for the "uses of life." The star-thrower he describes is possessed by a passion — the passion of a knowledge which is disciplined, which requires obedience and responsibility, Here "obedience" means being able to listen to what speaks or to what is being said. And to be able to hear the stars, one must love their nature. From M. van Manen (1986), *The tone of teaching.* Richmond Hill, Ont.: Scholastic-TAB Press (in Canada); Portsmouth, N.H.: Heinemann Educational Books (in the U.S.), pp. 51 – 52.

21. A Dutch saying.

22. *The Oxford Dictionary of English Etymology* (1979), s.v. "educate" p. 238. See also van Manen (1982), Phenomenological pedagogy, *Curriculum Inquiry*, vol. 12:3.

23. See Max van Manen (1982), Edifying theory: serving the good. *Theory into Practice* (Columbus), vol. 21, no. 1, Winter.

24. See Stephen Strasser (1963), *Opvoedingswetenschap en opvoedingswijsheid.* 's Hertogenbosch: L.C.G. Malmberg.

25. See J. Bruner (1960), The process of education. New York: Vintage Books.

26. For example, in *Waarden in opvoeding,* Levering argues that we should not expect children to do something that they cannot do. However, this position would make all education and child rearing impossible. As educators we are constantly asking children to learn to do what they cannot yet do, to extend and stretch the limits of their knowledge and skills. As Merleau-Ponty (1964), so aptly says, the child always lives "beyond his means" (p. 138). Levering is correct, however, in cases such as toilet training: We should not expect that young babies hold their bowels and bladder as long as they are neurologically unable to control their muscles.

27. See also Max van Manen (1989), By the light of anecdote. In *Phenomenology and Pedagogy* (Edmonton), vol. 7, pp. 232–253.

28. See Stephen Smith (1989), *The pedagogy of risk.* Doctoral dissertation, Edmonton: The University of Alberta.

29. See Bruner (1982).

30. See, for example, Michael Rutter, Barbara Maughan, Peter Mortimore, Janet Ouston (1979), *Fifteen thousand hours: Secondary schools and their effects on children.* Cambridge, Mass.: Harvard University Press.

31. Martin Buber (1970), *Voordrachten over de opvoeding.* Utrecht: Aula, p. 29.

32. See O. F. Bollnow (1989), The pedagogical atmosphere. *Phenomenology and Pedagogy,* vol. 8, 1989, pp. 44–46.

33. *The Edmonton Journal,* Oct. 23, 1987.

34. Langeveld (1965), p. 144. See also Max van Manen (1979), The Utrecht School: a phenomenological experiment in educational theoriz-

ing, *Interchange: The Journal of Educational Policy Studies* (Toronto), vol. 10, No. 1.

35. See H.W.F. Stellwag (1970), *'Situatie' en 'relatie.'* Groningen: Wolters-Noordhoff.

36. H. Nohl (1970), *Die pädagogische Bewegung in Deutschland und ihre Theorie.* Frankfurt am Main: Schulte-Bulmke. p. 132.

37. See Nohl (1970).

38. See, for example, W.H.O. Schmidt (1973), *Child development: The human, cultural, and educational context.* New York: Harper & Row. pp. 23–26.

39. *The Oxford Dictionary of English Etymology* (1979). s.v. "mistake."

40. *The Oxford Dictionary of English Etymology* (1979). s.v. "failing."

41. An article by Horst Scarbath prompted some distinctions here; however, Scarbath simply equates disciplined understanding (such as "empathic understanding" in Carl Rogers' sense) with pedagogical understanding. See H. Scarbath (1985), What is pedagogic understanding? Understanding as an element of competence for pedagogic action. *Education,* vol. 31, pp. 92–128.

42. See Max Scheler (1970), *The nature of sympathy.* Hamden, Conn.: Archon Press.

43. See John Dewey (1916/1973), Experience and thinking. In J. Dewey (1973) *The Philosophy of John Dewey,* J. J. McDermott, ed. New York: G. P. Putnam's Sons, p. 502.

44. Of course, it often happens in schools in Canada and the United States that teachers are assigned to teach subjects that they know little about. This approach is justified on the mistaken assumption that teachers who know how to teach should therefore be able to teach anything. Teachers who are just one day ahead of the students in the mastery of certain subject matter have less facility to be open and dynamic in their teaching. They may need to plan their lessons with inflexibility for fear that otherwise they will not know what they are doing.

45. For a phenomenological analysis of decision, see Paul Ricoeur (1966), *Freedom and nature: The voluntary and the involuntary.* Evanston, Ill.: Northwestern University Press.

46. See chapter eight below, "The tactful structure of thoughtful action."

47. Of course, medical situations are often normative (moral) as well. However, the medical question of whether to perform an amputation on a gangrenous leg for example, is a purely medical decision for the specialist, to the extent that the specialist must know what alternative procedures are available and what consequences and possible risks are involved in the decision to amputate a diseased portion of a limb. The normative or moral dimensions of medical decisions usually have to do with considerations that non-specialists can participate in as well, for example, is life worth living with an amputated limb?

48. It is fascinating how some of the dominant models of "reflective teaching" or "teaching as reflection-in-action" curiously wind up looking suspiciously similar to the process of scientific inquiry itself, complete with "rigor in on-the-spot experiment," "hypothesizing," and "testing." See, for example, D. A. Schön (1983), *The reflective practitioner: How professionals think in action.* New York: Basic Books; and (1987), *Educating the reflective practitioner.* San Francisco: Jossey-Bass.

49. Indeed, etymologically the term *secret* means "separated, divided, set apart."

50. This awareness may be like the kind of checking on the acting self that characterizes stage actors. They often report that they somehow remain aware of their acting behavior even though the acting itself should be a total immersion into the spirit of the role that they are creatively assuming. But in acting, a role or persona is in some way, of course, an assumed and "false" self. In contrast, the pedagogue (teacher or parent), in acting with children, needs to remain true to his or her own being.

51. For additional epistemological comments on thoughtful action, see the section in chapter eight entitled "The tactful structure of thoughtful action."

52. I thought that I had coined the notion of "pedagogical thoughtfulness and tact." See for example: Max van Manen (1984), Theory of the unique: thoughtful learning for pedagogic tactfulness. In G. Milburn and R. Enns, eds., *Curriculum Canada,* University of British Columbia. Also: Max van Manen (1986), *The tone of teaching.* Richmond Hill, Ont.: Scholastic-TAB Press (in Canada); Portsmouth, N.H.: Heinemann Educational Books (in U.S.). However, I became aware of the discussion of "pedagogical tact" in the older German literature, especially after my German friend and colleague Helmut Danner sent me the booklet by Jacob Muth (1982), *Pädagogischer Takt,* Essen: Verlagsgesellschaft. Muth's text distinguished certain categories of pedagogical tact further developed in this book. Muth's review of the notion of tact contains the 1802 lecture by Herbart (Herbart in Muth, pp. 54, 55).

53. The best historical reference is probably the small but excellent book already referred to (Note 52) on the role of tact in German educational theory by Muth (1982). I have been guided by several insights in Muth's text on the history of tact in education.

54. William James (1962), *Talks to teachers on psychology.* New York: Dover Publications, p. 29.

55. Muth cites the early works of Herbart's predecessors, such as Campus (1783) and Knigge (1788), to show that the feeling of "sensitivity" and the action of "holding back" in tactful action was already being discussed. See Muth (1982).

56. H.-G. Gadamer (1975), *Truth and method.* New York: Seabury Press, p. 17.

57. See O. F. Bollnow (1987), *Crisis and new beginning.* Pittsburgh: Duquesne University Press.

58. See Muth (1982).

59. *The Oxford Dictionary of English Etymology,* (1979), s.v. "tact."

60. For a discussion of the nature of otherness and the human responsibility that flows from the experience of otherness, see especially Emmanuel Levinas (1969), *Totality and infinity.* Pittsburgh: Duquesne University Press, and (1981), *Otherwise than being or beyond essence.* The Hague: Martinus Nijhoff. In this section I also benefitted from some nice illustrative discussions by Jan C. M. Engelen (1987), *Het gelaat: jij die mij aanziet.* Hilversum: Gooi & Sticht.

61. See O. F. Bollnow (1989), The pedagogical atmosphere — the perspective of the child. *Phenomenology and Pedagogy,* vol. 7, pp. 47–51.

62. It is quite common to refer to the "art" of teaching (in contrast to the "science" of teaching), however this is probably an unfortunate conception. If teaching were an "art" then the classroom would be like a "play," an "act" or some such artistic performance or production. But teachers do not teach in order to be watched and admired for their artistic "acting" ability. The purpose of teaching lies in the intent of the pedagogical relation between adult and child, or teacher and student.

63. J. H. Pestalozzi (1799/1954), *Ausgewählte Schriften,* W. Flitner, ed. Düsseldorf/München. p. 103.

64. See also van Manen (1986).

65. O. F. Bollnow (1982), On silence—findings of philosophico-pedagogical anthropology. *Universitas*, vol. 24, no. 1, p. 57.

66. In this section I borrow ideas from Cornelis Verhoeven (1980), *Tractaat over het spieken: Het onderwijs als producent van schijn.* Baarn: Ambo.

67. See M. J. Langeveld (1953), De pubescent en het orde probleem: enkele aspecten. *Paedagogische Studiën*, 30, pp 369–388.

68. In this section I borrow from M. J. Langeveld (1954), Humor in de paedagogische ontmoeting. *DUX*, vol. 1, no. 5, pp. 230–233.

69. For a discussion along these lines, see van Manen (1989).

70. See also M. van Manen (1977), Linking ways of knowing with ways of being practical. *Curriculum Inquiry*, vol. 6 no. 3, pp. 205–228.

71. See the discussion of orientational skill in M. van Manen (1977), p. 211.

72. Michael Polanyi has argued that we learn all kinds of details about ordinary things but that these details form a silent or tacit knowledge. We have a hard time expressing how we know these things. For example, I recognize the face of a friend out of a crowd of passers-by, yet I would have difficulty telling what it is about my friend's face that makes it possible for me to identify this person. Polanyi argues that this proves that "we know more than we can tell." Somehow we are able to integrate our many impressions and particular experiences into holistic intuitions; these intuitions Polanyi calls "personal knowledge" that each individual must acquire in order to gain competence at certain tasks. For example, a doctor cannot just learn from a book how to recognize certain symptoms. The doctor has to learn these often subtle diagnostic skills through experience or apprenticeship.

Personal knowledge is a process of moving from a subsidiary awareness of particulars to a focal awareness of an integrated whole. Polanyi distinguishes between four analogous structures of tacit knowledge: understanding physiognomies, performance of skills, the use of the senses, and the mastery of tools. Although Polanyi's analysis of personal knowledge as a from–to function of the relation between particulars and whole may be somewhat mechanistic, his notion of tacit knowledge is experientially appealing. It is similar to the idea of embodied-knowledge and bodily skills that also emphasizes the importance of the personal, embodied nature of knowledge. See M. Polanyi (1958), *Personal knowledge.* Chicago: University of Chicago Press.

73. Langeveld identifies four anthropological assumptions that must exist for pedagogy to be possible at all. In the following discussion I am guided by his distinctions. See Langeveld (1965), pp. 76, 77.

74. See for example the work of Paulo Freire, e.g., P. Freire and D. Macedo (1987). *Literacy: Reading the word and the world.* South Hadley, Mass.: Bergin and Garvey.

75. See Note 12.

Bibliography

Arendt, H. (1978). *Between past and future*. Harmondsworth: Penguin Books.

Blum, A. (1970). *Socrates*. London: Routledge and Kegan Paul.

Blum, A. and McHugh, P. (1984). *Self-reflection in the arts and sciences*. Atlantic Highland: Humanities Press.

Bollnow, O. F. (1982). On silence — findings of philosophico-pedagogical anthropology. *Universitas*, vol. 24, no. 1, pp .

———. (1987). *Crisis and new beginning*. Pittsburgh: Duquesne University Press.

———. (1989). The pedagogical atmosphere — the perspective of the child. *Phenomenology and Pedagogy*. (Edmonton), vol. 7, pp. 47 – 51.

Bruner, J. (1960). *The process of education*. New York: Vintage Books.

Bruner, J. (1982). Schooling children in a nasty climate. *Psychology Today*. January 1982, pp. 57 – 63.

Buber, M. (1970). *Voordrachten over de opvoeding*. Utrecht: Aula.

Buytendijk, F.J.J. (1947). *Het kennen van de innerlijkheid*. Utrecht: N. V. Dekker & van de Vegt.

———. (1947/88). The first smile of the child. *Phenomenology and Pedagogy*. (Edmonton), vol. 6, no. 1, pp. 15 – 24.

Calderhead, J. (1989). Reflective teaching and teacher education. *Teaching & Teacher Education*, vol. 5, no. 1, pp. 43 – 51.

Compact Edition of the Oxford English Dictionary. (1971). Oxford: Oxford University Press.

Dewey, J. (1902). The relation of theory to practice in education. *The relation of theory to practice in the education of teachers.* Third Yearbook of the National Society for the Scientific Study of Education. Bloomington, Ind.: Public School Publishing Company, pp. 9 – 30.

———. (1916/1973). Experience and thinking. In J. Dewey (1973), *The Philosophy of John Dewey.* J. J. McDermott, ed. New York: G. P. Putnam's Sons.

Eiseley, L. (1978). *The star thrower.* London: Wildwood House.

Engelen, J. C. M. (1987). Het gelaat: jij die mij aanziet. Hilversum: Gooi & Sticht.

Flitner, A. (1982). Educational science and educational practice. *Education,* vol. 25. pp. 63 – 75.

Freire, P. and Macedo, D. (1987). *Literacy: Reading the word and the world.* South Hadley, Mass.: Bergin and Garvey.

Gadamer, H.-G. (1975). *Truth and method.* New York: Seabury Press.

Hawking, S. W. (1988). *A brief history of time: From the big bang to black holes.* New York: Bantam Books.

Imelman, J. D. (1977). *Inleiding in de pedagogiek.* Groningen: Wolter-Noordhoff.

James W. (1890/1962). *Talks to teachers on psychology.* New York: Dover Publications.

Klein, E. (1971). *A comprehensive etymological dictionary of the English Language.* Amsterdam: Elsevier Scientific Publishing Company.

Langeveld, M. J. (1953). De pubescent en het orde probleem: Enkele aspecten. *Paedagogische Studiën,* vol. 30, pp. 369 – 388.

———. (1954). Humor in de paedagogische ontmoeting. *DUX,* vol. 1, no. 5, pp. 230 – 233.

———. (1944/65). *Beknopte theoretische pedagogiek.* Groningen: Wolters.

———. (1983). The stillness of the secret place. *Phenomenology and Pedagogy.* (Edmonton), vol. 1, no. 1, pp. 11 – 17.

————. (1984). How does the child experience the world of things? *Phenomenology and Pedagogy.* (Edmonton), University of Alberta Publication Services, vol. 2, no. 3, pp. 215 – 223.

Levering, B. (1988). *Waarden in opvoeding en opvoedingswetenschap: Pleidooi voor een uitdagende pedagogiek.* Leuven: Acco.

Levinas, E. (1969). *Totality and infinity.* Pittsburgh: Duquesne University Press.

————. (1981). *Otherwise than being or beyond essence.* The Hague: Martinus Nijhoff.

Litt, Th. (1927/67). *Führen oder Wachsenlassen.* Stuttgart: Ernst Klett Verlag.

MacIntyre, A. (1989). *Recoiling from reason.* South Bend, Ind.: University of Notre Dame Press.

Marcel, G. (1978). *Homo viator.* Gloucester, Mass.: Smith.

Merleau-Ponty, M. (1964). *The primacy of perception.* Evanston, Ill.: Northwestern University Press.

Miller, A. (1983). *For your own good: Hidden cruelty in child-rearing and the roots of violence.* New York: New American Library.

————. (1984). *Thou shalt not be aware: Society's betrayal of the child.* New York: New American Library.

Mollenhauer, K. (1974). *Het kind en zijn kansen: Over de plaats van individu en maatschappij in het opvoedingsproces.* Meppel: Boom.

Muth, J. (1982). *Pädagogischer Takt.* Essen: Verlagsgesellschaft.

Nohl, H. (1967). *Ausgewählte pädagogische Abhandlungen.* Paderborn: Ferdinand Schöningh.

————. (1970). *Die pädagogische Bewegung in Deutschland und ihre Theorie.* Frankfurt am Main: Schulte-Bulmke.

Ondaatje, M. (1979). *There's a trick with a knife I'm learning to do.* Toronto: McClelland and Stewart.

Oxford dictionary of English etymology (1979). London: Oxford University Press.

Perquin, N. (1964). *Pedagogiek.* Roermond: J. J. Romen en Zonen.

Pestalozzi, J. H. (1799/1954). *Ausgewählte Schriften.* W. Flitner (ed.). Düsseldorf/Munich.

Polanyi, M. (1958). *Personal knowledge.* Chicago: University of Chicago Press.

Ricoeur, P. (1966). *Freedom and nature: The voluntary and the involuntary.* Evanston, Ill.: Northwestern University Press.

Rutter, M.; Maughan, B.; Mortimore, P.; Ouston, J. (1979). *Fifteen thousand hours: Secondary schools and their effects on children.* Cambridge, Mass.: Harvard University Press.

Scarbath, H. (1985). What is pedagogic understanding? Understanding as an element of competence for pedagogic action. *Education* (Tübingen), vol. 31, pp. 93 – 128.

Scheler, M. (1970). *The nature of sympathy.* Hamden, Conn.: Archon Books.

Schleiermacher, F.E.D. (1964). *Ausgewählte pädagogische Schriften.* Paderborn: Ferdinand Schöningh.

Schmidt, W.H.O. (1973). *Child development: the human, cultural, and educational context.* New York: Harper & Row.

Schön, D. A. (1983). *The reflective practitioner: How professionals think in action.* New York: Basic Books.

————. (1987). *Educating the reflective practitioner.* San Francisco: Jossey-Bass.

Schubert, W. H. (1982). The return of curriculum inquiry from schooling to education. *Curriculum Inquiry* (Toronto), vol. 12, no. 2, pp. 221 – 232.

Shorter, E. (1977). *The making of the modern family.* New York: Basic Books.

Smith, S. (1989). *The pedagogy of risk.* Doctoral dissertation, Edmonton: The University of Alberta.

Spiecker, B. (1984). The pedagogical relation. *Oxford Review of Education.* (Oxford), vol. 10, no. 2, pp. 203–209.

Stellwag, H.W.F. (1970). *'Situatie' en 'relatie.'* Groningen: Wolters-Noordhoff.

Strasser, S. (1963). *Opvoedingswetenschap en opvoedingswijsheid.* 's-Hertogenbosch: L.C.G. Malmberg.

Van den Berg, J. H. and Linschoten, J. (eds.) (1953). *Persoon en wereld.* Utrecht: Erven J. Bijleveld.

Van Manen, M. (1977). Linking ways of knowing with ways of being practical. *Curriculum Inquiry.* (Toronto), vol. 6 no. 3, pp. 205–228.

———. (1979). The phenomenology of pedagogical observation. *The Canadian Journal for Studies in Education,* vol. 4, no. 1, pp. 5–16.

———. (1979). The Utrecht School: A phenomenological experiment in educational theorizing, *Interchange: The Journal of Educational Policy Studies.* (Toronto), vol. 10, no. 1.

———. (1982). Edifying theory: serving the good. *Theory Into Practice.* vol. 21, no. 1, pp. 44–49.

———. (1982). Phenomenological pedagogy. *Curriculum Inquiry.* (Toronto), vol. 12, no. 3, pp. 283–299.

———. (1984). Theory of the unique: thoughtful learning for pedagogic tactfulness. In G. Milburn and R. Enns, eds., *Curriculum Canada,* Vancouver: University of British Columbia, (pp. 63–87).

———. (1986). *The tone of teaching.* Richmond Hill, Ont.: Scholastic-TAB (in Canada); Portsmouth, N.H.: Heinemann Educational Books (in U.S.).

———. (1989). By the light of anecdote. In *Phenomenology and Pedagogy* (Edmonton), vol. 7, pp. 232–253.

———. (1990). *"In loco parentis."* The M. J. Langeveld Lecture, The University of Utrecht, April 26.

————. (1990). *Researching lived experience: Human science for an action-sensitive pedagogy.* London, Ont.: Althouse Press (in Canada); Albany, N.Y.: State University of New York Press (in U.S.).

Verhoeven, C. (1980). *Tractaat over het spieken: Het onderwijs als producent van schijn.* Baarn: Ambo.

Waldenfels, B. (1985). *In den Netzen der Lebenswelt.* Frankfurt am Main: Suhrkamp.

Index